Equus Phasmatis

Paperback publication February 25, 2015.

ISBN 13: 978-0692390122

ISBN 10: 069239012X

Bisac: Biography & Autobiography/Personal Memoir

Cover Photo taken by Kimberly Sue McLaughlin.

Back Cover photo taken by Alden Cole.

Dedicated to all the wonderful people
who helped me along the way,
to all the loving and loyal horses
who bring out the best in their humans,
and to the most beautiful, special,
and precious horse in the whole world,
Trixie.

Table of Contents

7/2/16

To Connor,

Always believe in yourself and run towards love!

Kim McLaught

Chapter # 1   A Momentous Meeting

The door lay in pieces scattered across the floor as my father flipped back his vest to reveal the gun he always carried. "I'm tired of you being so mouthy. You better learn to watch your tone with me."

I stuck my face right in his, leaned in, and yelled at full volume. "Pull the gun!" There came a point when living no longer mattered. It didn't matter if you lived or died, as long as the torment ended.

I never knew if it was Dad's joy of intimidation, his apparent need to push the boundaries of society as far as possible, or his mental illness that brought him to that moment in the spring of '91. But I knew what had brought me there.

It all started on June 1 of 1979, when my mother drove me down to Woody and Mary Browns' house, a fairly close neighbor of ours in rural Dayton, Maine and my life was forever changed. At the age of nine, I fell irrevocably in love with the horse who'd become my steadfast companion for the next twenty-five years.

On that so long ago day, I set my eyes on the most beautiful, precious, and special creature in the whole world. A delicate new-born, filly afire with the life that surged within her tiny body; she frisked and spun around her pinto mother, her dam.

A copper, red bay with three white socks and a blaze, she sported a black mane and tail, both of which fluffed out bushy and short. I imagined them growing to be long and beautiful when she got older. Her nose gleamed a beautiful, rose-petal pink, beneath her white blaze. She frolicked and pranced around her mother. She danced like a flame and her coat shined like fire, so I thought she'd be hot to touch. Instead, she felt warm and soft, like a pillow. But I sensed the strength under the softness, the boundless energy. She emitted a life force more dynamic than anything I'd ever experienced before.

My eyes stayed locked on her. Her beauty made me think of the mirror-smooth pond, dappled with autumn leaves, reflecting a robin's-egg blue sky and snowy clouds, which had caused me to stop and gaze in wonder at nature's splendor. Her zest for life reminded me of a spring stream, sweetly singing a bubbling, rippling melody, prompting me to take joy in the moment. I watched her, unable to tear my eyes away and my mind overflowed with dreams. I dreamt that the best horse ever belonged to me and that I belonged to her.

Mr. Brown stood leaning against the fence beside my Mom, his straight, brown hair blowing in the breeze while Mom's curly, black hair never even rustled. He towered over her, taller and leaner than my father. He smiled widely, with his lips parted and his teeth sparkling in the summer sun. I knew not to trust that grin because sometimes Dad smiled with delight but he was only playing a trick on you and he'd explode into anger if you grinned back.

I couldn't tell the difference between Dad's true and fake faces, but Mom and my brother Ev could, so I learned to watch their eyes. If Dad was happy their green eyes lit with the bright green of wild clover, but if Dad only pretended, their eyes darkened to granite green, speckled with black and brown, stone-cold, sad eyes. Today, Mom's eyes glimmered spring-warm, glad eyes. I realized Mr. Brown really was nice and cheerful, so I asked. "What's her name?"

"Trixie," he said with his deep, vibrant voice. He chuckled when she bucked her way around in a tiny circle.

"Like a trick, with an e?"

"No, Mary wanted her name to be spelled like her mother's. Her mother's name is D-i-x-i-e, so we named her T-r-i-x-i-e. She surprised us, because we didn't know that Dixie carried a foal until I saw Trixie following her in the pasture this morning."

My smile grew even bigger. "She's the most beautiful horse in the whole world," I told Mr. Brown.

Mr. Brown and my Mom smiled at each other. I knew that look; the smirk adults used when they thought kids said something foolish. In that moment, I realized they didn't see Trixie's uniqueness; maybe because Mr. Brown leased pastures to people who wanted rough board for their horses. The animals stayed in a mixed herd that varied in size from year to year. To me Trixie's birth in such a setting meant she was extra special, unplanned and unexpected, like finding a four-leaved clover when you never even searched for it. "What do you plan to do with her?"

He shrugged. "We'll wait until she grows up a little bit, and then sell her. We didn't plan on having another horse."

I kept quiet about it, but I decided that somehow I must buy Trixie. Realistically as a child, I had little chance of raising enough money to purchase such a beautiful foal. But Mr. Brown said she needed to grow up some first, so that gave me time to earn money.

My birthday was on June twenty-third. Once in a while, I got money as gifts. This year, I planned on saving it all. Mom gave me money occasionally for helping around the house. Not an allowance like other kids bragged about having, but money for helping with an odd job or a reward for being real good.

Trixie ran around her mother. She turned and circled her again. And as I watched this tiny, delicate creature prance and caper around her dam, an immense, overwhelming feeling, too profound for me to then understand welled up inside me. A belief, a conviction surged to life throughout me. With Trixie and me, together, everything became possible; from the mundane to the unbelievable, from the simple to the inconceivable, from trials to triumphs. I stood transfixed in that moment, knowing that somehow Trixie and I needed to be together and in my head I started to plan.

Dad preferred children to be seen not heard. If both Ev and I silently stayed out of sight, especially when Dad thought, worked, or relaxed. He appreciated it and we might get rewarded.

Over the next few weeks, I really tried to behave properly; when I competed with Ev it became especially difficult. A year and nine months older and much smarter than me, Ev figured out all the games we played faster than me. Occasionally he let me win, but that usually only happened when he got bored and gave up trying. Lots of times I wished to find something, anything that I excelled at better than Ev, but so far it remained undiscovered.

Whenever I felt like stomping off, crying, or screaming because I never managed to win against Ev, I pictured Trixie in my head, playing beside her mother. Her dainty white socks flashing up and down as her tiny hooves danced her around in circles, her fiery coat shining in the sunlight. It calmed me down and reminded me that if I refrained from getting upset, I might get rewarded, and that meant I really did win, by earning money for Trixie. As the days went by, my brother and I got along better. Together, we managed to convince Mom to sometimes let us babysit ourselves when she went to work.

In the weeks preceding my birthday, we watched ourselves five or six times. My brother gave a huge concession by doing so. Normally, our great Aunt Irene babysat us and her son Buddy was Ev's best friend. Ev and I enjoyed going over and playing with Bud, but now I wanted to earn money. When Mom agreed to give us a little money if my brother and I succeeded in not fighting or making a mess while she worked, Ev joined my campaign for earning cash.

Mom always paid us each the exact same amount. That change tempted me so much. She'd place it in my hand and I'd think of penny candy and toys. I'd stand there almost tasting that candy. An image of Trixie running around her mother would pop into my mind and I'd walk down the hall to my room and set the change on top of my bed, arguing with myself in my head, my childish greed for candy duking it out with my overwhelming wish for Trixie.

"Here you go." Ev and I looked at each other's coins. His hand held two quarters. Mine cupped a quarter, two dimes, and Mom placed the last nickel in my outstretched hand.

"Wow!" Ev proclaimed.

"I asked Dad. He said he heard nothing from either of you all afternoon. He didn't even realize you stayed home, the kitchen looks and smells clean, and no games litter the floor." Mom smiled widely.

"Ev made us our afternoon snack. He ate peanut butter on crackers. I had jelly."

Taller and thinner than me with long skinny arms dusted with freckles, Ev had to stretch to his fullest to reach the top cupboard; his eyelids squinted nearly closed barely allowing his eyes darkened to granite green in concentration to show, his arm knocked his thick glasses askew as he strained upwards with his fingers scratching and scrabbling through the shelf contents, searching for the container that felt right. Ev's coordination also made him much better at spreading stuff without leaving drips. He handled utensils and containers better than me. We'd learned to compromise. In trade for Ev doing the girly stuff of preparing snacks, I cleaned up the games we'd played, putting every checker and domino back in their boxes and placing them neatly on Ev's closet shelf.

"You both did very well." Mom said proudly, her whole face smiled as she pulled us each into a hug. Most people called Mom short and a little on the plump side, but both

Ev and I agreed Mom was perfect for hugging. We could reach her without having to stretch every muscle in our bodies and she felt soft and cuddly, not all hard, poky bones like the people who called her plump.

Ev and I raced across the living room, our fingers clasped tight around our precious loot. He, as usual, beat me to the stairs and I followed his thumping sneakers up the treads. Right now, Dad worked out in the garage so we raced without the fear of angering him with our noise. The sunlight shining down through the little square window at the top of the stairs made Ev's dark brown hair glint with red streaks.

Both Dad's hair and beard grew a bright carroty red, not at all like the dark apple red that shined in Ev's hair. But even though Ev's color looked much prettier, he disliked being called a redhead or even told that he had red highlights, so I only teased him about it when I thought he really deserved it.

At the end of the hall, Ev turned left and I went right into my room. I looked at my two piggy banks - well, one piggy bank and one doggy bank. The piggy bank locked closed and opened with a little key. I kept the key on the top of my bureau mirror. I needed to climb to get that key. Savings went into the piggy bank. Mom had taught me about savings. She opened bank accounts for my brother and me and told us when we planned to go to the bank so we could take our piggy banks with us.

I considered my doggy bank. Pushed against my wall, made of white and black molded plastic, he sat on the floor, hiding the big hole in his bottom. I picked him up and shook him when I wanted the money to fall out. He held money for candy and toys, not savings. I looked at the change on the bed. Fifty cents was a lot. Sometimes when Ev and I barely behaved, we only got rewarded a dime each, or fifteen cents.

Fifty cents. I thought about putting twenty-five cents in each bank. Twenty-five cents bought a lot of candy. Some money still remained in doggy bank. While good, candy disappeared so quickly. I looked at the change again. Then I thought of it. I picked up the dimes and put one in each bank. Next I put the quarter in piggy bank and the nickel in doggy bank. The more important thing, Trixie got more. Plus, fifteen cents still bought a lot of candy.

The next morning dawned clear and bright, I laid in bed, stretching under the covers and then I heard banging, echoing down from the garage on the hill as Dad worked. I jumped out of bed and pulled my clothes on as quickly as possible. Today, Mom intended to take us to town, first grocery shopping and then the bank. When I arrived downstairs, Ev already sat at the table. I ran over, shook myself out a bowl of fruit loops, and started eating. Mom had to leave for work by noon, so we needed to hurry into town and get the shopping done quick, or she wouldn't have time to stop at the bank.

I ate fast and brought the bowl to the kitchen where Mom washed the pans from Dad's breakfast. "Are you all set to leave?" I forgot things quite often and frequently ran back into the house to get this or that. To prevent delays, Mom started getting me prepared before herself or Ev.

I ran upstairs and got the piggy bank. He weighed a lot not just because of the change inside him, but because a dark brown metal that shined a bright orangey-red if rubbed hard enough made up his body. I wrapped my hands around his belly. I trotted downstairs and placed him in the back of the car. Then I remembered that I needed his key. Back upstairs, I stood on the edge of my bed and stretched my arms out, leaning over towards the bureau top. With my fingers firmly grasping the sides of the bureau, I pushed off with my toes, wriggling and slithering until I lay belly down on top of the bureau. I stood up with my head now brushing the ceiling and plucked the little key off of the very top bureau shelf. I sat down, leaned over and jumped down to the floor. I stuffed the key firmly down into my pocket and ran to the car.

Sitting in the backseat already buckled in, I remembered my candy change. I could buy a soda to drink while Mom shopped. Once again, I left the car door open and sprinted up the stairs. I grabbed the doggy bank around his neck and shook him hard. Change scattered everywhere. I heard Ev across the hall getting his own bank off his bureau. They were almost ready, so I scrambled around the floor and gathered up the change, squeezing under the bed to get the ones that rolled away the farthest. I trotted down the stairs, double-checking to make sure the piggy key still lay in my pocket. As usual, Ev beat me to the car.

When we first got to the grocery store, I bought a Welch's grape soda. Then I bustled around trying to help Mom hurry up the shopping, but mostly getting in her way. By the time we got to the checkout, Mom alternately bit her lip and wrung her hands while holding her breath and grinding her teeth. Ev and I fished items out of the cart. I dropped about half of mine before they made it to the counter. With a long drawn-out sigh, Mom pointed to the other side of the checkout right by the doors. "You go stand there in my sight and don't move. This won't take long."

I trudged over to the designated spot, dragging my feet. Why was I always the clumsy one? While I stared down at my soda morosely, a hand slid in front of me and a nickel dropped with a plunk and fizz down into my soda. My startled eyes shot up to meet the gaze of an elderly lady. "Why'd you do that?" I asked.

"You're not collecting change?"

"Ah…. No. I' m just waiting for my Mom." I pointed her out at the cashier's counter.

The old lady looked down at my soda. "Well, if you're not collecting money, can I get my nickel back?"

I didn't dare drink my last gulp of soda for fear of choking on the nickel. So the last of the soda drizzled all over my fingers as I upended the can and shook it. But the doggy bank cooperated more than the soda can. No matter how hard or fast I shook the can; the nickel refused to drop out. It just bounced around inside the can, clinging and clanging.

With an exasperated sigh the elderly lady shook her head and tottered off, leaving me with sticky, purple streaked hands to follow Mom and Ev to the car explaining what happened. Both Mom and Ev laughed. On the way to the bank, Ev took the can and tried to get the nickel out for me. After all, I deserved it for losing the last of my soda. But even though Ev managed to do many things better than me, no matter how many different ways he tilted and thumped the can, the nickel refused to drop out.

Mom unlocked piggy for me and we walked into the bank. I ran to the bathroom to wash my sticky hands and then joined Mom and Ev in line, where Mom handed me my change. The teller counted out my three dollars and thirty-five cents, typed it in my book, and then let me pick out a lollipop. So even when I saved the money, I got some candy.

Plus, it remained my money, I could go to the bank and ask for it back. You only used savings for something real special. My brother talked about saving for a motorbike. I saved my money for Trixie. Mom needed to okay what you took out. That worried me a little; she didn't realize Trixie was the best horse in the world. But she admitted that Trixie looked beautiful, so she'd probably let me take out my money for her.

Chapter # 2   **The Value of Money**

I woke up, rolled over, and smiled. Today, on the 23rd of June, I turned ten. Two cards sat on my bureau top, one from Grammy and Grampy Knowlton, and one from Grammy and Grampy McLaughlin. Each came with ten dollars tucked into it. I wrote them each a thank-you letter without Mom telling me to.

Ten whole dollars each. I placed them both in piggy bank. I refused to break a ten dollar bill for candy. Uh-uh. Something that big was extraordinary. That meant I could only use it for something special - Trixie.

I stopped staring at the cards, jumped out of bed, pulled on my favorite jeans and T-shirt, opened my bedroom door and listened. Snoring, I heard snoring. No running, I didn't want to wake Dad up. He severely disliked waking up. If I woke him up, he yelled and swore, cursing so hard and fast that spittle flew from his lips. Sometimes he got so mad, he shook me. Dad got up when he wanted to and I'd learned it was best to leave him alone until after breakfast, even on birthdays. I tiptoed down the hall. The floor held two boards that squeaked. They lay right in front of Mom and Dad's room. I stretched my leg out and stepped over them. I walked slowly down the stairs because they noisily echoed the smallest sound. Once I got downstairs, I ran to the kitchen.

The kitchen smelled like sausage, my favorite. Mom gave Ev and I each a piece, the minute it cooled. I really, really liked it with maple syrup. When Dad was in a good mood, I sometimes even asked him for a piece of his and he'd split one and give me half.

Mom gave me a big hug the minute she saw me. "Happy Birthday! You're up early. Your brother's still asleep. The smell will wake him up."

I nodded as she handed me a sausage. I'd woken up to the smell of breakfast cooking before. Waking up that way started the day off nicely.

Mom baked my cake in the morning. The whole house smelled sweet, dark and rich. I only had to close my eyes and I saw the chocolate cake, moist and inviting me to eat it. Mom served my favorite dinner, macaroni and cheese. In the afternoon, she frosted my cake. I opened my presents. I got two pairs of pants, one green and one red, a red plush long-sleeved shirt as soft as dandelion fluff, and a white tank top trimmed in red with a picture of a seal balancing a ball on his nose. All of the clothes looked as good as new and I realized Mom had spent a lot of time shopping at Goodwill to find ones I liked.

Ev gave me a stuffed dog, not a soft and cuddly toy, but one made out of canvas, tough and strong. I knew instantly why Ev picked him out. Tan and white, he looked like Major, Dad's dog. A German Shepherd/Collie mix, working dog, Major bulged with muscles and had long legs covered with a thick wiry fur. He raced along a wire run in front of Dad's garage, barking and growling at any stranger who came in the yard. But he loved Ev and me and licked us as quickly and eagerly as any soft, cuddly puppy.

I carried my new clothes upstairs and put them carefully away. The stuffed dog lay on top of my pillow, so he could see and guard my whole room and also be close enough to hug. I knew Major's secret, the one Dad never let us tell strangers about. Thunderstorms terrified Major. He whined and cried whenever he heard them in the distance. Bringing him into the house quieted him down and once there, he promptly crawled under the nearest bed and shook so hard that the mattress bounced. He only stopped shaking if Ev or I crawled under the bed and hugged him.

When I went back downstairs, Mom and Dad gave me a card with five dollars in it. Then I got a last present from Ev; two water pistols, a lime green one that looked like a real gun and a pretty lilac purple one shaped like a laser from STAR TREK. Ev and I spent the rest of the afternoon chasing and shooting each other. I let him use the green pistol and retained the pretty one for myself. But the choice backfired on me because my purple gun leaked badly and the green one not at all. I kept running out of water while Ev had loads left to douse me with.

That afternoon, Ev ran out to get the mail and sprinted right back, waving an envelope in the air. "Another card came from Missouri."

"Aunt Connie!" I ripped it open. Inside the card lay a crisp, new five dollar bill.

"A total of thirty bucks! That's more than I've ever got for my birthday," Ev said in awe.

I stared at the card, frozen in shock at receiving so much more money than I'd even dared hope for.

Carl Harris came over after we ate supper. He and his wife Wilma lived one street away from us. He told me to call him Carl not Mr. Harris. Carl never talked to me and Ev or gave us anything in front of Dad. But if Dad wasn't around, he went down on one knee, looked us in the eye, asked how we felt, and patiently listened to all our childhood woes. Then he'd give us each a piece of gum or hard candy before he left. While Carl talked to Dad, I ran outside to play by his car, hoping to see him alone before he left. I wanted to tell him how great my birthday turned out to be.

When he came out, Carl walked up to me, squatted down, reached in his back pocket, pulled out a card, and handed it to me. It contained two dollars.

I gave Carl a hug. "Thank you. I got lots of money this year."

Carl's lips turned up into a wide smile. "How much did you get?"

"Thirty-two dollars," I said proudly.

Carl rocked back on his heels so quickly he almost over-balanced. "Thirty-two dollars could buy a lot of toys." I shook my head. "Why not?"

I leant forward and said quietly. "I'm saving it all."

Carl held perfectly still. "All of it?" I nodded. "What are you saving it for?"

I liked Carl. He never laughed at what I said or put on that adult smirk. I motioned him closer and whispered,

"I'm saving it to buy a horse."

Carl slid his right foot back and rested his knee on the ground, raising his head up a couple of inches so he looked down at me. He hesitated for a minute. "You know you need to have a lot of things to take care of a horse properly."

"Like brushes?" Carl bobbed his head in a quick nod. "There are brushes at the Goodwins Mills Store, back in the corner with the saddles."

Carl leant back, pulled out his wallet and took out another dollar bill. "Let's make a deal. I'll give you this dollar, if you promise to use it and those two to buy some brushes. Then you've got to keep saving your money, because you have to get a horse to use the brushes on."

I grinned and nodded. It made sense to me. I held out my hand and shook Carl's.

"Deal," we both said.

I hugged him again. "Thank you. I'm going to go show Mom." I ran to my mother and showed her the card and my three dollars.

* * * * * * * *

A week later Mom and I went to the bank. I took my thirty dollars with me. Before we entered she asked, "Are you sure you want to put all thirty dollars in the bank? You can only take it back out for something real special."

"Mom, if I save up enough money, would you let me use it to buy Trixie?"

Mom stared at me. Her eyes colored a rich, summer grass green, not stone-cold sad and not her happy clover green either, but somewhere in between. "You want to buy Trixie? Kim, it takes a lot of money to buy a horse. Plus, you need to have the money to take care of the horse. They require hay and grain in the winter."

I swallowed hard. "But if I save up enough, would you let me buy Trixie?"

Mom sat absolutely still for a moment, her dimples disappeared, her green eyes darkened. She closed them, took a slow, deep breath and let it out in a long sigh. I smiled to myself, she always sighed before she gave in. "If you saved up enough money to buy her and take care of her, yes, I'd let you."

I'd need way more than thirty dollars to buy and take care of Trixie. But if I started saving now, I'd raise the cash eventually. "I want to put the whole thirty dollars in the bank." Mom nodded and got out of the car.

*   *   *   *   *   *   *   *   *

On a Tuesday afternoon, two weeks after my birthday, I stood in the back right corner of the Goodwins Mills Store, my favorite part of the store, even better than the shelf of penny candy. I knew this corner inside and out because every time we came to the store I ran here first. Only after my eyes covetously scanned every inch and my heart near overflowed with secret longing did I trot back to the front aisle and its row of penny candy.

High up near the ceiling, two Western saddles stretched spread-eagled and tacked to the wall, their leather carved into intricate interweaving flowers and swirls. One shined a bright, reflective black and the other a deep, rich brown;

between and around them dangled an assortment of beautiful bridles. Below that at finger-tip grazing height hung pegs full of halters, red, blue, green, and yellow.

Three shelves made of rough plywood with splinters sticking out of their edges measured a foot wide and reached out four feet long. The top one held fly repellants, bag balms, liniments, and a box of hoof picks. The middle one barely contained a pile of lead ropes in a variety of lengths and colors. The bottom shelf cradled boxes full of an assortment of brushes.

I pulled out the boxes and rifled through them. Mom stood behind me waiting patiently with a wide smile on her face. I really liked two of the brushes. The oval, red, wooden one with a leather strap stapled to its back to help you hold it bore one inch long, short, hard bristles. The tan plastic one measured eight inches long and three inches wide with grooves in its sides to make it easier to grip. It erupted with three inch long soft, flowing bristles. But they added up to more than three dollars and my doggy bank change remained at home.

"Mom, can I borrow what I need to buy both? I'll pay you back. I'll need this red one with short, coarse hair to get off mud. And this silky one is nice and soft to gently brush Trixie's face." I held up the larger tan one.

Mom unzipped her purse, pulled out her wallet, counted her money, and then nodded. I held the brushes close and rubbed my hand back and forth over the bristles of the soft one. It felt like rubbing my hand over a freshly washed plush blanket, the whispery touch as soft as a kitten's fur.

"Kim, you know you might not earn the money in time to buy Trixie. You might have to wait and buy a different horse," Mom said as we walked towards the front of the store.

I stopped walking. "I don't want another horse. I want Trixie."

Mom leant down and looked me in the eye. Her dimples disappeared as her cheeks dropped, her nostrils narrowed, and her brow creased. "I know you want Trixie, but sometimes we don't get what we want."

I closed my eyes as I realized that lots of times, I didn't get what I wanted. I rubbed my hand slowly over the brush; it felt rougher now. The day no longer felt warm and happy. I remembered once again, the feeling that made my whole chest swell up and my heart thunder, when I first saw Trixie. I couldn't figure out how to explain it to Mom. I didn't just want or need Trixie. We were supposed to, we had to be together; she belonged with me. Determination welled up in me and I opened my eyes and stared back at Mom. "If someone else buys Trixie would they keep her forever?"

"Maybe, maybe not, sometimes people keep horses. Other times they sell them after a couple of years."

I pondered that and a solution popped into my mind. "So if I fall short of enough money to buy Trixie from the Browns, I can buy her later from someone else."

"Maybe you could if they want to sell her, but they might want to keep her. Do you still want to buy the brushes?"

I clutched the brushes close to my chest. They symbolized my hope. They showed that I wouldn't give up until I succeeded. "Yes." Even if the Browns sold Trixie, I could purchase her later. Deep down inside, I sensed the importance of us being together. Partnered we became something special. Somehow, I needed to earn enough money to buy Trixie from whoever had her.

*   *   *   *   *   *   *   *

All that summer, I pestered Mom to let me go visit Trixie. No alarm clock shocked me awake in the dark, no morning rush to get ready for school, no homework, no report cards for Dad to scream over, or school trips for him to complain about, I became totally free. I wanted to spend all my time with Trixie. To just stand at the edge of the fence and watch her made me happy.

When we visited Trixie, Mom drove us down to the Browns' with me fidgeting the whole way. She parked the car in the shade of the big red barn. We rolled down the windows and left the doors open for Ev, who disliked horses, even Trixie. Visiting horses ranked near the top of Ev's lets-not-do-it list and he sat in the car reading a book, refusing to walk down to the fence line with us.

Mom and I walked to the pasture fence. A friendly, curious foal, Trixie quickly gamboled across the field. Her thin, delicate foal body perched incongruously atop her gangly, long legs. When she ran, she reminded me of my young cousin Virginia capering around her house in her father's rain boots with a wide grin splitting her face. They both radiated the pure joy of a youngling imagining that they had grown big.

Trixie accepted the pats and the wisps of grass, we picked for her. She tried to squeeze her head between the strands of barbed wire to get closer to us. Fearing she'd get cut, I quickly thrust my arms between the strands and held her off with my hands. Bending over a little let me look her directly in the eye and she seemed to get taller every day. After staying with us for a little bit, Trixie realized that she stood alone, far away from her mother's protection and she dashed across the pasture to rejoin her. "She didn't squeal, this time, Mom." I announced as the bright summer sun warmed the back of my t-shirt, making my muscles loosen into tranquil relaxation.

"Maybe she's beginning to realize, she doesn't need to always be close to Dixie."

As the summer progressed, time proved Mom right, because day by day Trixie stayed with us longer and longer. Drawing out Ev's torturous sessions of boredom in the car until he trudged down to the pasture fence and begged. "Can we please go home now?"

I dove into whatever chores Mom assigned me around the house to earn money. I even worked some for Dad in the garage, picking tools up, wiping them clean, and sweeping the floor. Even with all the lights brightly burning, the garage felt like a dark place. The air weighed down heavy, musty, and dank with the stink of burnt motor oil, axle grease, and Dad's tobacco smoke over-layed with the acrid tang of welding fumes.

A well-driller, Dad worked with the old rig drilling artesian wells and invested the money he made in building the new rig. He labored to build a pneumatic well-rig, an ingenious concept never seen in Maine before. With no blueprint or model to guide him, using what he'd learned about oil-rigs as inspiration Dad built the new-rig piece-by-piece. He'd been working on it for years. He also did metal fabrication work, repairing farm and yard equipment, or building something totally new for customers. When desperate, he took work as an automobile mechanic.

The whole time I worked in the garage fear gnawed at me, twisting my guts into knots and tightening my chest so that every breath became a struggle. My fingers trembled and my legs quaked.

Because I knew what would happen. If a greasy tool slipped from my grasp to fall with a clatter, if I happened to set a metric wrench mistakenly with the standard ones, if the broom pushed too much dust up into the air, if I sneezed or my shadow fell into Dad's light, he'd pick up the nearest thing to him and hurl it at me. I'd have to dodge and race as quick as my terrified limbs could carry me; out of the garage's grasping heaviness, barrel down the tree shadowed hill, sprint across the rock pebbled driveway, and duck into the relative safety of the house. All the way Dad's thrown curses slapped against me as fast as a downpour and as hard as stones. "Damn idiot! Fucking moron! Absolute imbecile! Stupid useless brat!"

I'd run all the way to my bedroom, find a hiding place, curl up in a ball, and cry. I never did understand why Dad acted so mean. But sometimes if I thought about it hard enough, I figured out what happened to make him get so mad. It took me three times doing it the wrong way to figure out that the wrenches with the mm's(metric) after the numbers, went in a separate place from the ones with the /(standard) in between the numbers. Other times what set Dad off remained a perpetual mystery.

On good days though, I made it all the way through the process without doing anything wrong. On those days, Dad came into lunch and set a quarter or two beside my plate and rewarded me with a gruff, "for the work."

Once while I cleaned, a mechanic friend stopped by to visit Dad. I instantly knew that meant I'd get rewarded. Dad always treated us nicely when other people watched on. That day when I finished sweeping, Dad beckoned me over, handed me a dollar, gave me a hug, ruffled my hair, and proudly said, "Good job! Now go on back to the house with your Momma."

With the tantalizing possibility of fifty cents or maybe even a dollar egging me on, every couple of days I worked up my courage and braved the ordeal of cleaning the garage for Dad.

In pity of my fear and in admiration of my determination, Mom asked the neighbors if they needed any chores done that I could handle. I accepted and did any job offered to me, joyful of finding a way to earn money while avoiding Dad's mercurial rages.

When school started, I looked for Trixie every time the school bus drove by the Browns'. I asked Joanna a girl at school who owned horses. At what age was a horse sold and how much did a horse cost? She told me that most horses got put on the market in the fall before they reached a year old and a grade horse like Trixie usually got purchased for a hundred and seventy five dollars.

Miss Waterhouse, who lived one house up from us, hired me to rake leaves. The job demanded hard work. A couple of feet taller than me, the rake kept whacking me in the ears as I struggled with its wide tines. Within Miss Waterhouse's yard, seven huge maple trees grew and shed their colorful foliage. The leaves lay so thick on the ground that they buried my sneakers with every step.

Worse of all, it rained on the second morning and the leaves got water-soaked. My hands blistered so badly from the first day's labor that Miss Waterhouse brought out a pair of gardening gloves for me to wear. The rain-washed leaves weighed so much that I struggled to pull the rake, sweeping the multitude of sodden, shriveled forms into a pile.

I labored hard, scooping the leaves up into the wheelbarrow by the dripping armfuls. She kept me working at it for three days after school. After the second night, my arms hurt even when I took off my shirt. Pleased with my work, Miss Waterhouse occasionally called with other odd jobs after I finished with the leaves.

Fall came and my bank account held only fifty-six dollars. Every day when the school bus went by the Browns', I looked for Trixie. We traveled down the Buzzell Road and I stared at the big red barn on the hill and searched for the horses in the pasture. My stomach got all queasy and jumpy as my eyes searched for a familiar bay form. Then I'd see her and suddenly anything and everything became possible again. She continued on un-sold, a chance for me to buy her remained.

One chilly, early winter morning, Trixie disappeared. The pasture no longer held her or Dixie. I worried all the way to school, had someone bought them both. Two days later, I spotted Dixie back in the pasture, but Trixie remained missing.

Day after day we drove by the Browns' house and Trixie didn't return. After a week it overcame me, the bus rolled by the Browns' and I searched uselessly for her with no positive results. I burst into tears.

"Why are you crying?" Joanna asked from the seat behind me.

"Trixie's gone." I snuffled and gulped, scrubbing my tears away with my jacket sleeve. I turned to look at Joanna. "I wanted to buy her, but I didn't have enough money saved yet."

Joanna rolled her eyes at me and then shook her head. "There'll be other horses." She turned away from me and began speaking with her friend Angela.

I twisted back forward in my seat and vowed to never speak to Joanna again. She'd acted like she knew and agreed that Trixie was special. But evidently she failed to understand that Trixie occupied a unique place in my heart, irrevocably stamped there, unforgettable and irreplaceable.

That winter trudged by slow and unrelenting for our family.

It started with the furnace. When the cold weather hit and it turned on, it unexpectedly died every couple of days. Requiring Dad to shut off its power every time and re-start it to get it going again. And then after weeks of that, it started rattling. Mom, Ev, and I hardly noticed the tick-tack, tick-tack sound. It infuriated Dad. He obsessively looked for the cause of the rattle and the unexpected shut-downs with no luck in finding them.

Again and again Mom pleaded with Dad, trying to convince him to call a repairman. But Dad proclaimed. "If I can't figure the damn piece of junk out, no one can."

Then to make matters worse, the phone bill came. The phone company installed a phone in the garage at Dad's request so that he no longer needed to walk down to the house to make a call. Unfortunately, he neglected to reckon on how much an extra phone would cost and became furious when the monthly bill went up.

While we ate supper in fearful silence, Dad screamed in rage at the operator on the phone. "My bill doubled this month, without a good reason. I'm not fucking paying this bill, unless you lower it." As Ev and I snuck up to bed, Dad's ice-blue steely eyes stared at the phone as if his gaze alone could bore through it to freeze the operator dead. His face turned a bright, angry red and spittle flew from his lips as he vented his fury.

The next morning, we waited for the school bus standing under the big oak tree in front of the garage. Ev blew clouds of his frozen breath into my face from four feet away. No matter how hard I tried, my billows of fluffy white never got close to him. "It's because you're bigger and older."

Ev shook his head. "Nope, it's 'cause I'm smarter."

A brr... brr... bring noise above my head in the tree diverted me from arguing. I looked up and stood transfixed by what I saw. Hanging from its cord tangled in the tree branches, the garage phone twisted back and forth. With every wind gust, it vibrated harder and emitted a weak brr... brr... bring.

Ev looked up at the phone and his jacket hitched up as his thin shoulders twitched up and then down. "The phone company won't fix that."

After that, it became a monthly ritual. The phone bill arrived and the next morning the phone dangled from the tree. It hung there for about a week until Dad got tired of traipsing down to the house. Then he'd take it down and wire it back into the garage, until the next bill showed up.

After the first couple of times, we got used to it and spent our morning waits counting how many rings the phone gave out before the bus came. But then in late February, we arrived home from school to find a scattered field of dented metal in the house driveway.

The furnace had finally irritated Dad beyond reason. Ev and I easily identified the damage. Dad reverted to the use of his trusty, never-fails, adjustment tool, his thirteen pound sledgehammer. Long ago, I'd learned the only steadfast rule about the mass of steel that Dad called his favorite tool. When he picked it up he always smashed, flattened, or pulverized something. Once the sledgehammer played a part, the furnace stood no chance of survival.

I looked over at Ev. "It lasted for over four months before he killed it."

Ev's forehead crinkled into his I'm thinking face. "Maybe Dad's learning patience."

Chapter # 3   Happy Easter!

I got up real early on Easter morning in 1980. Because Mom told me, I'd get a surprise that I really liked for doing so. We sometimes attended our churches' sunrise service. I thought Mom meant that as the surprise. Because while I disliked getting up early, I really enjoyed watching the sunrise and we seldom got to see it, because we lived in the woods.

But when I went downstairs, Dad stood leaning against the kitchen counter watching Mom sweep the floor. I knew from the way that Dad's hair lay smooth and flat under his baseball cap that he'd combed it instead of letting it stick out in all directions like usual. He'd also trimmed his beard down to about an inch in length. He wore his normal Dickie's pants.

Dad only wore the "old style" of Dickie's pants. I learned this when I spent a whole day with Mom going through over a dozen stores to find him new ones when the old ones wore out. Dad rejected both the painter style with the extra pockets to put brushes in and the carpenter style with the loop to hang a hammer in. Dad required the pants to have four pockets and five belt loops. He refused to wear anything else, threatening to go naked, if Mom didn't find him 'his proper pants' when Mom tried to get him to switch to the new easier to acquire styles.

But today, Dad didn't wear his normal grease-stained T-shirt. He sported the special dress shirt that he wore when we took Grammy and Grampy McLaughlin out to dinner. I realized that meant our day included Dad but not sunrise service, because Dad never went to church.

I sat down on the couch and pretended to watch Mom but really kept glancing at Dad. He didn't seem mad or upset. I wondered what motivated him to put on his fancy shirt. He ran his right hand through his beard over and over, feeling its new shape with his fingertips.

At five foot nine, Dad stood shorter than my male teachers and my friends' fathers. He wasn't a huge man, although the muscles in his chest, shoulders, and arms rippled every time he moved. Even standing quiet and still as he did at that very moment, he reminded me of a powerful race car idling; the thrump-thrump-thrump of its engine warning everyone that it simply waited for an occasion to squeal its tires and make some noise. Dad lived and breathed like that ever ready to explode into action.

Mom looked up, saw me, and put away the broom.

"Okay, let's go." Dad said. I got up and followed them to the car. Dad drove. When we turned up the Brown's driveway, my heart started pounding faster and faster. Could it be?

As soon as the car stopped, I jumped out.

Trixie stood, shining like a copper penny in the sunlight.

Woody Brown held the lead rope on her as she danced circles around him. She'd grown six inches since I'd last seen her. Now, I needed to tilt my head back to look her in the eye. At her shoulder she stood an inch or two taller than me, but her gracefully arched neck held her head high above mine. Woody switched the lead rope from one hand to the other as she whirled around him.

All the breath in me came out on one word, as I dashed forward.

"Trixie!" Mom grabbed me by the shoulder and held me back.

"You need to stay away unless she calms down and holds still."

I squirmed under Mom's hand, urgent to get free. Mom tightened her grasp. "She's nervous and might hurt you without meaning to."

"I... I thought you sold her," I said to Mr. Brown. "She wasn't in the pasture."

Mr. Brown chuckled. "Nobody wanted to buy her." He spun about, preventing the rope from winding around him and started trading the rope from hand to hand again. Trixie continued circling. "We put her in the back pasture behind the house to wean her from Dixie. She stayed out of sight back there," he added. "Are you sure, absolutely sure, you want this horse?"

All of the air rushed out of me. Unable to speak, I nodded so hard my teeth clacked together. Worried he wouldn't see me; I croaked. "Yes!"

He smiled at me. "Okay, she's yours."

"Really?" I asked breathless. "But I only saved up seventy-two dollars."

"Really. She's a gift, keep your money. Trixie belongs to you now. She can stay here in the summer, free for two years. We'll also give you winter hay for two years, but you have to take her home for the winter. Plus, you've got to help put the hay in."

"Yes! Yes! Yes!" My throat clogged up as I realized my hugest wish was coming true. Mom rubbed my shoulders, slowly back and forth, just like she did when she hugged me, smoothing the tension away. Unobtrusively, not wanting anyone to notice, I pulled my arms in tight around my ribs and pinched myself. Nothing changed. Suddenly, my lungs worked normally again.

"I'm going to put Trixie back in the pasture." Mr. Brown said as he led her off. "She isn't used to having this many people around or being taken out so early."

Once Trixie left my sight, I peered at Mom, wide-eyed and hesitant. When could we come see her again? Mom saw the naked yearning in my eyes and answered it.

"We'll come down and see her this afternoon. But she stays in the pasture because she's had enough excitement today already."

The mornings chilly air spilled into my mouth as my face cracked open in a wide grin. "Mom, what about grain? You said horses need hay and grain. Can we take out some of my money to buy grain?"

"We can do that. We'll go to the feed store tomorrow." I craned my head in the direction Trixie went and watched Mr. Brown leading her through the pasture gate beyond the trees. When he unhooked her lead rope, Trixie stood there for a moment, shining brilliantly against the background of young green grass. Then with a snort and a toss of her head, she whirled and raced off to join the other horses. I watched her every stride possessively as she galloped away. Mine. Trixie was mine. I felt like the luckiest kid in the whole world.

*   *   *   *   *   *   *   *

By May of 1980, Mom established a routine with Ev and me. We went to see Trixie every other day. No matter how much I pestered Mom, it remained every *other* day. She explained to me that it wasn't fair to always do what I wanted. Since my brother disliked going to see Trixie. Every other day offered the only way to reach a fair compromise.

It'd be mean to make Ev sit in the car every day waiting for us. Then I got an idea. "Mom, can I go to see Trixie by myself?"

Mom thought about it. "Kim, you can't take Trixie out by yourself. The other horses crowd the gate. You need two people to get her out. Plus, she still pulls too much for you to lead her by yourself."

I nodded as my shoulders slumped forward. Trixie loved to come out. She relished the attention of being brushed and talked to. Occasionally when you tried to set a brush down, she twisted her back legs around and stood over the brush box so you couldn't put them away.

Trixie enjoyed being cared for so much; sometimes she wanted to stay with us instead of going back to join the other horses. She walked slower and slower until her hooves scuffed furrows in the dirt when we tried to lead her back to the pasture. She leant back against the lead rope.

Her head crept up higher and higher, as her rump sank lower and lower. Mom and I talked to her, and patted her, and told her it was all right. Sometimes it took quite a while to get Trixie back in the pasture. I think it amused Mr. Brown. He said he knew plenty of horses who dragged their feet coming out of a pasture, but Trixie was the only one who dragged her feet going back in.

But when Trixie got told to stop, she kept right on going. Plus, sometimes she pulled me where she wanted to go. When she pulled, Mom helped to control her, because Trixie's strength outstripped mine by a huge margin.

"What if I leave her in the pasture?" I pleaded. "Sometimes she stays in the paddock beside the barn all by herself. If I closed that gate, it would keep the other horses out, allowing me to brush her in there."

Mom continued to wash the counter. Her hand slowed until it barely moved at all as she considered my suggestion. She turned her head to glance at me and I froze in place, trying to hold her gaze. If I got Trixie by herself, away from the other horses, it'd be easy to brush her.

"Okay, but you only get to go to see Trixie if you behave and you only get to go into the pasture if she is alone. Don't try to get in the pasture with the other horses there. You don't know what they will do. And you close that gate right off."

I agreed with her rules. Sometimes the other horses pushed me around, unaware of their strength and more interested in possibly escaping the confines of the pasture than worried about my getting in the way. Plus, Dixie always bit and kicked Trixie, her own foal. I knew as Trixie's mom, I should like her, but sometimes she acted so mean to Trixie; I disliked her fervently. I looked at my mother.

"I've been good today, right?" I smiled widely, showing off all my teeth and trying to appear innocent of any and all wrongdoing, both imagined and real.

She laughed. "Other than being a pest, yes. I plan on going to the store. Are you sure you don't want to wait 'til after?"

I knew Mom meant Goodwins Mills Store and that imparted a real special treat. When you walked into it, you instantly knew it'd stood there for a long time. Every grain of wood in the worn floorboards made its own little ridge and in the summer when you knelt on them in shorts your legs became imprinted with dozens of wavy lines. Your first inhalation brought the scents of apples, cigarette smoke, and ham into your lungs. The light bulbs on the ceiling hung far apart, so bright circles marked the aisles then shaded gradually to dark before you reached another circle of light. The most popular aisle stood in the very front of the store. The topmost shelf contained the cigarettes and tobaccos. The next two down cradled the bagged chips and pretzels.

The bottom shelf held a long line of plastic containers and usually at least one kid dug through them, because those canisters contained a treasure trove. They overflowed with penny candies of every sort, Tootsie rolls, Mary Jane's, Bits of Honey, taffies, caramels, and every other kind of candy imaginable.

The hardest decision became what to get because so many options existed. Mom watched on waiting patiently while you picked out what you wanted. "I'll go see Trixie.

Ev going to the store alone with you will make up for all the times he sat in the car while we took care of Trixie." Ev really did deserve a treat. He never complained to me even once or tried at all to get back at me for the time he spent alone in the car, while I cared for Trixie. I headed for the door.

"You be careful, riding your bike. Watch for cars! Make sure there are no other horses in the pasture!"

I ran out before she changed her mind. I rode my bike as fast as possible down to the Browns. I saw no horses in the pasture beside the barn, not even Trixie. I pedaled up the driveway looking in the other pasture for Trixie. Where was she? Then when I arrived at the top of the driveway, a familiar beautiful head, leaned out the barn door.

Trixie stood inside the barn in the shade. I sprinted into the shadowy interior, the light spilling in from the open main door, dimly lit even the furthest corners. The smell of hay, tractor grease, and dust filled my lungs as I checked to make sure no other horses accompanied Trixie inside. She stood alone. I trotted through the pastures ankle-high, shorn grass, stumbling over hidden clumps of dirt, down the slight slope to the gate and swung it closed as it squeaked and groaned in protest.

Trixie came out of the barn, hesitantly followed me for a few feet, and then stopped and watched me trip along. She stood frozen in place with her ears twitching back and forth at the gate's noise making. I walked up to her.

"It's okay beautiful. I get to visit you by myself today." I patted Trixie's neck with long gentle strokes. Trixie turned and followed me back into the barns cool interior.

"You stay right here and wait for me." I ducked through

the slats and went to the tack room, talking as I went.

"How did you get all dusty? Have you been rolling?" When I returned, Trixie stood with her neck propped up and over the wooden boards watching me. I carried the brushes into the middle of the stall.

"Move over here, so I can brush both sides of you, girl." The moment I picked a brush up in my hand, Trixie ambled over, stopped when the bristles touched her hide, and gently leaned into the brush.

I laughed quietly, not wanting to scare her. "I promise I'll do a really good job. You'll sparkle when I get done." It took a long time to brush Trixie's mane and tail, which flowed down in long, thick cascades.

Mr. Brown told me that the luxurious, thick mane came from Trixie's father, a purebred Tennessee Walker. I never met him. Mr. Brown said that he'd been a yearling that only stayed in the pasture for a little while.

I so enjoyed those days when I got to go down to see Trixie by myself. I'd jump on my bike and coast down the driveway, listening for anything on the blind corner beyond the drive. At the bottom I nearly stopped; to stand on my pedals and look left up the hill for traffic. If none came, I pedaled hard down to the first corner, then folded myself up as low as possible, coasting fast down the hill with the air whistling in my ears and my hair flying back, tugging on my scalp. I always stopped at the intersection with Waterhouse Road, but after that, I pedaled fast, coasted, pedaled, coasted. Next, I turned into the Browns' driveway and pedaled hard up their small hill, making my own miniature rooster tail with the dust flying up from my wheels, all the time looking to see if Trixie stood alone in the pasture. If she did I dropped my bike over next to the barn and sprinted down to close the gate without stopping to catch my breath.

Then panting, with my beautiful girl watching my every move, I retrieved her brushes and carried them out into the pasture. She always remained perfectly still and let me brush and rub her. I used a cloth to wipe her down. When I finished, her bay coat shined a coppery red with golden highlights in the sunlight. As I brushed her, she nodded off to sleep. Before I left, I said goodbye and she'd open one eye, look at me, and then slowly close it, giving me a slow-motion, sleepy wink. As time passed, she got a little better at being led. She still pulled sometimes and windy days seemed to be the worst.

*   *   *   *   *   *   *   *

Mom let me go down to see Trixie by myself quite often in the summer of 1980. If she grazed with the other horses, I lay down spread-eagled in the grass on the edge of the Brown's lawn and watched her for hours. Once, I stayed so long, arriving in the morning and staying through to the late afternoon, that Mr. Brown's mother came out to see me. She made me a cucumber sandwich and gave me some cookies and a big glass of ice cold water.

One day, I tied Trixie to a post to brush her, not realizing that Dixie stood nearby, behind some bushes in the pasture. Dixie trotted over and nipped at her daughter. Trixie pulled the rope knot so tight that I had to ask Mr. Brown to untie it for me. When Mom heard, she made me promise to make sure, by counting the horses, that none hid in the pasture out of my line of vision.

Another day, Mom took me down to the Brown's to take Trixie out of the pasture, she told me to call Trixie. At first I wasn't sure what to call out, but then I thought of the perfect call.

"Trixie girl! Come on, beautiful!" Trixie's head snapped up out of the grass. She sprinted across the pasture, darting around the other horses. We quickly snapped on her lead rope, opened the gate, and led her out. Closing the gate behind us before the other horses meandering towards it took the opportunity to escape. Then we stopped and lavished Trixie with attention.

"You're such a good girl, Trixie." I praised her as I ran my hands all over her head and neck, smoothing her forelock and mane into an attractive sweep.

Before half the summer sped by, Trixie came running every time I called. Some days she already stood waiting at the gate for us. Mom told me Trixie heard our car and knew it was us, when we drove up the driveway.

When it came time to start haying, Mom, Ev, and I helped Mr. Brown bring in the hay. Ev and I tried to drag the hay bales closer to the wagon, so Mom wouldn't have to walk so far. Sometimes we succeeded. Other times, we pulled the strings off the bale. Mr. Brown never got mad. Instead, he showed Ev and me how to roll the bales.

We lined up facing each other with the bale lying lengthwise between us. Ev took the right side of the bale and I took the left. We flipped the bale over a couple of times, building up momentum and then we got behind it and kept pushing on the upward side. Flip, flip, flip all the way up to the wagon. Mom lifted the bale onto the wagon, and Mr. Brown stacked them. The work dragged on through the heat of the day, exhausting us.

The sun beat down on us, unrelenting in its full unclouded power. We learned to wear light colored t-shirts, because the dark ones got so hot from the sun's rays, they felt like they scorched permanently into your shoulders and back. Mom always brought plenty of Kool-Aid in the car for when we got thirsty.

In July, I joined an all-girl 4-H group. Everyone owned a horse and we specialized in just horse stuff and called ourselves the Riverdale Riders. I learned many things relating to horses that I previously knew nothing about. Mrs. Allen and Mrs. Hussey ran the group. Jane Allen gave riding lessons to earn money and she didn't mind answering my numerous questions. Overjoyed to have an experienced horsewoman to advise me, I queried Jane about hoof care, fly repellants, grain portions, and everything else horse-related that popped into my mind. A truly generous person, Jane never grew impatient with my relentless inquiries.

Summer, as always, went by too quickly. When school started back up, Dad took most of my money out of the bank to make the old garage into a barn for Trixie. Then in the last week of September, the time arrived to bring Trixie home for the winter.

Chapter # 4   The Benefit of Going in Circles

The day we planned to bring Trixie home. The wind blew in strong blasts, rattling tree branches and howling across the fields. Dad drove Mom and me down to the Brown's to drop us off and bring the car back home. When we took Trixie out of the pasture, she pulled Mom around. Every time the wind gusted, Trixie went in a different direction.

Dad stood in the middle of the driveway with his arms crossed and his eyes narrowed. Glaring as Trixie sidestepped to the left and then the right, tugging Mom along with her. His left hand tilted his baseball cap back and he ran his right hand through his hair. Then he tugged the cap down hard on his head, pulled his shoulders back, and stepped forward with his right hand outstretched.

"She pulls too strongly for you to handle her. I'll lead her home." Dad walked over and grabbed the lead rope out of Mom's hands. He looped the end of the rope around his left hand and gripped the halters chin strap tightly in his right hand. With a jerk, he flexed his arm and pulled

Trixie's head in snug to his side.

"I'll go with you Dad," I volunteered. I noticed Trixie rolling her eyes away from Dad and tilting her head to the side, trying futilely to loosen his tight grip on her. The wind scared her and Dad's tight clasp worsened the fear.

"No, you go home with Mom. I'll handle Trixie." Dad said as he pulled her forward into a walk.

I didn't want to get in the car. The way Trixie kept looking at Mom and me and edging her body sideways towards us as Dad pulled her away showed me that she wanted to be with us, not Dad.

"Get in the car, Kim." Mom locked her eyes on mine and jerked her head towards the passenger side of the car.

"But Mom…." My gaze swung free of hers and zeroed in on Trixie, as Dad led her down the driveway. Dad walked on the gravel. But Trixie's neck twisted sideways with her head still firmly grasped by Dad and her body pulled away with all four hooves scuffing across the Brown's lawn. I swallowed the lump rising up in my throat.

Mom re-captured my gaze. Her eyes flicked to the passenger seat. "Now."

My sneakers left furrows in the Brown's driveway as I trudged unwillingly to the car. Only a short car-ride home loomed ahead of me, but I felt as if I was being forced to embark on a journey that I desperately wanted to avoid.

"Trixie isn't used to Dad. She's scared and he doesn't know how to calm her down. I should go with them."

"Your father said no. That's the end of the discussion." Mom started the car and drove us home. Then we waited. The Browns' house stood not even a mile from ours. It seemed to take a long time.

"Stop pulling!" We finally heard Dad yelling, his voice hoarse and anger-filled. "I said to stop, stupid! Stop, you fucking dumb horse!" The yelling got louder. I realized Dad must be screaming at full volume.

"They sound pretty close. Don't they?" I looked at Mom, hoping she'd agree with me.

Mom quirked her eyebrow up and I understood what she meant. The volume of Dad's voice echoing off the trees had no connection to his actual distance, but instead related to the level of his anger. The screaming and swearing got louder and louder. We saw them come around the corner. Trixie walked nearly sideways, trying to pull away from Dad. He held the halters chin strap in a clenched fist and every time he yelled at her, he punched her in the neck with his left arm. WHACK! "I said, stop fucking pulling! You have to be the dumbest fricking horse ever born!"

Trixie's eyes wheeled wildly, darting from side to side. Her ears swiveled around. Unfamiliar with being yelled at, and never hit before in her life, Trixie's muscles trembled under his blows. Her nostrils flared widely. And her sides heaved with every breath.

Anger swelled up in me. He was hurting my girl. I took a step forward and a deep breath to tell Dad to stop yelling at Trixie and hitting her. Mom put her hand on my shoulder, grasping me firmly. My eyes swung to hers and she shook her head.

"But Mom, he's hurting her." I ground out between my teeth. Mom shook her head again and squeezed my shoulder harder.

I sighed in resignation. Mom understood Dad well. Once he started yelling and swearing, nothing made him stop. If anyone said anything to him or tried to stop him he just got madder. He'd just hit Trixie more, if I said anything. Trixie saw Mom and me and she pulled Dad right across the street to us.

He screamed in her ear, "Stupid damn horse! What if a car drove by? Stop pulling, you fucking dummy!" WHACK!

Mom tugged on my shoulder and started backing towards the barn, with Trixie pulling Dad right in after us. She went into the stall and tried to walk straight out into the paddock. He forced her back, his feet scrabbling for purchase as he tried to hold her still.

"Just let her go, Evans," Mom said. But he refused to listen. Trixie gave a snort and charged forward. The door opening measured too narrow for them both to pass through. She made it. He hit the wall with a loud thump, but stubbornly held firmly onto the halter, his knuckles bleached ivory white from the tightness of his grip.

I stood frozen in place by my inner turmoil. I wanted my father to remain unharmed, but I felt like cheering Trixie on. I believed she deserved to be rewarded for the courage she showed in demanding Dad let her go. Even though he scared her, she bravely fought for her freedom.

"Let go, Evans," Mom near hollered. Dad swore and yelled, so loud he didn't hear her. Trixie backed up and ran for the door again; he hit the wall a second time. Trixie shook her neck angrily, her mane tossing up into the air. She pawed the ground, then backed up for another try and darted forward. Dad swore and finally let go of the halter.

Trixie ran out into the paddock and wheeled around, glaring at my father with her ears pinned back. She looked real mean.

"Stupid horse!" Dad yelled one last time. He stomped out of the stall and threw the lead rope on the ground as he headed up to the garage, swearing as he went.

Mom showed me how to close the stall by sliding the three boards across and putting them in their grooves.

"How about you stay out here and talk to Trixie until suppertime. Stay out of the paddock. She's scared and confused. Just talk to her and see if you can calm her down." I remained with Trixie talking to her, until suppertime. She continued to be jumpy all evening. Deep into the night, I heard the sound of hoof beats trotting about interspersed with an occasional snort of alarm.

Trixie paced nervously around the edges of the paddock for a couple of days, carving a path down into the dirt. She skittishly darted back and forth every time the wind gusted through the large oak that overhung the fence line.

Mom decided not to take Trixie out so I brushed her in the paddock. She wouldn't let me touch her face and shied away when I brushed her neck. I knew from my 4-H classes, that my silly, filly was now head shy from Dad hitting her.

As I brushed my girl lovingly every day, I talked to her gently, running my hands tenderly all over her back, sides, and legs. Jane Allen had told me that training abused horses took time and patience. Dad had abused Trixie and that made me very mad at him. But it also made me more determined to give her everything she needed to regain her trust. My Dad had hurt her, but I'd make it better.

*   *   *   *   *   *   *   *

Mom hired Charlie Hussey to work with Trixie and me in the spring of '81. She paid for him out of her own part-time job money. Charlie looked closer to my grandfather's age than Dad's. His shoulders slouched over slightly, his belly hung down over his belt, and his pants draped loosely on his skinny legs. He wore a red baseball cap, smoked cigarettes, and habitually rubbed his chin in thought.

Charlie decided that teaching me to lunge Trixie would be the best way for her to learn word commands. We used the bottom of the garage driveway as our training area. The thirty foot, sparsely graveled area that served as a staging area for the well rig was the closest thing to a flat spot on the property.

Charlie asked me to stand beside him as he put Trixie on a really long lead rope so she could circle around us. He slowly fed the rope out, letting the circle get bigger and bigger. He held an eight foot long whip with a dangling six foot braided leather tip, but he never hit her with it. He slapped it on the ground behind her to keep her going, showing me how Trixie responded to it.

Trixie held her head high, flashing her hooves quickly up and down as she paraded around us. I smiled to myself, as I realized that she was showing off. The closer the whip got to her, the faster she went. Even now in the midst of her growth spurt with her rear quarters taller than her front ones, my beautiful girl managed to look elegant as she trotted around and around. Her mane and tail flowed back. Her ears pointed forward and her neck arched proudly as she pranced about. When Charlie pulled the whip back away from her, she slowed down to a walk.

"Yup, she's a smart one. She catches on quickly and works willingly. She just doesn't know what you want her to do." Charlie handed me the whip.

"Now, you take control of the whip. Bring it closer to her rear end and say 'Trot!' when she speeds up into one." I did as he said. Trixie trotted for three circuits as Charlie rubbed his stubble beard and I struggled to keep the whip in the right position.

"To slow her back down to a walk, you back off the whip. Let her trot away from it until it points about ten feet behind her. When she slows down to a walk, you say 'Walk!'" I followed his instructions and smiled widely as my beautiful girl slowed to a walk.

"Lunge her every day and in a week or so, she'll understand what 'walk' and 'trot' mean."

"How do I get her to stop?"

"You do this. Let go of it and drop the whip on the ground." Charlie said. When I did, he gave a tug on the lead rope. Trixie turned towards us, walked a couple of steps, and stopped just as Charlie said "Whoa!" Charlie smiled widely and I got a glimpse of his yellowed teeth.

"Yup, she's real smart. Now, you stand beside me." Charlie handed me the lead rope, showed me how to position it in my hand, and bobbed his head.

"Go on now. You can do it. Say the words like you mean them and speak them right after she does what you want. You work at it every day. In next to no time, she'll respond to the words not the whip."

Charlie made it look easy. I, on the other hand, struggled with the constantly tangling rope, the tip heavy whip, and continually tripped myself up as I turned around and round in the same spot. He stayed for an hour. By the end of it, I managed to get Trixie to walk, trot, and whoa. She responded to the whip not the words.

I worked with my girl every day, as long as the weather held clear. Charlie came over once every couple of weeks. Sometimes he smelled funny and showed up at the wrong time or even on the wrong day. None of that mattered to me. I really liked Charlie and looked forward to him showing up. He always praised Trixie and showed me something new; like how to get her to switch directions, how to get her to back up, or lower her head so I could put her halter on by myself.

Then one day, Charlie said we no longer needed his help. "You'll do fine. She knows how to walk, trot, canter, and whoa to word commands. She picks up her feet for you to clean, and lowers her head for the halter. If you need help when it comes time to ride her, you get your Mom to call me."

Charlie left and my mind got stuck on one thing: riding Trixie!

I never thought of it much before. I always enjoyed myself just being with Trixie. Riding her, could only be better. A horse needed to be at least two years old before they carried a rider's weight. While Trixie was nearing her second birthday, both she and I needed to learn a lot before we could safely have our first ride. And I knew everything must go right, because if anything went wrong Mom wouldn't let me back on Trixie for years.

I brushed Trixie down and gave her some attention. She now let me brush her face again. Happily, she no longer pulled anymore; Dad wouldn't have to lead her again. She still pinned her ears back, whenever Dad walked by the paddock. I doubted if she'd ever like or trust him.

*   *   *   *   *   *   *   *

For Christmas, Mom had given me a new halter for Trixie and some riding lessons from Jane Allen. In April of '81, it warmed up enough for me to take the lessons. I rode an Appaloosa named Eagle and part of the lesson was to catch, saddle, and bridle her.

The main pasture always had at least four or five horses in it, happily grazing away. It covered a hill and gully across the road from the training paddock and barn.

On the side of the road by the pasture gate I stopped and called. A car drove by and I smelt the oily, burnt-wood fragrance of a leaking engine gasket. I exhaled hard a couple of times as I opened the pasture gate, hoping to clear the stink from my nostrils.

No horses stood in sight on the hill top. I walked over to the solitary, scraggly, aged and drooping apple tree that crowned the crest of the hill. The sweet, smell of its newly unfurled leaves flushed the oil stink from my nose. I stopped under its dapple shade and turned in a slow circle, looking for the horses. I spotted them at the bottom of the hill, grazing beside some young poplars. The land lay low down there, prone to flooding in heavy rain. Because of that the grass grew lush and thick, much to the horses delight. Amongst the bay and black coats Eagle's white hide glimmered like a beacon.

"Eagle, come on girl."

Eagle continued to graze. She declined to leave her

succulent spring feast for an unknown person who might not gift her with a rewarding treat.

"Eagle, come on. Please. I've got an apple for you in the barn." I pleaded. Eagle remained unmoved.

Short cropped grass covered the top of the hill. But as I plodded down the hillside, the myriad weeds and brambles soaked my pants through to mid-thigh by the time I reached the poplars.

Jane's Morgan mare Silkie grazed closest to me. Her head popped up out of the grass and her eyes darted to the dangling lead rope in my hand. A highly intelligent, beautiful black with elegant white markings, Silkie earned her keep as a show and breeding animal. She need not deal with amateurs like me and she knew it. With a snort for my so rude interruption, she turned and trotted off. All of the other horses except for Eagle followed her.

Jane used Eagle as her lesson horse for beginner and intermediate riders because of her gentle, forgiving nature and her rock-solid training. Eagle trained the riders as much as Jane did. Leaving the pasture voluntarily went above and beyond the call of duty, something Eagle abstained from doing. She gobbled up the thick grass in quick bites until I got the lead rope snapped on to her halter. Then with just one last snip of her teeth to the succulent green, she raised her head and followed me up the hill.

Very thorough in their training, Jane and Eagle put me through a series of pre-riding tests. Not all horses lowered their heads as Charlie had helped train Trixie to do. Jane trained Eagle not to lower hers. Learning how to adapt became my first lesson.

"Most horses stand above fifteen and a half hands, Kim.

If you only grow to your mother's height, you'll need to know how to bridle and saddle horses that stand higher than your arm's reach." Jane explained as she passed me a milk crate.

As I stood on it, stretching to my fullest height to get the headstall over Eagle's ears, Jane continued. "You're too new to this to try to saddle a horse that refuses to stand still. But before I finish with you, you'll learn to."

Tottering on my toe-tips as the leather finally, thankfully slid behind Eagle's ears, I realized that riding lessons were not going to be the fun and games that I imagined them as. I needed to learn a lot about riding and quite a bit of it happened on the ground instead of on the horses back.

Luckily, Jane patiently explained things. Eagle kindly ignored some of my mistakes and stoically endured the others. Jane recommended getting Trixie used to a saddle and bridle months before I attempted to ride her. She suggested lunging her with the saddle on to get her used to wearing it. She sold Mom a used youth saddle for thirty-five dollars, so that I could start training her.

We brought Trixie back down to the Browns' on April 15. Mom led her and she hardly pulled at all. In her excitement, she kept prancing like a parade horse. When we let her out into the pasture, she immediately ran straight up to her mother, whickering softly. Dixie turned around and kicked her. Even though, she followed her mother around all day nickering softly while opening and closing her mouth with her lips smacking together looking like she was mouthing "mama-mama", whenever she got too close, Dixie bit or kicked her.

In normal horse behavior, a dam chased their yearling

foal away from their side to earn its own spot in the herd. Her instincts urged Dixie to tell Trixie in impossible to ignore horse language. "Take care of yourself." I knew Dixie was only following nature's laws, but I couldn't help but dislike her for doing it.

It took weeks of laying the saddle on the ground next to Trixie before she stood calmly beside it. Then I got her used to the smell of the saddle by lifting it up and letting her sniff it all over. Trixie ran her nose across the suede seat, inhaling and exhaling deeply, pulling in the dark, loamy scent of the aged leather overlaid with the tang of glycerin. She nipped the saddle leaving a small scar beside the pommel and then made a funny face. Her nose curled up and twisted to the right, her left eye squinted near closed while the right hitched up, and then she let out a huge sneeze. She followed that with shaking her head vigorously with her ears flopping loosely about. I took the perform-ance as a sign that saddles tasted bad.

After a week of attempts to lick, taste, and spit out the saddle blanket, she let me rub it on her neck and lay it on her back. I brushed her with the blanket lying over her body, so she got used to it staying on. Finally, she accepted it.

The first few times, I lifted the saddle onto Trixie's back she sidestepped right out from under it. Two weeks later, she began to allow it to stay on. I took the process slowly because I knew we continued to make good progress. Plus, Jane said training slowly and thoroughly increased the horses trust in the trainer which helped prevent injuries if anything ever went wrong. My biggest fear for our future involved one of us getting hurt, because that'd bring out

Mom's protective side and she'd restrict my freedom with Trixie as a result.

Eventually, Trixie learned that enduring the presence of the saddle and blanket brought her no pain. She felt no fear of them. This counted as a great accomplishment for both of us because sometimes a horse's instinctual response to remove an object from its back before it bit or clawed them eroded their training and made them hard to handle under saddle.

Currently, Jane worked at re-training a horse with severe saddle fear. I watched one session where Jane spent hours simply putting on and removing the tack again and again while patting and talking gently to the horse until saddling no longer induced eye-rolling, muscle quivering, side-heaving terror. Jane followed that routine with weeks of lunging the horse with the saddle on while constantly praising it before she ever rode the horse. Overcoming that horse's saddle fear allowed it to think instead of instinctively react and it became a fine riding animal.

To learn that a saddle meant her no harm from the very beginning and building slowly on that meant Trixie and I dodged a lot of problems that might crop up later on in her training.

*   *   *   *   *   *   *   *

Near the end of the school year in '81, Mom picked me up early one day from school. She said Trixie got spooked in the night and went through the barbed wire fence in the Brown's pasture. The vet stitched her up and said she needed to take it easy for quite a while. They trailered her to the vet's and then home. She needed to stay in the small corral at home, until she healed up.

The ride home from school only took about five minutes. I worried every second of the way. How badly was Trixie hurt? Was she in pain? Would she heal up okay?

I jumped out of the car the moment it stopped and raced out to the paddock. My girl stood out in the open, soaking up the afternoon sun. I ducked under the fence and rushed to her side.

"Beautiful, are you all right?" I ran my hands over her as I examined her. I carefully traced the stitches on her upper right front leg.

"Oh Trixie, you silly girl." I took a deep breath and exhaled it slowly when I realized only one wound cut her deep enough to require stitches. Fortunately, it went into the muscle avoiding her tendons and ligaments that I'd learned about just last month in 4-H. If one of them happened to get severed, it crippled the horse for life.

"You're a lucky silly filly." I leant closer to her and rubbed behind her ears. She lowered her head and tilted it towards me to induce me to keep scratching. Her shoulders and mine met up at the same height, making us a perfect fit for each other. When both of us, tired of the scratching, I lay my arm over her back. She leant lightly into me and I into her. We stood there held up, comforted, and supported by each other.

The balmy afternoon sun shined down on us, seeping into our muscles and bones, loosening, relaxing, and melding us together. We inhaled the scents of loamy sun-dried mud, the rich heaviness of Miss Waterhouse's freshly mown lawn, and the hint of oil seeping from the old well-rig parked beside the paddock. We breathed in and out at the same time. Two separate beings sharing the moment, the air and sun, and each other.

Two weeks later, Trixie returned to normal. At her last check-up, the vet said she inherited her growth pattern from her Tennessee Walker blood because of its slow progression. While the vet only expected her to gain another inch or two at most, her bones hadn't fully matured yet and therefore could incur damage easily. He recommended that we wait until next spring to ride her.

Mom happily agreed, because she wanted me to be older when I first rode Trixie.

Disappointment welled up in me. My riding lessons with Jane revealed to me how fun it was to ride a horse. I knew riding my silly filly would far surpass riding Eagle, because Trixie belonged to me.

I looked forward to riding away from it all, but my girl wasn't ready yet. Riding her before she finished growing might warp and weaken her bones, making her prone to injury. I never wanted to hurt my girl.

Next spring wasn't that far away, nine months, less than a year, and after that came years, decades even of riding together. Plus, currently the oldest horse on record was a Tennessee Walker who lived to the age of forty-one. If my girl took after her father, maybe she'd live to be that old. Nine months barely counted when compared to forty years.

*   *   *   *   *   *   *   *

Tiny rivulets of water seeped out of the snow banks. Day by day, the piles of snow sank lower and lower. The water running out of them carved down through the winter's accumulated ice until it reached the ground. The sides of the road, the paddock, the hills and fields blanketed with white cracked open, becoming seamed and riddled with patches of brown dirt, shriveled piles of rusty leaves, and yellowed mats of old grass that sprouted tiny clumps of new green life.

The warmth of the sun shining down overpowered the cold of the winter-frozen ground creeping up. The trees, the land, the world revived. The air carried a heady mixture of scents, the sharp cold bite of ice and snow, the musty tang of old leaves, and the green minty aroma of new grass. Spring arrived with an abundance of growth and renewal.

I asked Mom, if I could ride Trixie now. I'd been putting the saddle and bridle on her, slipping her halter on over the bridle, tying the reins to the saddle horn, and lunging her. She no longer got the least bit nervous about it.

She disliked the bit, even though I used a gentle on her mouth, snaffle bit. She never got really upset; she just kept working it around in her mouth until she drooled all over the place.

Mom decided to wait until the snow melted out of the driveway, before she'd condone our first ride. That way, we need not worry about Trixie slipping. I hoped it'd melt quickly. When I took Trixie into the barn to unsaddle her, I stepped up onto a pail and leaned on the saddle, hoping it helped her get used to the idea of me getting up there. Jane Allen suggested that I tie a bag of grain on the saddle and lunge Trixie with it on her. The grain bag weighed too much for me to lift it up into the saddle, though.

I hoped Trixie would remain calm when I rode her. I

wanted her to enjoy it as much as me. Nothing could go wrong to scare Mom or my girl. I needed to do everything right, the training, the saddling, and the first-ride. If it went wrong, I'd have to start over.

Chapter # 5   Stormy and Sheba

Winter's cold no longer rides the wind, biting at unprotected flesh. Instead spring flourishes, grass once again colors the fields in shades of green, flowers decorate gardens, and the trees bud out, new leaves unfurling throughout the woods. Today, my life and Trixie's will enter a new season in our partnership. Today, I'll ride my girl for the first time. We'll embark upon our journey as horse and rider, together, closer than ever before.

I unsnapped the second cross-tie and lowered it to the ground. Trixie stood stock still watching me. But Mom holding on to the bridle reins shuffled her feet back and forth, kicking last year's dead dry leaves around the sparse grass growing beneath the oak.

This was the very spot where we waited for the school bus and today here I was going to mount Trixie for the first time. I walked over to the left hand stirrup and took a deep breath.

"What if she bucks?" Mom asked.

"She won't. Trixie's a good girl. Aren't you, my silly

filly?" I patted Trixie's neck to reassure both of us. Before Mom worked herself into a panic, I put my foot in the stirrup and swung up into the saddle.

Trixie's ears pinned back and she froze in place, holding her breath. I leaned forward and patted her. "Easy, beautiful. Easy, now. I'm not going to hurt you at all. Let's just stand here and enjoy the moment, girl."

I continued to rub Trixie's neck, working my hand under her mane until I reached the itchy spots. This time of year Trixie shed her winter coat, the long, coarse dark brown hair falling out by the brush-fulls. Soon, only her coopery summer coat would remain sleek and brilliant.

Breath by breath, Trixie relaxed. "See, beautiful. There is nothing wrong." Her ears swiveled back and she pulled her head sideways. Mom held on to her tightly.

"Mom, let her see me. She hears me back here and wants to know where I am."

Mom loosened her hold and Trixie turned her head to look at me. Her eyes went wide. "Easy, girl. Everything is all right, girl." I reassured her as I patted her some more, she let out a sigh and straightened her head back out.

"We can head out now, Mom."

"Are you sure?"

"Yes. Trixie's a brave girl."

Mom looked at Trixie shrewdly and then nodded. "Walk," she commanded and stepped forward. Trixie stood unmoving. Mom stopped and turned to look with her arm stretched back, pulling the reins forward. Trixie only moved her nose, which she pushed forward by lowering her head. The rest of her remained absolutely still.

I barely managed to stifle a laugh!

"Let me try, Mom. Trixie, walk." Trixie stepped forward and then stopped. She seemed to notice my weight in the saddle more when she moved, which explained why Jane Allen recommended that I tie a full grain bag in the saddle to accustom her to this different feeling.

Both Mom and I said "Walk" at the same time. Trixie's left ear pointed sideways at Mom and her right one swiveled back to face me. She took two hesitant steps forward and then stopped again.

Slowly, step by step, we walked up the road until we reached Miss Waterhouse's house. The traditionally built, big house, little house, backhouse structure bore an unconventional soft yellow paint and three trellises overgrown with flowering vines. Encompassed and surrounded by nearly a dozen granite edged luxuriantly blooming flower gardens, the house emitted a fairyland quality that always sets my eyes searching for pixies, dragons, and unicorns. The short trip of about two hundred yards took us a half hour to travel.

"Let's head back, Mom." Trixie quickened her steps on the way back, but she still stopped and started frequently. By the time, we get back to the cross-ties she lengthened the intervals to six steps between stops.

At the cross-ties, I dismounted carefully. "You're such a good girl, Trixie. See, Mom not even one buck."

I stepped in close to my girl, wrapped my left arm under her neck, my right arm over it, and gave her a hug. She tucked her chin in tight so that I felt her cheek and jaw resting against my back. I weaved my fingers into her mane and inhaled her musky scent. She bobbed her head against my back, once, twice, and then exhaled a flood of warm air over my lower spine. I chuckled, let her go, and stepped back.

She lowered and tilted her head and I scratched behind her ears. She rubbed up against me. I knew this meant she wanted me to scratch the base of her neck. She stretched out her neck, cocked her head sideways, and rolled her eyes. Her ears pinned back and her nostrils flared, but she wasn't mad. She just made those faces when I reached the right itchy spots.

*   *   *   *   *   *   *   *

Mom has always loved horses but never owned one. For the past couple of months, she's saved up part-time job money to buy a horse. In the spring of '82, a couple of horses went up for sale, so we headed out to look at them.

We drove past the house and down the dirt road to Mr. Robert's barn. A simple one-story structure with a hayloft in its peak, the road-facing front bore clapboard siding painted a sun-faded dull red. Rough-hewn boards covered the sides of the barn and a small pasture butted up to its left side. When Mom talked to him on the phone, he agreed to meet us at the barn, but no one joined us.

In the field, a buckskin walked out from under some haggard pine trees and up to the weathered and sagging three-board fence line. We peered out the windshield at him and he gazed back at us. He looked thin.

"We might as well get out and take a look at him. Maybe Mr. Robert's running late."

As we approached the fence, the buckskin leant against the boards, stretching towards us. He eagerly sniffed our hands when we got close enough and let us pat him. We barely managed to see the other horse, a bay, hiding in the dark shade between the trees and the barn wall.

Churned up mud filled the pasture which enclosed an area so small it resembled a big paddock. No grass or hay lingered in sight. As we moved around the fence to look at the buckskin from the side, we realized how pitifully thin he looked.

Mom gasped in horror. "Why would anyone let this happen? Only skin and bones covers this poor fellow. Do you think he's sick?"

"I don't know. His eyes look clear. His breathing sounds normal. His hair looks fine with no bald patches, so he hasn't got mange or ringworm. We need to ask Jane Allen." I looked from the fence leaning precariously in some spots while appearing sturdy in others, to the dark, slimy puddles of water that pervaded the muddy paddock, to the scraggly, young hardwood trees dotted throughout it.

"Those trees look weird. No new leaves grow on them and the bottom of their trunks look white."

Mom squinted at the trees. "They appear gnawed on."

I agreed with Mom; the horses had chewed off the tree bark. Some things that I'd read about horses, clicked together in my mind. "That's not good."

"Why?"

"I've read about horses that got so hungry that they eat tree bark. But they have to be really hungry for a long time to do it."

Mom's eyes turned stone-cold sad. She reached through the fence and patted the buckskins side. He slowly turned around to face us and leaned his head over the fence.

Mom's eyes teared up as she gently patted his face. "Who would be so mean to you?"

"Who keeps horses if they can't afford to feed them?"

"I don't know. But it's inhumane and cruel and wrong."

"What can we do?"

"Let's drive down to Jane's and see if she'll come look at this fellow. She can tell if he's sick, starved, or both."

Jane was giving an English riding lesson when we reached her place. We stood beside the paddock gate waiting to talk to her. When she spotted us, she called out, "Sarah, switch to a trot. Post around for three laps, and then do three more laps in the opposite direction. I'll watch from the gate." Jane walked over to us. "Did you go look at those horses, Gloria?"

Mom's head bobbed up and down in a slow nod. "Could you go take a look at them? The buckskin looks horribly thin. And the other horse completely ignored us."

Jane looked at me. "How skinny is he, Kim?"

"All his ribs and both hip bones stick out. Plus, no grass is growing in their paddock and they chewed the bark off the trees."

Jane sighed. "They told me that Mr. Robert conducted honest trade and that his horses always stood in good condition. I should have checked myself before I told you about it, Gloria. I'll go look at them after this lesson gets done and call you in, let's say two hours."

"Okay, that sounds good to me."

Jane called us at the appointed time. Mom and I huddled together so we could both hear her.

"I found nothing wrong with either of those horses, other than the fact that their owner doesn't feed them. By the looks of their teeth, the buckskin appears to be the older of the two, between six and nine years old. Their owner came out and said the buckskin rides well in both English and Western tack. The bay has no saddle training at all."

"Did he say why he was starving them?"

"No. He got real defensive when I asked why they carried so little weight. He said he only ran out of hay yesterday, which is bull. Those horses haven't had a decent meal in weeks. He finished up with the fact that I need not recommend the sale. And honestly, I can't. Neither one of you has the experience needed to train that unbroken four or five year old bay, and the buckskin's malnourishment will take a couple of months to recede enough for him to get in riding condition."

Mom pulled the phone away from her ear, stared at it for a moment, and then leaned back over it. "But Jane, we can't just leave them there to starve. We have to at least call the humane society."

"That man won't give up those horses without a fight unless he gets paid for them. He claims that he wants to keep one, but doesn't care which one."

"That poor buckskin acted so friendly." Mom choked out.

"Yeah, but he also appears skittish. He's had it rough and he may actually get harder to handle when he regains his strength. He will remember being that hungry for a long time and I think he suffered physical abuse at one time or another."

Mom walked around the house after Jane got off the phone. She swept the kitchen floor and then paced. She loaded some laundry into the washing machine and then paced. She wiped down the counter and then whirled around and threw the dishcloth into the sink. It landed with a loud pop.

"We can't leave that poor horse to starve." Mom stomped over to the refrigerator and pulled out all the carrots that we had. She put them and our apples into a lunch bag. She picked up another bag and passed it to me. "Fill it up with some of Trixie's grain." I filled it to the top and stuffed my pockets full of Trixie's sugar cubes.

When we got to Mr. Robert's barn, the buckskin once again walked over to the fence to see us. He crunched down the carrots as fast as possible. By the time we got to the apples, the bay had ambled over to join us. He looked just as skinny as the buckskin. I fed the bay and Mom kept feeding her new friend. The apples and sugar cubes disappeared quickly.

The grain took longer. Not because the horses ate any slower but because we failed to find any pails around and we only managed to hold a couple of cups at a time in our hands. They licked our hands clean after every handful. Their desperate determination to get every morsel triggered tears in both Mom and me. After they consumed the grain, both horses stayed at the fence. Repeatedly, they stretched their heads out and accepted our pats with obvious joy.

"They're happy." I said in amazement.

Mom snuffled as she rubbed the buckskins blaze. "They haven't eaten in so long that that little bit probably seemed like a feast to them."

"His name's Stormy." A loud voice boomed out. Mom and I whirled to look at the approaching man. Short and stocky with a protruding beer-belly, he wore jeans, a chambray shirt, dark-brown scuffed and scarred cowboy boots, and a multi-stained tan cowboy hat, a fat cigar sagged from between his lips. His face carried a multitude of wrinkles and was tanned several shades darker than the hat. Both horses looked at him, turned, and slowly trotted off.

"The buckskin," the man pointed. "His name's Stormy. A right, big, handsome lad, ain't he? Trained up good too, rides fine in English and Western. Seven or eight years old, can't remember which, for sure? You interested in him?"

Mom's eyes turned as dark as I'd ever seen them. "He's a fine horse."

"'hat he is. Sell 'im to you cheap. No need for me to keep 'em both. Ran out of hay yeste'day. Will use what I get from one to buy for t'other."

Mom's eyes squinted nearly closed. "I need to call around and see if I can get some hay myself. My daughter only has enough for her horse. How about I call you this evening with my offer?"

"T'at be fine, mighty fine." The man smiled widely, turned, and walked away.

Mom called up Woody Brown when we got home. She asked to buy some more hay from him and to put another horse in the pasture. He sold Mom his extra twenty-five bales of hay and said the pasture could easily handle another horse.

Mom called the man back up and bought the horse named Stormy. She paid Jane to trailer him to our house and only then did we notice that his tail was half gone from the other horse chewing on it. His mane lay down thin and wispy in some spots and stuck up in short spikes in others.

His black knees and hocks made the bones of his half-starved body seem even larger. His ribs showed up from twenty feet away and his hip bones jutted up like tent poles trying to poke through canvas.

After Stormy entered the paddock with Trixie and happily worked away at gobbling up a pile of hay, Mom called the Humane Society. She told them about the bay that the man still owned, his starved condition, and the fact that she doubted that the man really intended to buy hay for him.

Stormy stood about eight inches taller at the shoulder than Trixie. Plus, his boning and body width far outstripped hers. We spread the hay out into three piles, every time we fed them. Stormy ran back and forth between two of the piles, eating as fast as he could. Trixie ate at the third pile.

Trixie soon learned to eat fast, too. If she ate slowly, Stormy finished one of his piles and then chased her off and claimed the two remaining piles of hay. It only took one day for Trixie to realize Stormy outweighed and overpowered her. She learned to keep the peace and stay out of his way.

*   *   *   *   *   *   *   *

When we brought the horses down to the Browns', Mom still refused to let go of the bridle when I rode Trixie. Stormy put on weight quickly, once he went out to pasture. I argued and pleaded with Mom. Finally, she let me ride Trixie by myself, up and down the Brown's driveway. She watched like a hawk for a couple of days. We both soon realized that Trixie responded better to word commands without someone leading her.

I rode Trixie every day that the sun shined, going further and further down the road headed towards Biddeford. We spent rainy days in the barn, avoiding the dangers of slippery paths, tack damage, and calming Trixie to nature's fury by grooming her lovingly. Inhaling the comforting scents of hay, grain, and horse I brushed her to perfection. Her wavy black mane and tail contrasted her copper coat shining brightly red-gold. And her dark knees and hocks allowed her pure-white socks sparkling like fresh snow to pop out in breathtaking detail.

I learned that Trixie disliked being ridden on trails. Closed in areas scared her; making her jump at the sound of creaky branches, spook at the sight of shadows shifting in the breeze, and bolt at the crunching of undergrowth. She behaved better riding on the side of the road, although she got spooked by motor-cycles and anything hauling a trailer. But she tensed up as soon as she heard those sounds, so at least I got a warning that she was going to spook.

*　　*　　*　　*　　*　　*　　*　　*

In the summer of '82, at age thirteen, I helped a lot more with the haying. I easily dragged a hay bale by myself and managed to even lift the light ones up onto the hay wagon, which surprised Mr. Brown. Saddling Trixie increased my strength because while the saddle weighed less, I had to lift it higher. I also succeeded in working longer before I got tired.

It was Trixie's last year of free pasture and hay. I needed to save all my money and find more odd jobs.

Hopefully, Miss Waterhouse knew some people looking for help. I'd probably have to gather up my courage and go door to door asking for work. News spread fast in our small community, if I asked just a couple of people; everyone would soon become aware that I wanted work.

I didn't want Dad to pay for Trixie's food or any of her care. He'd hold it over me, saying that meant he owned Trixie. It'd be like the time I got the electronic game Mr. Wizard for Christmas. The moment I opened the box and plugged it in, Dad took it from me so he could "figure it out". After all, he paid for it and therefore he owned it and wanted to make sure I used it the "right way".

Four days later, after he figured out how to consistently beat it, he returned it to me. But every time I played with it and it let out a negative "you failed" bleep, Dad would scream. "You stupid girl, can't you even figure out a simple game?" and snatch it away to show me how to win.

Within a couple of weeks, the game that I'd so fervently begged for and still continued to be the hottest fad became a torment to me. I stopped playing it voluntarily and only picked it up when Dad complained about wasting money on it. When Mr. Wizard and its cost faded from Dad's memory in early March, I joyfully stuffed it in the back of my closet to gather dust.

I learned from my experience with Mr. Wizard to never ask for a game and to always remember that if Dad paid for something even as a gift, he retained ownership of it and would proceed to ruin your enjoyment of it. I wanted him to have no claim on Trixie. I'd ask Mom for help out of her part-time job money, if I needed it.

*   *   *   *   *   *   *   *

Summer went by too quickly. School started back up and I entered the eighth grade, my last year at Saco Middle School. The time came to bring Trixie and Stormy home for the winter. In September of '82, on a chilly clear morning, we undertook the task of leading Stormy and Trixie home from the Brown's. Ev usually avoided anything and everything to do with the horses. But Mom needed to pick Dad up in town and give him a ride home so Ev manfully volunteered for the job.

Mom dropped us off at around ten in the morning. Trixie already stood at the gate waiting for us. I took her out of the pasture and tied her at the barn door. Then I measured out a portion of grain as her reward and poured another portion in a battered red bucket with a hay bale string as a handle to tempt Stormy out of the pasture.

"We'll have to get Stormy out quick when he comes to the gate Ev. Because all the horses will try to get out once they smell grain."

Ev straightened his shoulders and then tugged his ball-cap down tight over his ears. "What do you want me to do?"

"You open and close the gate. I'll get the halter and lead rope on Stormy." I said as we walked back to the pasture.

"Stormy! Come on, boy!" I hollered. Stormy looked up at me and I shook the bucket. His ears pricked forward as the grain rattled around and he sprinted towards the gate, beating the other horses by a wide margin. He cooperated well, letting me get his halter on before he buried his head deep into the bucket and following me willingly out of the pasture as I carried it. I heard the reassuring snick as Ev hooked the gate behind me scarce moments before the thundering hooves of the rest of the herd reached it.

"That was easy!" Ev exclaimed.

I decided not to regal him with stories of all the times that simple feat had gone so very wrong.

Halfway across the yard, Trixie took umbrage to the fact that I was leading another horse. She trumpeted fiercely, stamping her hooves, and her mane flipped in violent arcs through the air as she tossed her head.

Ev stopped in the middle of the yard, his eyes wide and bright as he watched Trixie throw her temper-tantrum. His head swung from her agitated stomping hooves and bobbing head to Stormy placidly clomping along with his head buried eye-deep in the grain bucket.

"I'll lead Stormy." Ev volunteered with a wide smile.

"Are you sure? This will be the first year we lead him home and I'm not sure how he'll behave."

"He's minding his manners a lot better than T is. I'll take him. You're stuck with her."

"Okay." I handed the weathered yellow lead rope to Ev and set the bucket in the barn door, then walked over to Trixie. By the time, Stormy finished licking out his bucket she calmed down, happy once again from regaining my attention.

We headed down the Brown's driveway with Trixie and me in the lead. She arched her neck and her hooves flashed high in full parade mode. I looked back over my shoulder and saw Stormy trotting to catch up with Ev.

Once he reached Ev's side, Stormy stopped and Ev continued to walk nearly turned sideways, never taking his eyes off Stormy until the fifteen foot lead rope stretched out between them, then Stormy once again trotted to catch up.

I shook my head in exasperation. "Ev, you're supposed to hold the lead rope near the horses head not by the very end."

Ev's head snapped around to face me. "You lead your way and I'll lead mine." He spit out and swung back around to watch Stormy.

Trixie pranced on and I kept stealing looks over my shoulder to see how Ev proceeded. All the way down the Brown's driveway, in front of the pastures, across the stream, and up the hill to the intersection with the Waterhouse Road, Stormy held back. He waited until Ev stretched the lead rope to its full length, then thought it over for a few minutes before he surged into his clomp-clomp-clomp trot to catch up to Ev.

But Trixie refused to hold back and the distance between Ev and us stretched out further and further. When we crossed the Waterhouse Road and headed up the upper Buzzell Road, Stormy and Ev lagged about thirty yards behind us.

Stormy decided he disliked the separation and when the lead rope stretched out between them, he broke into a trot straight at Ev and didn't slow down. Ev broke into a jog to keep some distance between him and his charge. Stormy's ears pricked forward, his tail flagged up, and he clomped along a mere two feet behind Ev with the lead rope swaying and bouncing between them.

I wanted to yell back and warn Ev that the lead rope could trip and panic Stormy. But when I saw Ev's flushed cheeks, wide eyes, and quickened jog, I realized Ev was close to panicking himself. And while a huge part of the problem lay in Ev's inexperience, I honestly had to admit that Stormy's eight inches and four hundred pound advantage on Trixie made him look intimidating. Let alone the fear his huge dinner plate sized hooves invoked when they clomped down in near vicinity of your feet.

When we rounded the corner and home loomed in sight, I was happy to see that Mom waited for us. She met us at the bottom of the driveway, took one look at Ev jogging along with Stormy clomping after him and headed down the road to take over leading Stormy. Surprisingly enough, Dad lounged leaning against the barn wall watching Mom and Stormy approach.

Mom rode Stormy very infrequently because he easily spooked and acted unpredictable in his fear. Dad claimed that Stormy just needed to be taught who was boss and lately hinted about family rides together. Both Mom and I knew aggressive handling was the wrong attitude to take with a previously abused and neglected horse. But Dad thought horses were just dumb animals to be ruled and controlled by brute force.

When Mom started saddling Stormy, I realized that her love for animals subjugated her fear of Dad's temper. Tired of his harping about Stormy, she had decided to let the dumb animal settle the matter.

So far, Woody Brown had been the only one able to ride Stormy without fear. Woody talked to Stormy, his low, melodious voice even and calm. He also always used smooth, slow motions. When he rode, he used a firm but gentle touch and Stormy obeyed him without hesitation. He calmed the panic and fright out of Stormy with his relaxing voice and easy-going presence. I believed that Dad with his loud, brash voice and sharp, violent motions would have the opposite effect and set Stormy off.

I put Trixie in the paddock and listened to Mom and Dad talk.

"He is very strong, Evans. He overpowers me. But he stops when I ask him to."

"I used to ride my sister's horses. He won't be too strong for me."

No longer able to resist, I walked out of the barn to watch. Mom patted Stormy's neck and head to keep him from shying away as Dad swung up into the saddle.

Dad settled down in the saddle and she stepped away from Stormy. The big buckskin stood perfectly still, waiting to see how this human decided to treat him. Dad tightened his hold on the reins and kicked his heels back hard into Stormy's ribs. Stormy exploded forward. Dad shrieked "Whoa!" Stormy banked left and charged up the hill. Dad leant right, clawing at the saddle pommel, and yelled "Whoa! Whoa!" at the top of his voice.

As Stormy crested the hill, he went beyond our sight for a couple of minutes. But Dad remained in hearing range. "Whoa! Damn it, whoa!" Then Stormy returned, flying downhill with no regard for how he was going to stop. Dad now leant far to the left. The reins flapped loosely about. Dad clutched the pommel with both hands.

"Whoa! Whoa!" Stormy reached the bottom of the driveway, performed a spin tight enough to make a barrel racer proud, and headed back up the hill. Dad's voice screamed in desperation. "Whoa! Whoa!" My jaw hung open. How did Dad manage to stay on through that spin?

Stormy made another run up the hill and out of sight. Dad's squeals became so high-pitched, he sounded like a woman screaming. "Whoa! Whoa!"

Stormy barreled back into sight, ran full steam downhill, and swerved towards the barn. I sidestepped in a hurry. Dad saw the barn coming and wailed. "Whoa! Whoa! Whoa!"

Gravel flew through the air as Stormy came to a bouncy, shuddering halt. "WA...... WA.......... WA-WHOA!" Dad's voice vibrated. Mom stepped forward and took hold of the bridle. She whispered soothingly in Stormy's ear, while patting his neck. Stormy's sides billowed in and out frantically. His muscles quivered in barely contained fear.

Dad swung off the saddle, faster than he had mounted. His voice reeked with his normal venom, but lacked its usual volume as he swore. "Damn fucking horse!"

I waited until Dad stomped off to the garage, before I went out to see how Stormy and Mom were. Mom smiled as she unsaddled the big buckskin and walked him cool. Sweat steamed from his hide. Mother and I grinned at each other as we put Stormy in the paddock, giving him an extra ration of grain with his supper.

For the next couple of weeks, we all walked on eggshells. Dad lingered in a foul mood, on the edge of erupting into a towering rage, but by sheer luck, a lot of avoidance, and a slew of fearful, deathly quiet meals, we managed to dodge the bullet. Never again did Dad mention family rides. And he took to avoiding the horse barn and paddock altogether.

*　　*　　*　　*　　*　　*　　*　　*

Winter arrived and on a nice day, a week from Christmas, I decided to deliver presents the old-fashioned way. I braided some bells onto ribbons and tied them to the bottom of the stirrups, the bridle reins, and one around each of Trixie's pasterns. She seemed unsure about them. She high-stepped her way up the road, tossing her head at the jingle-jangle sound that accompanied her every step. Of course, the head tossing only made the ones on the reins ring all the more, so we created a loud, merry noise as we went. I talked to Trixie and patted her neck.

"Easy, beautiful. Christmas means bells and decorations. Count yourself lucky. I refrained from even trying to stick a bow on you." She shook her head and flicked her ears frantically about trying to hear every little rattle. I laughed as I imagined her asking. "What will she come up with next?"

By the time we got to the house of Miss Waterhouse, Trixie realized there was no way to avoid the ruckus of the ringing bells. I tied the reins to the rail, and carried Miss Waterhouse's present up onto the porch. Trixie stepped onto the first riser. I twisted around. "Whoa! You stay right there!" A rough-hewn granite block stood in as the first step and it could handle the weight of a horse. After that wood construction made up the porch. Not okay. "Whoa! Not a step further, Trixie. I mean it." I pivoted away and headed for the door. I heard a tinkle and whirled around. "Don't you dare!" I pointed at her. "Back... zzz.... zzz.... zzz.... Back.....zzz ......zzz .....zzz." Trixie exhaled a long drawn out breath like a kid giving a raspberry to show displeasure and edged back a step.

She abided on the granite step, eyeing the porch with

obvious longing when I twisted and looked at Miss Waterhouse's door. Half of the porch remained in front of me. "Trixie, whoa!" Trixie shifted her weight around like a kid squirming in a seat. She watched me and slowly lifted her hoof. I pointed at her again. "No, you stay right there! Whoa!" Her hoof slowly lowered back to the granite.

I turned back to face the door. I stretched as far as possible to reach and grab the leaf rake leaning against the wall and used it to stab at the door bell. Doing this took three tries. Trixie watched my antics, standing frozen in place.

Miss Waterhouse opened the door dressed in a long-sleeved, ankle length teal dress. Her curly gray hair haloed her head attractively. She smiled widely showing off twin dimples and laugh lines accenting her eyes when she saw my silly filly at the edge of her porch, one hoof once again raised, with bells jingling on it.

I held out her wrapped gift. "Merry Christmas."

"Thank you. I'll get yours." She stopped in mid-turn and cocked her head. "Can I give a carrot to your horse?"

"Trixie would like that very much." I joined my girl on the edge of the porch to keep her out of further mischief. Miss Waterhouse soon returned.

"Here you go." She handed me a plastic bag containing a gift for me and one for my brother and mother.

"Thank you." She stood tall enough on the porch to look Trixie square in the eye as she held out the carrot.

"Hold your hand out flat with the carrot resting in your palm." I suggested as she hesitated.

"She is so lovely." She exclaimed as Trixie stretched out her neck. She giggled like a young girl as Trixie gently feathered her rose-petal, pink lips across her palm, caressing the carrot before delicately picking it up and loudly crunching it to pieces.

As we rode away jingling a tune, I waved back to Miss Waterhouse who watched from the edge of her porch. My girl tossed her head energetically and I laughed in joy as I recollected that none of our other destinations had wooden porches.

*   *   *   *   *   *   *   *

In January of '83, winters grasp firmly held us in its clutches. The ground hid beneath drifts of snow. The air crept coldly through every crack in clothing and shelter. And gray clouds loomed perpetually overhead.

I had hoped that with time and patience Stormy would learn to trust us, but he still remained possessive of his food. I needed to put out three piles of hay for Trixie to get one. And I needed to be careful when I put the hay out. Sometimes, Stormy nipped at me, if I moved away from his hay too slowly. After being so starved, he acted afraid of losing even a wisp of his precious food.

On that day, I was setting out Stormy's second pile when he caught me by surprise. He trotted over to the pile. I backed up, but evidently not fast enough. He shoved his head forward and clamped his teeth over my left shoulder, where the muscle connected to my neck. I felt myself being lifted off my feet and screamed.

"Stormy, let me go!" He shook his head and mine bounced off his. I literally saw stars bloom to live and explode in flashes so brilliant they stunned me. Stormy shook me harder.

I screamed again, "Stormy, let go!" Tears streaked down my face; my left arm felt aflame and my shoulder pounded.

Stormy shook me again. Then I heard a squeal of anger and a hoof hitting flesh. Stormy dropped me. I cradled my left arm with my right. It took four tries to get to my feet. Squeals of pain made my head snap up. Stormy pushed Trixie tight into the corner of the stall. She tried to fight him off. Bigger, stronger, and with more reach, he nipped her again and again, pummeling her with his bared teeth.

I knew that if Stormy turned and kicked Trixie, his powerful hindquarters could kill her. I stumbled out of the stall and grabbed Trixie's lunging whip. I needed to drive Stormy away from her. Reaching him required a climb to the top board of the stall partition. I gripped the whip between my teeth, and clambered up the partition with my right arm. My left one throbbed when I tried to move it. I balanced standing on the middle board, leant over the top board, and took the whip to Stormy. He shrieked with rage. As I whipped him, Trixie continued to fight back. I kept on, until he wheeled and charged the partition.

I jerked my body back as his bared teeth swung over the top board. I overbalanced, dropped the whip, and fell over backwards to the floor. I saw Trixie streak out to the freedom of the paddock as I hit the ground. I lay there crying for a couple of minutes until I realized I needed to check on her. I was hurt, and she might be badly hurt, too.

I managed to make it outdoors. Trixie stood in the center of the paddock with her legs spread wide. Her head hung low and she shook all over, wavering back and forth on unsteady legs. I stumbled my way to the house, crying and incoherent.

"You gotta check Trixie?"

Mom took one look at me clasping my left shoulder and rushed over.

"What happened?" She started unzipping my jacket.

"Stormy shook me." I snuffled into my shirt collar. "He hurt Trixie. You gotta check her."

"You first." She slipped off my jacket. "Did he bite you?" She unbuttoned my shirt.

I flicked my eyes up and down because my shoulder hurt too much to nod. "He clamped on, lifted me up, and shook me." I bit my lip as Mom pulled my shirt away from my left shoulder. "Trixie?" I caught her eyes.

"All right. You're not bleeding. I'll check on Trixie." She quickly returned.

"I can't see any blood on her. She's supporting her weight on all four legs. She looks scared." Mom slid my sleeve arm off. "Once Stormy finishes eating, we'll take Trixie out and check her over real good." She gently moved my arm around. My shoulder hurt real bad, but it didn't creak, catch, or pop in any one spot.

"It's not broken. We'll ice it."

My whole shoulder ended up bruised, dark purple, from my collarbone, up over my shoulder, and down my back. The bruise covered an area from my neck to the top of my left arm, and wrapped all the way around to my spine. Trixie, sore in dozens of spots, trembled with pain when I ran my hands over her. I brushed her very gently and took her for slow walks, so her muscles stayed loose. Two weeks went by before I became capable of lunging her, and a month before I managed to lift the saddle onto her back again.

The most difficult thing in the following weeks proved to be hiding my injury from Dad. Mom and I agreed, Dad must not find out. He still held a grudge against Stormy for his rough ride and we knew my injury made the perfect excuse to shoot Stormy and tell everyone he only did it to protect his child. Mom and I both comprehended that Stormy only attacked me because he feared losing his food. He seemed to think of every meal as possibly his last one, which caused him to guard his food ferociously.

Stormy and I trod carefully around each other after he bit me. I knew he felt unsure of me. He exhibited almost equal measures of trust and fear for me. I fed him and talked nicely to him but I had whipped him and I felt horrible about further traumatizing him. He behaved like an overgrown terrified child. I believed I had no other choice. I no longer felt any anger at him or fear of him, I just took extra care from then on to throw his hay over the fence, so that I never actually got close to him when he ate. I wanted to avoid injuries to all three of us.

Early on in my life, I realized that physical pain wasn't really that bad because I knew eventually it'd stop and heal. Invisible wounds caused far more damage. In Kindergarten, when I got my first report card it fell far short of Dad's expectations. Mom, Ev, and I had been lined up against the wall that became Dad's favorite yelling spot over the years and he let loose. Whenever Dad lined us up there, he started with berating and belittling my mother. When he got bored with yelling at Mom, he moved on to Ev and then me. I usually began crying before he even finished with Mom.

"I know she's dumb. How could she be anything but stupid, when you're her mother? But both your sister and brother have nice looking girls. Not you. You give me not only a stupid daughter, but an ugly one too. She's too dumb to figure anything out and too ugly to ever be worth anything. She's useless and that will never change."

Ever after that, whenever my friends showed off a pretty dress their Dads bought them, or talked about going to zoos, picnics, and vacations with doting fathers, or even worse, their fathers picked them up at school with hugs and love shining out of their eyes, my heart stopped and then jolted back to life with a stab of pain that time never lessened or healed. Both Stormy and I knew that far worse things than mere physical pain existed.

*   *   *   *   *   *   *   *

Even after the February thaw in '83, a lot of snow still covered the ground. I woke up hearing rain falling in the middle of the night. When I went out to take care of Stormy and Trixie in the morning, they both stood in the center of the paddock. The barn roof pointed in the wrong direction with the peak lying in a shattered mess in the middle of the stall under a huge pile of snow. Saturated beyond belief, the snow shed snowmelt into streams that collected into puddles behind and under the snow-banks. The barn roof had collapsed from the sheer weight of the water-logged snow.

I went and got Mom. We entered the paddock and checked on the horses. We found no cuts anywhere on them and neither limped at all. They stood heads down, ears cocked half-back, and sopping wet out in the slushy snow, looking thoroughly disgusted with their lot in life. The looks on their faces said quite clearly "Enough is enough!" Mom said they probably heard the roof creaking and ran out before it collapsed, avoiding physical injury. But their demeanor showed that they remained thoroughly upset about it.

Dad called up Carl Harris. He came over and helped Dad salvage some of the wood and build a lean-to on the back side of the paddock.

*   *   *   *   *   *   *   *

Spring seemed to come late in '83. The warm days melted the snow into puddles. The paths turned into ankle deep morasses of slush. And every night the temperature plummeted and froze everything back into place. My morning journey to the paddock became an expedition of sliding across ice patches and tripping over hummocks formed from yesterday's frozen slush tracks.

In April, the warm days incrementally made headway against the cool nights. The puddles of snow melt succeeded in carving their way through the snow-banks and joined into rivulets that coursed downhill to the stream. The slush melted away, freeing the long cloaked ground to absorb the sun's heat.

I came home from school on the last Wednesday in April and found Stormy gone. I didn't even know Mom wanted to sell him. When I asked her about it she explained that she put him up for sale when he bit me. Only the meat factory showed an interest in him during the winter. But an experienced horse trainer up mid-state offered to buy Stormy in the spring. He re-trained starved and abused horses on a frequent basis. Stormy wasn't a bad horse, just fearful that he might get starved or beaten again. Mom and I both hoped that the trainer could help him.

My bank account held enough money to pay for Trixie's pasture and her shots this spring. I worked twice a week for Miss Waterhouse after school, and once a week for Charlotte Cole, and earned between fifteen and twenty dollars every week.

All of the other girls in my 4-H group showed their horses. Three of the girls lived in families where they all owned horses and they didn't have to worry about any bills. They kept pure-bred horses and looked down on the mixed breeds. They didn't seem to love their horses and appeared not to care if or when their parents sold them or to whom they went, as long as they got a replacement horse. But the other three girls from 4-H felt like me, they loved their horses. Two of these girls also owned purebreds. While they understood my love for Trixie, they believed that purebred horses offered a 'better quality experience of horse ownership' than grade horses. But then again, I thought Trixie's 'quality' far outshined all of their horses and even a few of the owners themselves.

I wanted to show Trixie some, just to get a chance to psychologically knock the spoiled girls off their high horses. I knew mutual love made a difference in horse performance, and if Trixie and I got in the ring together, we could prove it to them. There was just one problem. I felt unsure that I'd have enough money for Trixie's hay, if I spent some on shows. Mom encouraged me to show Trixie.

She said she'd help me buy Trixie's hay in the fall.

In '83, I entered Trixie in two horse shows, one in July and one in August. The morning of the first show, Jane Allen showed up with the horse trailer at seven. My first class started at nine. Forty-five minutes later, Jane and her husband still struggled to get Trixie into the trailer. They tried leading her in. She pulled them backwards. They tried getting her to follow a bucket of grain in. She lost her appetite at the edge of the trailer ramp. Then they tried putting a rope behind her rump and winching her in. Trixie sat down in the road like a mule.

Finally, Jane prepared to leave without us. She had other horses, already loaded and they needed to get to the show on time. I asked her to let me try to get Trixie into the trailer. She gave me one chance to get my girl to load up.

I walked over to Trixie, pulled her head down, and looked her straight in the eye. "I've already paid the entrance fees, Trixie."

She tossed her head up, tugging on the lead rope. I gave the rope one quick jerk to get her attention. "If you don't get in this trailer, I'm going to saddle you up and ride you all the way up to that show."

Her ears twitched back and forth. I tucked my chin down, narrowed my eyes, and glared at her. "Then I'm going to ride you in every class we entered in. After that, I'll ride you all the way back home."

Her head slowly lowered and her ears stayed pointing at me. I turned to face the trailer. "So you better get in the trailer or you're going to be some tired by the time the day is done." I gave the lead rope a shake and walked into the trailer. Trixie followed right behind me. I tied her in the trailer and climbed out the side door.

When I exited the trailer, I found Jane and her husband staring at me open-mouthed and slack-jawed. I jerked my shoulders up and down in a quick shrug. "You need to say it like you mean it."

Jane nods. "I believed you."

Mr. Allen shook his head. "You wouldn't have ridden her way up there, would you?"

"Yeah, I would've." I picked up my saddle and carried it to the pick-up.

"It cost me twenty-five dollars to enter those classes." Jane helped me lower the saddle into the back of the truck.

"Plus, my Aunt Connie in Missouri bought my show shirt and belt and sent them to me."

I jumped in and buckled my seat buckle. Mr. Allen cocked his head at me and motioned for me to continue talking. "And Mom got me a new bridle for Trixie for my birthday, so Trixie is going in those classes, one way or the other."

Jane nodded, laughing. "Say it like you mean it and mean what you say. It works every time."

The three classes before lunch went by fast. We placed fourth in barrels and fifth in poles. I thought that was pretty good considering Trixie and I never practiced at either of them and we went up against Quarter Horses, the fastest breed of short distance sprinting horses in the world. We won sixth in open equitation. But as Jane put it first, second, third, and fifth in that class went to the "professionally trained". A stable out of Old Orchard Beach offered free daily equitation classes for their "Jr. Riders". The lady who gave the classes just retired from the national circuit. Four of her "Jr, riders" trailered in to this show together. They consistently won the top ribbons in all the " Jr." English and open classes.

The "Obstacle class" took place after lunch. I only entered Trixie in that class because if you paid for four classes, you got a fifth for free. Trixie disliked trails and hated obstacles. We stood next to no chance of placing in the class. Plus, those four pro-trained "Jr's" signed up for it. I heard one of them bragging that they set an obstacle course up in one of their extra outside arenas. I flinched at the thought of having "extra" arenas available. "Extra" arenas meant big money, lots of land, and not having to worry about wasting either the money or the land on something not used on a daily basis.

The course started with the competitor weaving through some safety cones, riding their horse up to the arena corner and then backing up ten feet. Next, take a left and ride over a blue tarp held down flat with rocks. After that, line up over a ground log and side-step down the length of it, through some more cones decked out with trash bags on sticks flapping from their tops. Then walk over various rails and sticks criss-crossed on the ground, do a figure eight around two poles, turn around and go through the course in the opposite direction. This timed event, allowed walking or trotting but no cantering. Bypassing any obstacle added a minute to the time. The time only counted for half of the score. Jane explained to me that the other half of the score related to how well a spooked or skittish horse responded to the riders commands. Horses that tried to toss their riders would lose points from the judged half of their score.

One of the pro-trained riders went first as Trixie and I

stood beside the arena and watched. She made it look easy. The bay mare trotted calmly over the tarp. Her ears didn't even twitch at the crrr... crrr... crrsh noise of the tarp crinkling under her hooves. The rider stayed in perfect balance and form as the mare side-stepped down the log.

They went through the flapping cones with dust puffing up all the way to the rider's knees, stirred up by the mare's brisk trot. Without a single misstep or stumble they navigated the criss-crossed sticks and then sent the sand afloat again with the mare's pristine, elegant show trot.

It amazed me that the mare showed no reaction to any of the obstacles. No hesitation. No fear. No snorts. Nothing but calm. To that horse it was just another walk around the arena. Meanwhile, outside it Trixie's ears pivoted wildly at every snap and crinkle. Her muscles quivered and shook. Her nostrils flared wide snorting the drifting clouds of airborne sand into miniature dust devils beneath her nose.

Our turn came and Trixie went through the first set of cones without a problem. She backed up quickly and in a straight line. The moment we started heading for the blue tarp, the hooves flashing high and head throwing started. I tightened my knees and headed Trixie straight at the tarp. She waited until her next step would put her on it and then she spun to the left and pranced away from it. I circled her and tried again, same thing. On the third try, I waited until I felt her start to spin and I yelled "Whoa!" I didn't care about winning a ribbon at this point; I just wanted Trixie to learn that the tarp posed no harm to her. She stopped in the middle of her spin and her front right hoof landed on the tarp. Her head shot up and she snorted, with her left foreleg hanging in mid-air, paralyzed in fear, muscles quivering under me, Trixie froze. I leaned forward and started patting her neck. "It's okay, beautiful. I won't let it hurt you. I promise."

Slowly, Trixie relaxed. When her quivering stopped, I tightened my heels and asked her to "walk" in a firm but gentle voice. The moment she took a step; I told her "Whoa" and reassured her that the tarp wouldn't eat her left hoof. Once all four feet landed on the tarp and I encouraged, patted, and talked to her enough, she high-stepped her way across it, head-tossing and snorting the whole way.

After the ordeal of the tarp, Trixie side-stepped happily away from it. She navigated the cones with flapping trash bags with a series of full body swings as she tried to stay away from first one, then the next trash bag while alternately stomping her feet and tossing her head. She walked over the criss-crossed sticks without a problem. Mundane in comparison to the rest of the course, Trixie showed no fear of them at all.

Trotting through the figure eight, Trixie willingly continued over the branches and with a lot of tail-swishing and excessively swinging hind-quarters around the detested trash bag cones. Her side-stepping over the log got slower and slower as she got closer to the hated tarp.

I stopped Trixie about three feet away from the tarp. I patted and reassured her and then asked her to "walk". She high-stepped her way onto the tarp. Her strides became an un-coordinated mix of mincing in fear and trying to keep her feet from touching the tarp. If a horse could spontaneously sprout wings, Trixie would have done so about mid-way across that tarp. She trotted willingly into the arena corner, backed up at high speed, and trotted quickly through the last cones.

The moment we got outside the arena gate, I stopped Trixie and dismounted. She took a huge breath and sighed loudly. A couple of the spectators broke out laughing. I walked my girl out into the back field and stopped under a big oak tree. I lavished her with attention and told her what a clever, brave horse she was.

I wanted to remain there until our mid-afternoon class, but our number called out over the intercom. They wanted us back in the arena. I wondered why they bothered to call us back. I hoped there hadn't been a tie or judges who disagreed. If they asked us to re-do that course, I'd forfeit. Trixie had gone through it once and I refused to ask her to face it again. While I felt extremely proud that Trixie trusted me to such a degree, it wouldn't be right to put her through such fear unnecessarily.

It stunned me when we won second place. The rest of the day went by in a fog of befuddlement. How had we placed second in obstacles? On the ride home Jane explained that Trixie's judged score topped out way higher than all of the other competitors. Obviously terrified, she never disobeyed a command, bucked, panicked, or bolted.

Her performance impressed all three of the judges. The high scores they awarded us had brought us in at second place, even though our slow time placed us seventh out of nine competitors.

Best of all my fellow 4-H members watched the show. They witnessed how well my "little grade mare" performed. None of their pure-breeds won more ribbons than my girl and we'd beaten two of them in the obstacle class. I smiled so widely all the way home that Jane kept breaking out into laughter every time she looked at me.

After we unloaded Trixie and let her out in the paddock. Jane clapped me on the shoulder and pointed at her.

"She'd try to climb a tree if you asked her to."

Somehow, my smile got even bigger.

*   *   *   *   *   *   *   *

Gordon Cole called my mother and asked if I wanted to work on his haying crew through the summer of '83. He'd only need me on days when he put in a lot of hay. Mom knew I wanted the work, so she said yes.

The Coles put in hay differently than Woody Brown did. Equipped with a kicker, their baler threw the hay bales into the wagon. I took the bales off the wagon and put them onto a conveyor. The conveyor carried the bales up into the loft of the barn. Two or three people worked in the hayloft, stacking the bales.

I only worked up in the loft a couple of times. Monumentally huge, the barn sported red clapboard siding, a metal roof, and a big front door hung on a rail inside the barn, so that the door slid out of the way between the outer wall and the stairs up to the lofts. The stair-steps were worn smooth; tread upon so often that time abraded shallow scoops out at every footfall. Hay dust wafted up with each footstep and the sunbeams slanting in from the high windows illuminated every dancing dust mote. You needed to walk up two sets of stairs to reach the catwalk to the main loft.

Because it measured only thirty inches wide, I found the

catwalk scary to walk across. An eight foot drop to the side loft on the right made my knees quiver and the sixteen foot drop to the barn's main floor on the left caused my feet to fumble. No railings lined it and at the end of the walk, stood a ladder to climb and step off at whatever height the hay reached to. I froze up my first couple of times across the walkway.

Stacking the hay bales required hard work and stamina. I lacked the strength needed to stay in the loft for more than thirty minutes at a time, so Andy Cole took pity on me and left me on the trailers mostly. I think he did it because he witnessed first-hand my overwhelming fear of heights.

*   *   *   *   *   *   *   *

Even with working for Gordon Cole, I fell short of having enough money to buy Trixie's hay in the fall of '83. Mom paid for almost half of it. Showing Trixie had used up all my cash. Mom said she didn't mind. But I felt horrible about it.

Mom worked hard for her money. Dad always screamed at her and called her fat and ugly and stupid and he made her cry a lot. She only got away from Dad when she worked. She always spent all her money on me and Ev. She bought Christmas presents, birthday presents, and special treats with her own money. She deserved to have that money to buy herself something special. But she always spent it on us without a complaint or any rewards. I vowed to myself, that next year I wouldn't show Trixie unless I'd already saved up her hay money. It wasn't fair to use Mom's.

Beauty flowed out of Mom when she smiled or laughed, you couldn't help but be happy too, because her whole face lit up. Her eyes sparkled and her laugh sounded sweet and contagious. When she sang, I thought she sounded like an angel, sweet, strong, and overflowing with love.

"I come to the garden alone, while the dew is still on the roses." Mom sang as she passed me another supper plate to rinse and dry.

Her voice rose and fell as beautifully as Patsy Cline's and Loretta Lynn's playing on the tape cassette. "And the voice I hear falling on my ear, the Son of God discloses."

Even though my voice sounded horrible compared to Mom's I joined her in the chorus. "And he walks with me and he talks with me."

She flicked me playfully with water. "And he tells me I am his own."

I retaliated with a towel snap to her backside. "And the joy we share as we tarry there."

We synched together perfectly for the last chorus line. "None other has even known."

Mom sung on through the next two songs as we finished the dishes and wiped down the counters and stove. I flipped the cassette over for her and we brought in the clothes off the line as the next song began.

Mom and I were belting out. "Then sings my soul, my Savior, God, to thee, how great thou art," when Ev came in from working with Dad in the garage. He washed up and headed up to his room to work on his homework.

When the song finished, Mom waved me towards the cassette player. "Flip it over for me."

I quickly trotted into the kitchen to do as she asked,

because if I flipped it now it re-started playing *In The Garden* again which was my favorite song on the tape.

"Go on up to bed. I'll finish folding the clothes." Mom said when I rejoined her in the living room.

When I got upstairs, I wasn't surprised to see Ev stretched out in his bed asleep with an open school book fallen onto his chest. When Dad got into full swing on a project, he only allowed Ev time to race to the house and change into work clothes after getting off the school bus. Since Dad years ago proclaimed me to be a useless girl, he never asked me to help in the garage.

So while I did homework and spent my afternoon free hours with Trixie, Ev labored in the garage. He came in for supper with Dad, grease-smeared and drooping. And after the meal, they went back to work. He got released to the house between 7:30 and 8:30. He tried to do his homework, but usually fell asleep before accomplishing much.

I stood in the hallway and pondered reaching into his room and switching off his light. Sometimes, that simple action startled him back awake and I didn't want to wake him. I heard a soft snore drift up from his half-open mouth and realized sleep already held him deeply. I flicked out his light, crossed the hall to my room, closed my door, and got changed and into bed as quietly as possible.

I turned out my light. Mom's voice drifted up from downstairs, "And he walks with me and he talks with me." Through my window curtains, I saw flashes of blue spear out of the garage windows and up into the night sky as Dad welded away on something.

I sank down into my bed, happy to have had a peaceful evening with Mom. A pang of guilt stabbed into me, because while these days when Dad immersed himself deeply in a project meant peaceful interludes for Mom and I. They dealt out laborious bouts of work for Ev that resulted in his homework getting done on the bus rides to and from school.

"And the joy we share as we tarry there," gently reached my ears. All my thoughts and worries seeped away and sleep overtook me.

Since we no longer had a barn, we used Dad's old broken down cube van to put Trixie's hay in. The van was painted mustard yellow with rusty patches surrounding the wheel wells and on the bottoms of the doors. I placed Trixie's saddle, bridle, and brushes in the passenger seat. We could fit about seventy bales inside. The floor got extremely slippery from the loose hay. The front cab retained an oily, greasy smell with a hint of Dad's tobacco smoke mixed in.

I thought the cab provided close to ideal living quarters for spiders. Luckily, I wasn't squeamish. Cobwebs decorated the inside of the cab. Narrow ones stretched out between the seats. Big ones spanned from the seat backs all the way up to the ceiling. Little ones hung from the rearview mirror. They even filled the gap between the gas and brake pedals. I used a broom stored in the back of the van to sweep the webs off the saddle and bridle. Even if I opened it every day, spider webs stretched out from the dash to spread over the passenger seat, dangling down on to Trixie's brushes.

Our neighbor two doors down gave Mom her horse, Sheba, because she ran short of money and time to spend on her. I always stopped and patted Sheba when I walked home from the bus stop, because her pasture lay just two houses down from ours. She was a dapple grey so light, she almost looked white. Her hair darkened and thinned on her nose, showing off her black nostrils and she loved to have her baby soft nose patted. Her mane and tail sheeted down in black strands thinner, straighter, and shorter than Trixie's. Sheba's face, knees and hocks were fine-boned, not as delicate as Trixie's but still allowing her Arabian lineage to shine through. I planned to lead her home for Mom today, the second Friday in October of '83. As always, Sheba let me pat her. She wore her halter and her lead rope hung from the corner post.

I felt tempted to hook on the lead rope over the fence, but Jane always told me that was real dangerous, especially with a barbed wire fence. If the horse got spooked, it could jerk you through the fence. If you let go of the lead rope, it could get tangled in the fence. Either way injuries could happen. So I picked the lead rope up and ducked into the pasture.

Sheba bit at me and I jumped back. She struck at me with her foreleg so I backed up further down the fence line. When she whirled to kick, I knew I had landed myself in big trouble. I couldn't duck under the fence quicker than she could kick. I did the only thing possible. I ran into the pasture far enough to the side to avoid her kick.

Within minutes, Sheba herded me out into the center of the pasture. Jane's words, "No matter what, never panic. Always talk in a calm voice. Never panic." kept going through my mind. I felt real close to panicking, but what good would that do? No one stood close by to help me. Whenever I had air to spare, I talked to Sheba. "Easy girl, easy. I'm a friend, remember, easy girl."

Finally, Sheba let me pat her neck. "Easy girl, easy, just take it easy." Sheba whipped her head around. I managed to avoid the snapping teeth, but her head slammed into me and I landed on the ground. I rolled and jumped back to my feet. She'd trample me if I stayed down. Sheba chased me around the pasture again.

Every time Sheba let me pat her neck, I got an inch or so closer to the halter. I lost count of how many times she let me pat her, how many times I hit the dirt or got chased around the pasture. But finally when dusk started setting in, Sheba let me work my hand all the way up to her halter. I snapped on the lead rope and rubbed my hands softly, gently, over Sheba's neck and head. I patted her again and again. "That's a good girl. Good girl, Sheba, good girl."

Sheba acted fine on the way home. I let her loose in the paddock with Trixie and trudged into the house. Mom called out when I walked in the door. "What took so long? It's getting dark out." She turned and looked at me. "What happened? Are you okay?"

I peered down at myself. Covered with a mixture of mud, grass stains, and smudge marks, I looked horrible. "Sheba dislikes having people in her pasture."

"But I thought she was friendly!"

"She is until you get into her pasture. Then she turns into Miss Demented Horse. If you can avoid being bit, struck, or kicked long enough to catch her, she behaves fine again." I sunk into a chair.

"Are you really okay?"

"She didn't hurt me. I'm just going to be sore tomorrow. She chased me around that pasture, again and again." I waved at my clothes.

"I don't know how many times I hit the ground. She kept catching me with a head swing. I'd almost get my hand on the halter and BAM, on the ground I'd go."

"Is she all right now?"

"Once I got the lead rope on her she behaved like a perfect angel. I'd rather not go try to catch her again, though. Let's give her a couple of days and hope for the best."

Mom worked with Sheba practically every day, lavishing her with attention and time. She avoided working and riding her. She just brushed her, talked to her, and spent time with her. Sheba slowly improved and got to the point where she only challenged people when they first went into the pasture. If I held still and gave her time to relax and talked to her, she backed down.

Sheba stood about an inch taller than Trixie and weighed fifty to a hundred pounds more. It took Trixie a week to concede that Sheba as the older more experienced horse, now held the top spot in the paddock.

One day in early January of '84, I went into the paddock to fill up the water bucket. I carried a pail in each hand, one filled with cold water, one with warm. Trixie liked her water warm in winter. Sheba only drank cold water. I ducked under the fence and stepped into the paddock, right onto a sheet of ice. As usual, Sheba challenged me. Sliding on the ice and unable to hold still, I tried setting down the buckets to stop my sliding, only to lose my balance, having to twist frantically while shuffling my feet to stay upright. Sheba whirled to kick me, a flash of brown ran in front of me and I flew backwards.

I went through the electric fence and the pail of warm water landed on top of me. Trixie thrashed on the ground by my feet, her hooves slipping back and forth on the ice as she tried to get back up. Sheba stood back to us, contemplating kicking again. I surged to my feet, grabbed the pail of cold water, and doused Sheba with it. She ran off to the other side of the paddock.

Trixie managed to get to her feet. When I checked her over, I found two hoof prints impressed into her shoulder. I went into the house and called Jane. I never saw an injury like that before and didn't know what to do. Jane said to keep an eye on it and make sure no infection or abscess formed. She also said I should be very thankful that Trixie took that kick. I'd have ended up in the hospital with broken bones, if I received a kick that hard.

Chapter # 6   Calling from the Hill

Two things happened in the spring of '84. One, our neighbor called Mom and asked for Sheba back. She said she kept having nightmares about giving her away. Mom returned Sheba to her. I thought it was unfair. Mom had spent so much time working with Sheba and she improved so much with Mom's careful handling. But Mom appeared fine with it. She said sometimes people realized how much something meant to them after they lost it. She said it would have been wrong to keep Sheba. And secondly, I started riding Trixie down to D + M Quarter Horse on the River Road and training her in their arena. Julie Dearborn offered me a trade. If I would clean stalls for them throughout the summer, I'd get free pasture for Trixie.

I found it difficult to make a decision. Trixie had always gone to the Browns in the summer and I really liked them. But I could save up hay money easier if I got pasture for free. I wanted to be able to buy Trixie's hay this year without Mom's help. She said Trixie was my horse and my responsibility, so I needed to make up my mind.

I decided to bring Trixie to D + M Quarter Horse to summer in their huge pasture. It started out on River Road, went along the side of the barn, up over a hill, and down through the woods to the flood plains of the Saco River. Seven horses, counting Trixie and one calf stayed in the pasture. Every night the horses got put into stalls. Trixie got placed in the smallest box stall, at the end of the barn.

Located about two miles from our house D + M Quarter Horse specialized in training reining horses. I got up in the morning and rode my bike down there. Julie put the horses out in the pasture early, before I arrived and then she went to work. I cleaned the stalls when I first showed up. Afterwards, I walked back to the hill in the big pasture.

I stood on that hill and looked down to the flood plains of the river, a wide even plain of dark green that grew tall and lush every summer, no matter how dry the season. I looked down there and saw the horses grazing. They stood so far away; they looked like brown, black, and white spots, no bigger than my thumbnail, against a field of green. They stood so far away; I couldn't tell which of the five brown spots was Trixie.

I stood on that hill and called.

"Trixie girl! Come on, beautiful!" One of the spots got taller, as a head popped up out of the grass. Then a nicker, loud and strong, floated up over the hill as Trixie answered me. The brown spot sprinted to the right and disappeared into the trees.

I closed my eyes and listened with every fiber in me. Then I heard the hoof-beats, at first so quiet they sounded like someone tapping their fingers against their leg. Next, they beat out rhythmically like the drumbeat in the melody of a country song. When they reverberated as loud as clapping hands, I opened my eyes and looked to the left.

Trixie almost seemed to be flying as she came out of those woods, her legs surging powerfully, her muscles rippling, her neck stretched out, her nostrils flared, her tail streaming out behind her. I stood there and my whole body filled with joy.

On that hill, it didn't matter that my clothes were hand-me-downs, ten years out of style. There, where the sound of the distant river and the breeze through the trees mingled into a tranquil melody, it didn't matter that I was all knees and elbows, constantly tripping over my own feet. In that special place overshadowed by pine trees stretching up towards the open sky, it didn't matter that my Dad thought of me as stupid, ugly, and worthless. Standing there on that hoof worn path of fertile dirt that the grass struggled to reclaim, I knew I was special. Because in that place, on that hill, the most beautiful horse in the whole world came running to me.

Free in that pasture, Trixie easily eluded capture if she wanted to. No grain. No treats, no rewards called her in. On that hill, it was just me. And on that hill I felt glad to be me. Trixie refused to come to anyone else's call. Julie often complained that Trixie only came to her for grain. But to me, Trixie flew. I was Trixie's girl and because she was strong, beautiful and special, so was I.

I stood on that hill and my heart lifted up free of all its sorrow as Trixie ran to me. She skidded to a stop, nudged me, and whickered softly. And I threw back my head and laughed at fate and its cruelties. On that hill, the world became a sparkling jewel that I held in my hand. There, life existed as a wonderful, amazing gift wrapped up in bright paper with a beautiful bow and handed to me, for no other reason than the fact that I was simply me.

*　*　*　*　*　*　*　*

Gordon Cole hired me for his haying crew again in the summer of '84. Stronger now, I worked in the loft about half the time. Heat collected up there, gathering more strength than it accumulated outdoors and the higher the haystack got inside the barn, the hotter it became. The barn swallows twisted, swooped, and swirled above the beams. Their nests built tight up against the roof rafters. The sweat soaked through my clothes and dripped down into my eyes, stinging them. The dust and chaff from the hay bales shrouded the ladders, the edge of the loft, everything.

The dust stuck to me and when I climbed down out of the loft to get a drink of water. My face, arms, and clothes were turned a dark green. The dust itched and I rubbed it off constantly. I cooled off by rinsing down with the water hose and I got so thirsty that I drank and drank and drank and only stopped when my stomach protested. Then as I climbed back up into the loft, I literally heard the water sloshing around inside me. The hay smelt really good, rich and fresh, so good that I instinctively inhaled deeply, only to then sneeze out the dust.

Always smiling and laughing, Andy Cole made it fun to work. He showed me how to go hay bale surfing, balancing myself as the conveyor carried it the length of the barn. Having carried countless bales before, the old conveyor dipped down between the beams that supported it. The bale rolled up and down and swayed side to side as I tried to balance on it. Andy bale surfed when the hay pile half filled the barn and to fall off meant a ten foot drop. I put off trying it until the hay stack reached within a couple of feet of the conveyor. I fell off a lot, though I never saw Andy fall off. When I finally managed to stay on the bale for the whole length of the barn I felt awesome, like it was a huge accomplishment proving my physical prowess.

I kept getting sunburn and peeling. Half the time I looked like a lobster, the other half I looked like a snake trying to shed its skin. I never seemed to tan, just burn and peel, again and again.

Shocking Mom, Julie Dearborn asked if I'd mind taking care of the horses by myself for ten days. She and her husband David planned on taking a couple of horses out to a reining competition in Ohio. Mom dithered back and forth in her decision, unsure of my ability to handle the responsibility. But at fifteen, I had grown sure of my capability with horses and I convinced her to let me take the job.

Encompassing a huge amount of work, the first seven days flew by. In the morning, I gave the horses their grain, put fly repellent on them, lead them all out to their various pastures, filled the outside water barrels, fed the dogs, and then cleaned the stalls. In the evenings, I brought the horses in, gave them their nightly hay and grain, filled the inside water buckets, fed the dogs, and locked up the barn.

On the eighth evening, the horses acted nervous and jumpy. It took a lot longer to get them in than usual. Even after I fed and grained them, they snorted and paced around in their stalls, even Pete the workhorse, a creature as steady and bombproof in personality and training as a horse could get. When I realized that all of the horses including Trixie remained frightened by something they smelt or heard outside, I got real scared myself. When I went to the barn door and called in the dogs, Penny the Border Collie, and Bradley the beagle-mix ran in the second I opened the door. They literally fell inside, tripping over the doorstep and each other, whining in a continuous non-stop, vibrating buzz. Together, they dashed over and hid themselves in the hay pile. Where was Heaki?

Heaki, a German pointer that David trained as a guard and hunting dog failed to respond, so I mustered up my courage and stepped out into the barnyard. It had taken me so long to care for the horses that darkness now gathered outside.

I called for Heaki again, then heard growling coming from beside the barn. By the time I rounded the corner, I trembled with each fearful step. In the pasture beside the barn dipped a deep gully with poplar and birch trees growing in it. Staring down into that watercourse, Heaki growled. I looked down into it and fear swelled through me. My eyes struggled to see in the dim evening light.

I had watched enough National Geographic Specials to see lions hunting wildebeest and wolves preparing to attack a herd of elk. Looking down into the gully, I saw a gray shadow stalking through the trees, crouching low to the ground, creeping forward step by step, as if preparing to spring forward in a deadly burst of speed, filling my racing heart with fear. The gray shadow looked blurry in the low light, I could perceive only two things clearly. It stalked along on four legs and it was headed straight at Heaki and me.

I froze in fear. Heaki acted. He backed up until he bumped into my legs, then turned his head and growled at me. I stumbled back a couple of steps. Time after time, Heaki drove me back, stumbling, step by step. When we made it around the corner, and the gully faded out of my sight, I turned and walked to the barn door. I wanted to run, but to run invited a chase. I didn't want whatever occupied the gully chasing me.

I so wanted to slam and lock the barn door, but Heaki stood guard at the corner of the barn, alert, stiff and growling."Heaki, come," I managed to squeak. Heaki ignored me, not even twitching in his guard stance. I took a deep breath, "Heaki, come!" Heaki spun and ran for the barn door and I slammed it so quickly behind him I nearly amputated his short stump of a tail.

It took three tries, with shaking hands, to dial home on the barn phone. I cringed at the thought of going out there to ride my bike home. My voice shook so much that Mom barely understood me, while the horses continued to kick the barn walls, whinnying up a storm. Heaki stood in the center of the hall facing the barn door, growling. Mom headed right down.

Mom drove the car right up to the barn door and left it running with the lights on. As soon as she entered the barn, she asked. "What's wrong with them?" She waved at the horses pacing in their stalls, kicking the walls, her head swung quickly from one horse to another. The two horses in the tie stalls stomped their feet and tossed their heads.

"Something was lurking down in the gully. It upset the dogs and scared the horses." I pointed beside the barn. "The horses acted nervous when I brought them in. Heaki stood outside growling at something. None of the horses want to calm down. Even Trixie refuses to relax." Mom walked down to look at Trixie with me. She paced around in her stall, snorting and kicking.

Mom shook her head and rubbed her hands together, massaging her knuckles in a nervous habit. "You can't make them calm down, so we should just go. I'll drive you down tomorrow morning to take care of them." I nodded. After this evening, I feared being alone down at D+M!

As we walked down the hall, Mom looked at the horses in the left hand stalls and I watched the ones on the right. I saw that Goofy, whose real name stretched out longer than mine, thrashed about in his tie stall. Sent here only green halter broke, he gave a fine ride now. A sweet-tempered Palomino, who always clowned around, he quickly earned the nick-name. As I walked by he threw his weight from side to side. I saw that somehow the weighted tie rope had gotten wrapped around his neck and now it strangled him. I realized I had only moments before it became too late. I leapt into his stall.

Mom turned, not knowing what I tried to achieve, she made a grab for me. I felt her fingers graze down beside my spine, failing to get a grip on me. I jumped up and walked halfway up the wall, on the second slated board. Even when he threw his weight over to my side, Goofy just pinned my legs against the wall holding me in place until he threw himself against the other wall. I heard Mom screaming at me. I ignored her. She still failed to notice the rope around Goofy's neck. But growing up with Dad trained me to become real good at ignoring screaming.

It only took a minute to work my way up to Goofy's halter. Luckily, he remained good-natured even as he struggled to breath. I pulled up the slack from the bottom of the tie rope and down on his halter, getting just enough slack to unsnap the tie rope. I un-wrapped it from around Goofy's neck. He calmed down almost instantly, standing still and taking in huge, deep breaths.

"Mom, what should I do now?"

"Get out here!" Mom commanded in a no-nonsense voice.

I looked out at her and saw her pacing in a tight circle, her steps jerky and her hands constantly moving. *Oh-oh, Mom has reached hornet mad mode.* "But Mom, what about Goofy? Should I leave him untied?"

"I'm too mad at you to really care about him, right now. You scared me half to death. How did you see the rope around his neck? And who names a horse Goofy?"

If I managed to get her to laugh, Mom wouldn't be so mad.

"I just saw the rope when he tried to toss his head. And his real name is Golden something or other, blah - blah - blah. But he acts like a big clown, so we call him Goofy." Mom's mouth quirked up on the right side as she struggled between grinning and remaining stern-faced.

"Tie him up. If he likes to clown around, he'll get into everything." Goofy did like to play with stuff. I hesitated with the rope. What caused it to choke him?

Mom watched me standing there, indecisive about my choices. "Has he ever got caught like that before?"

My long tousled, hair slapped against my cheeks as I shook my head. "No, the design of the weighted tie rope supposedly prevents this. The weight on the end of the rope keeps the slack pulled out. I don't know how he managed to get it loose enough to wrap around his neck."

"That means he probably won't do it again." Mom stood still for a minute, thinking it through. "But a horse with a goofy personality would likely get into trouble loose."

I nodded and tied Goofy back up. Mom grabbed me the instant I got out of the stall. She gave me a little shake and then pulled me into a tight hug, quickly released me and shook me once again. "Never do that again. I shouldn't have let you take this job. You are only fifteen!"

"I handled it, Mom. Goofy is okay and so am I. It's only for two more days."

"It is thirteen horses, Kim, too much for a teenager to handle alone. You won't be doing this again," Mom announced. I sighed with exaggerated gusto, trying to show Mom that she was losing all perspective. But she barely even noticed. When Mom proclaimed something like that, she refused to change her mind. Oh well, Julie hadn't told me about any other competitions she wanted to attend. Maybe she didn't plan on going to any more of them.

Mom drove me back and forth, and hovered around every time I took care of the horses until the Dearborn's came back. Neither the dogs, the horses, nor I wanted to go down into the gully to investigate what lurked there. Julie tried to make light of it, when I told them. But upon hearing about how Heaki behaved David became obviously worried.

Three evenings after the Dearborn's returned, their next door neighbors Newfoundland got attacked right next to its owners back house steps. The man let the dog out before bed and heard one yelp. When he turned on his flood lights, he found his dog lying in a pool of blood, and rushed it into emergency surgery to get its neck and chest stitched back together. Theories ran rampant for months, coyotes, wolves, a cougar, wild-dogs. The only thing apparent to all was that nothing got trapped (though many tried various methods) and no one found tracks clear enough to pinpoint a species. The Newfoundland healed, but became forever timid afterwards and Heaki remained tense and edgy every dusk and dawn for weeks.

*   *   *   *   *   *   *   *

I bought all of Trixie's hay myself in the fall of '84. I also saved up the money for her spring shots. That year, I brought her home for the winter and started riding her bareback. Trixie always gave a big sigh, when I saddled her, and I always teased her about being such a poor over-worked horse. She put on the hang-dog, kicked-puppy look as well as an award-winning actress and used that expression every time she saw the saddle coming. I remained clueless as to why she suddenly disliked the saddle so much.

She didn't act mean or scared. She gave me the abused-puppy-dog look and exhaled a huge drawn out sigh. When I tightened the cinch, she jumped up with her rear end in a half-hearted lurch. Her feet barely even came off the ground, before she sighed and gave me the 'poor-me' look again. So I started riding her bareback, because she made me feel sorry for her, my silly-filly, the poor over-worked horse.

I wanted to train Trixie to parade dance on command, figuring out how to do it presented a problem. How could I get her to execute a spontaneous action on demand? She often paraded around, high-stepping with her hooves flashing prettily in graceful arcs. Usually she performed it when I wanted to go slow because of muddy, snowy, or rocky ground. Trixie never feared for her footing and tried to ignore my caution. She wanted to go full-speed ahead; no matter over what ground or in which direction, just as long as we headed there in a hurry.

*   *   *   *   *   *   *   *

When it came time to put Trixie out to pasture, Mom gave me permission to pasture her at D+M Quarter Horse. But she refused to allow me to watch the horses again if Julie went to a competition. She vetoed it every time, even just the short weekend shows. She even called up Julie and told her so.

Mom always said I got my stubbornness from Dad. I doubted that it came solely from him. Mom wasn't a pushover. Sometimes I managed to out-last her, but when she laid down the law, forget it. She dug in and refused to budge.

Julie conceded to defeat. She understood Mom worried about me and just wanted to protect me. They got in four more horses to train and ran short of stalls in the barn. Trixie, Gypsy, the pony, Pete, and the calf got turfed out into the big pasture. They stood under the trees for shade and if the weather got bad, Julie agreed to stable them overnight in the barn hall. But the rest of the time, they remained out in the pasture.

At first, I worried obsessively. I remembered how scared the horses acted about whatever lurked in the gully. But then I realized the next farm over left their mares and two month old foals out overnight. If anything decided to go after a horse, it would go for one of the foals, not the full-grown horses. I kept a close eye on those foals. I planned to take Trixie home or to the Browns', before the next sunset, if one of the foals got attacked.

But nothing happened. The horses no longer showed any fear of the gully. The mares and foals never get spooked or chased by anything. Whatever prowled in the gully last summer during those spooky weeks, vanished, just as it appeared, with no warning and left behind no clue of its identity or if it'd ever return.

$*$ $*$ $*$ $*$ $*$ $*$ $*$ $*$ $*$

The year I turned sixteen, Gordon Cole got rid of his cows and closed down the dairy. The monetary value of milk lowered too far. For years the dairy lost money. It cost more to feed the cows than the milk sold for. So, no haying crew would operate on Cole Farm that year.

I started working for Mr. Logan in Goodwin Mills. A tall, lean man with grey hair, bright, sparkling eyes, a deep, hearty laugh, and talented, artistic hands, he worked as a sign painter. He taught me how to select, sand, glue, and prime or stain wood, how to drill both metal and wood, and how to countersink the holes, so the screws lay flush with the surface.

At first, I worked for him after school twice a week and

on Saturday mornings. But when I finished my sophomore year and school let out, I worked two, three, or even four full days a week for him. I rode my bike over to his house, carrying my lunch in my backpack. His wife stored my lunch in the refrigerator for me. At lunch time, I got thirty minutes off. Sometimes, I ate inside with the Logan's. Other times, I walked over to the millpond and sat on the dam to eat, watching the reflection of the clouds skim across the pond's surface, as unhindered and free on the water's surface as they were in the sky.

Mr. Logan explained how to rip off old cedar shingles. I tore them off the whole backside of his huge barn. Then he showed me how to put up new cedar shingles, and I shingled the barn. He demonstrated how to scrape and paint the house. He applied the trim and I painted the rest.

I also still worked for Miss Waterhouse and Charlotte Cole and for the first time ever, I needed to plan when to spend time with Trixie. I tried to go see her every evening, but sometimes my exhaustion made it impossible to ride my bike down to D+M's. Other times, I managed to go see Trixie and give her some attention, but lacked the energy to ride her.

Mr. Logan always asked me. "How about starting tomorrow at eight?" Or he'd say, "Tomorrow, you work for Miss Waterhouse. Want to come the day after?"

By midsummer, I felt torn. Finally, I worked up the courage to talk to Mr. Logan. "I like the work, but I miss spending time with Trixie."

Mr. Logan stood quietly for a moment and I wondered about his thoughts and feelings. *Was he mad?* "Well, let's stop work at noon. Then the afternoon stands open to spend with your horse."

I nodded vigorously. "Thank you. I'll go down to D+M at about three, when the evening sea breeze starts to pick up and cool things off and spend hours with Trixie. Plus, I won't be tired."

Mr. Logan's right cheek creased with a deep dimple as he smiled. "It's okay to tell me if you don't want to work. Whenever you want to spend time with your horse, just tell me." I felt relieved, reassured that I worked for a good, kind man who cared about my wishes.

*   *   *   *   *   *   *   *

In mid-August, I went down to see Trixie early one morning. She stood right beside the woods on top of the hill, not in her usual spot down by the river. The minute she saw me; she whickered and started hobbling towards me, hardly putting any weight on her left foreleg. I found no cuts on her, and checked her hoof when she picked it up for me, to look for rocks or twigs. Nothing had lodged inside it.

I led her, limping into the barn. David went out into the pasture to check on the other horses. I called up my mother and then the vet. In a little over an hour, a different vet than normal showed up. He looked too young to be a vet to me, barely out of college, a tall, skinny boy-man.

He jumped out of the van wearing a thigh-length, white lab coat that flapped in the breeze and quickly walked over to us and grabbed for Trixie's halter. When she reared straight up and trumpeted, he backed up real quickly.

When I finally got Trixie calmed down a little, I quickly turned to him. I wanted to scream at him, but I knew that would only scare my girl so I managed to keep my voice level. I needed to tell this guy how foolish his behavior was.

"What's wrong with you? You never grab the halter of a horse unfamiliar to you, especially if they're hurt. You talk to a horse when you approach it, keep your voice calm and your tone friendly." I pointed at him and he backed up a step. "And you always refrain from wearing something like that around a horse. Horses get spooked by things that flap around. Lucky for you, Trixie has a gentle nature. Half the horses I know bite or kick when you do something that foolish."

He stood there gaping at me and Trixie. Maybe he was shocked that someone a foot shorter and probably ten years younger than him dared to lecture him on how to act around horses. He froze in place. His eyes widened, his brow wrinkled, and his mouth opened and closed slightly a couple of times. Then his mouth shut, his shoulders went back, and he cleared his throat.

"They told me an emergency had occurred."

"It has. Trixie barely puts any weight on her left foreleg. David found an overhang down by the river, collapsed, with a hoof print in it where a horse broke through and got caught in the roots. Trixie is the only one lame, so she likely fell through by herself."

The vet nodded. This time, he talked to Trixie as he walked up to her.

"You're a beautiful girl. So you got into a misadventure by the riverside, huh? Hmm, how bad was it though? That's the question." He bypassed her halter and ran his hands down her shoulder and leg, then lifted her hoof and looked at it. When he put it down, he asked. "Please, walk her once around the barnyard."

I waited for him to step back and then made a slow trip around the yard with Trixie. He watched, nodded, and went to the van, returning with a bottle of Bute and without his white lab coat. I smiled. At least, he learned not to make the same mistake twice.

He prescribed Bute morning and night for Trixie. By what he observed, he thought Trixie had badly pulled some muscles, and possibly strained a tendon. If she showed no improvement within a week, we should trailer her down to the clinic for some tests.

I read the dosage he prescribed for her. "This dosage amount goes to a thousand to twelve hundred pound horse. Trixie only weighs about nine hundred pounds."

"It won't hurt her. It's just a painkiller," he explained.

I cocked my head and thought about it. A vet needed to go through a lot of schooling before they got their degree, so he must know what he was talking about. I tied Trixie in the barn hall and gave her a pail of water, then went out and cut some grass for her, so she'd have something to eat. I hoped Julie decided to let me keep Trixie in a stall until she improved some. Over half of the summer remained ahead of us. Bringing my silly filly home now made no sense. Plus, I couldn't lead her home in her lame state anyway.

When Julie got home from work, I asked her for a stall to stable my girl in but Julie shook her head.

"We don't have a stall to spare, Kim. We accepted money to board and train these horses. They need to stay in at night. And Trixie can't remain in the hall during the day. We need to train five horses this afternoon and that requires the use of the crossties." Julie touched my shoulder gently. "You can keep Trixie in the hall at night, 'til she improves. But she needs to go out during the day. If you want, David and I will trailer her home for you after we work the horses. Put Trixie out for now. Call your Mom and see what she tells you to do."

I reluctantly lead Trixie out to the pasture. She limped less now. I couldn't make up my mind. If I brought her home, the paddock hardly grew any grass in it. She needed to eat, so that left me either buying hay or cutting grass for her. If I left her down at D + M, she fed herself. But if the other horses got to running, she'd try to run, too. I went back in the barn and called Mom.

Mom left the decision up to me. She didn't know what to do either? She ended the conversation with. "You have to decide, Kim."

Why was it, that when I didn't know what to do, everybody I asked for advice said it was my decision? And when I knew what to do, everyone said I made the wrong decision and gave me advice.

I sat on a bale of shavings and thought about it. Then it dawned on me. *Ask Jane Allen!* She knew everything about horses. She gave good advice. She always gave it nicely and explained why she suggested doing it that way. I picked up the barn phone to call her. But then I heard a trumpeting horse in the pasture, I dropped the phone and raced outdoors. That was Trixie! I sprinted out to the pasture in a total panic.

A cloud of dust rose down by the pond and the sound of hooves hitting flesh filled the air. Where was Trixie? The dust cleared a little and I screamed. "Jon, Trixie, no!" They danced around each other. The rest of the horses, except for Pete who ignored the commotion, milled in a circle surrounding them. I groaned. Gypsy lead the herd, but Jon policed it. Trixie stood near the bottom of the pecking order with only Pete, Goofy, the pony, and the cow beneath her.

I screamed and waved my arms. "Jon, get, leave her alone." I stood on the side of the fence, wondering how to get Trixie out of there. Part of me knew I couldn't. When together in the pasture, the horses ruled their world with instincts as old as time. I knew Trixie tolerated, even welcomed me into that world. But the other horses might not. Right now, Jon definitely wouldn't condone any interference in his control over the herd.

So I stood on the side of the fence, and watched as Jon and Trixie danced around each other. Even at a distance, it remained easy to discern the differences between the two bays because Jon stood six inches taller and his boning and musculature hugely outstripped Trixie's. She showed no pain at all now, an extremely, bad sign. No way had my silly filly miraculously healed in a mere couple of hours. She either possessed an ultra-sensitivity to Bute or she suffered from an overdose. Now, she felt no pain at all. That meant she could hurt herself even worse, and not realize it until the medicine wore off.

Jon and Trixie both squealed. The other horses milled around again. Clouds of dust spiraled up into the air. I heard impacts on flesh and Trixie squealed again. David and Julie came running out of the barn. They looked down at the dust cloud. "What's going on?" David asked.

"Jon and Trixie are fighting," I said and grimaced as Trixie squealed again. Then with a thunder of hoofs, Jon came running out of the dust cloud with Trixie a mere fifteen feet behind him. My jaw dropped. *What? How?* Jon sprinted away from Trixie.

The big bay wheeled on one back hoof, showing off his superb reining horse agility and screamed. Oh, geez, he was really going to pound Trixie now. She never faltered in her stride. She ran right into Jon shoulder to shoulder, pushing him back. He stumbled, trying to regain his balance. She reared up, striking her hooves down at his shoulder as he scrambled backwards and her head whipped back and forth full of flashing teeth. I gritted my own teeth and shuddered. Bloody heck! Jon outweighed Trixie by about three hundred pounds. He bulged with muscles, a Quarter Horse in the prime of his life and in working condition. Why did she ram him like that?

Jon shrieked in panic. His hooves churning up clods of dirt as he lurched away from her, turned, and ran.

Julie shook her head, her long, sleek blonde ponytail whipping back and forth. "That dosage of Bute should have just lifted the pain. She has got to be ultra-sensitive for it to do this."

Jon wheeled again. Trixie reared up and slashed her hooves at his face. I'd never seen any mare rear that high before. I groaned. "She thinks she's super-horse."

"Yup, she's definitely suffering from delusions of grandeur," David drawled as he rubbed a calloused hand over his stubble beard and lifted his right foot to rest his boot on the bottom fence board. He tilted his cowboy hat back allowing his coal black eyes to reflect the suns glare as his gaze followed Jon wheeling and racing up, over, and around the hill slopes, trees, and rocks in the pasture trying to evade Trixie's determined pursuit. "Wait until they calm down and then try to catch her. If you can capture her, put her in Jon's stall. You are going to have to take her home." I bobbed my head in agreement. Trixie had made that decision rather decisively.

I stayed out by the fence all afternoon. Twice, the horses calmed down. The first time, I went into the pasture and called her. As always, my beautiful girl came galloping straight at me. Unfortunately, terrified of Trixie's drug-altered personality the six horses between us took one look at her headed their way and sprinted away. I knew Trixie wouldn't trample me. Still, I choose to err on the side of caution considering the six horses racing in front of her and I made a hasty retreat out of the pasture. I suppose Trixie decided that since the other horses were running, she might as well chase them.

After the second time the horses calmed down, I decided to walk out and get her. Way up at the end of the pasture by the River Road, she looked up and spotted me, just as I walked past Jon. She made a sudden dash for me. When Jon looked up and saw her coming, he turned and ran for it.

Trixie's face glimmered with glee. She banked right, cut across the marshy area that any horse in their right mind avoided, and headed after him.

After dark, Trixie started limping again and we managed to catch the horses. David and Julie decided it had become too late to trailer her home. They were tired and hungry. David promised to haul her for me in the morning.

That night,I gave Trixie a quarter of her dose of Bute. I didn't dare to give her more, because she was going to spend the night tied in the hall.

The next morning, I found my girl in horrible shape. She braced her left shoulder and ribcage up against the wall and held her left front hoof up clear of the floor while her right front leg angled out, pressing her body's weight into the thick, cedar boards. Her sides heaved and she dripped sweat. She stood with her rear end tilted, the left hindquarter jutting up. I watched her right rear hoof drop down to touch the ground and she jolted, jerking it back up into the air. It slowly descended again as her left rear leg trembled with the effort of holding herself up. The wall supporting her barely kept her on her feet.

I called the vet immediately. He wanted her trailered to the nearest clinic to perform x-rays, but David lacked the time to trailer her to the clinic.

Tears streaked down my face. My girl needed help. I looked at her and shuddered as her pain slammed into me, making my heart clinch and my lungs squeeze. I paced back and forth. What could I do?

Suddenly, my lungs loosened and air entered them freely once more as I remembered Jane Allen. I raced to the phone and called her. When she heard how badly hurt Trixie was and how upset I was, she canceled the day's riding lessons in order to haul Trixie to the clinic.

Fifteen minutes later, Jane was backing her horse trailer into the yard. She parked, lowered the trailer door, and nodded to me. "Load her up, Kim."

I walked forward and Trixie's neck stretched out to its fullest length. She didn't want to move. "I'm sorry, girl. We need to get you to the clinic. WALK."

She wobbled away then against, then away from the wall and hopped forward on her right foreleg. She swayed and her belly trembled. Then, with a mighty heave, she hopped her left hindquarter forward. Somehow, balancing on two legs, hop by hop, Trixie walked.

Jane watched the first couple of steps and went to her truck. She closed the trailer gate, and backed across the yard until she reached the barn door, eliminating over half of the distance Trixie needed to traverse. Next, she lowered the gate into the barn hall and began arranging and tying straps up on the left side of the trailer.

Halfway down the hall, Trixie came to a stop, swaying unsteadily from side to side. Her every exhalation blew out in a loud snort as she gasped for air. I squatted down and put my right shoulder to her left, cupped her left knee in my left palm, and wrapped my right hand beneath her knee, holding her dangling hoof up free of the floor and helping to steady her. She leaned against me and her labored breathing quieted. After a few minutes, we began the hop-hop procession again.

Once Trixie finally stood in the trailer, Jane snapped two lead ropes onto her halter and pulled them up tight to opposite sides of the trailer walls. Then she passed three straps under her belly.

"Okay Kim, come over here to the other side of the partition." I stepped out the side door of the trailer and re-entered it from the back, walking into the other stall.

"Let's push the partition over as far as it goes. If we wedge Trixie in as tight as possible, it'll help support her." As soon as the partition touched Trixie, she leaned into it and we both shoved hard to get her standing straight upright. Then, we locked the partition in place.

Jane pulled up on the front strap under Trixie's belly

and fed it through a hook on the top right side of the trailer.

"I'm using these straps as an extra support." She explained. "If I cinch them up firmly under her belly, they'll take some of the weight off her legs." I helped pull up the last two straps and by the time we finished, Trixie stood easier, her breathing evened out and her legs stopped trembling. Lastly, we pulled the rump rope up tight and closed the gate. There Trixie stood, firmly squished into place, sandwiched from the sides and roped in tight from the front, back, and underneath.

Jane looked over the tailgate and nodded in satisfaction. "That'll keep her upright on the road. If she went down in the condition she's in, we'd never get her back up."

We headed out, with me sitting nearly sideways in my seat, straining to hear if any thuds or bumps came from the trailer. Both the trailer and pickup remained silent until we got halfway to the clinic, Jane was the first to speak. "I hate to say it Kim, because Trixie's a good horse. But if she fractured a bone, the only humane thing to do is to put her down. You don't have either the money or the facilities required to support her until a bone heals and she'd be in pain all the time if it doesn't."

I shuddered in my seat, not wanting to face Jane or the horrible decision that lay ahead of me. But Jane refused to let me hide from my responsibility. "It'd be cruel to let her suffer, Kim."

I shuddered again and gave a nod. *I'm not ready for this. We're supposed to have decades together. It can't end like this.* Jane gave me a quick, firm pat on the shoulder. The pickup cab once again filled with foreboding silence. My mind understood what Jane said and agreed with her. Trixie shouldn't suffer in vain, if she couldn't heal. But my heart screamed. "No, no, I won't put Trixie down!" So I rode down to the clinic in silence, dreading what was to come.

I didn't cry. I wouldn't cry. Tears were a waste and never benefited anyone or anything. Plus, when people saw what hurt you, they learned how to hurt you. I rode with Jane, quiet and dry-eyed on the outside, but inside my heart screamed and cried every mile of the way.

The vet did x-rays on Trixie's left foreleg and right hind leg. Thankfully, no breaks showed up, but copious swelling did. My beautiful girl had injured some tendons, possibly even overstretched some ligaments and the vet estimated she wouldn't be able to carry a rider for at least nine months, possibly a year. We were lucky. Trixie's youth benefited her. An older horse probably couldn't have healed after such injuries, especially with two damaged legs.

I gently patted Trixie's neck, as I leaned over to kiss her nose. She put her head over my shoulder and I stood cradled between her neck and head, staring at the vet, almost afraid to believe him.

"She will heal though?"

"Eventually, in nine months to a year," the vet's hand writing on Trixie's chart stopped moving and he stared at me with chocolate eyes. He cocked his head and his blonde bangs flopped down to his eyebrows.

I thought it over. "Good, that's good."

"Most people get terribly upset about being unable to ride their horse for that long. Do you own another horse?" He asked as he shook his head tossing his bangs back into place.

"No, but Trixie *will* heal, and I can still spend time with her. Just no riding." I shrugged. "That's okay, huh, beautiful? We'll take you home and you'll heal up. Then in a year, I can ride you again." I turned and looked the vet in the eye. "What about the pain? I don't really want to give her Bute again."

The vet's brow furrowed and his eyes narrowed for a moment, and then his face cleared and his lips turned up in a small smile. "I'll give her a shot for the ride home. After that, you might want to give her half doses for a little while. You want to give her just enough to take some of the pain away, but not all of it. You want her to feel some pain, so she doesn't overdo it. Try half a dose. If she starts to get too active, cut it to a third."

I agreed with a quick bob of my head. I never wanted Trixie trying to act like super-horse again. We might not be so fortunate twice. She was going to be okay. Plus, I'd saved a lot of money working for Mr. Logan. I used it to pay the vet.

I gave Trixie partial doses of Bute for two weeks. We cut grass for her on the side of the road and brought it home in trash bags. I gave her three trash bags full a day. We stocked up a couple of days' worth at a time and put it in the cube van.

At one point, I borrowed some money from Mom to buy Trixie's hay. The vet bill cleaned out my savings. But I kept working after school and paid Mom back.

Jane Allen arranged for our 4-H group to receive a guided tour of the vet clinic. The outside of the building had red metal siding, a big sliding door alongside the traditional 'house' door, and a wide gently sloped roof.

Inside, the veterinarian assistants showed us the pool

where the horses got exercised, and the operating room, which scared me with its four padded walls and huge operating table they'd constructed from a lift like mechanics used to work on cars. They used the lift to raise the horse up off the floor after they had knocked it out with anesthesia.

Walking through the clinic and seeing the sick and injured horses upset me the most. Some of them seemed almost normal. A couple of them had been operated on, and they looked miserable. They appeared pain-free, but twitched fearfully at every little sound. Their eyes darted from side to side in confusion. I couldn't imagine anything worse than going through an operation with no understanding of why it had happened to you.

I felt the fear pouring out of those horse's eyes. They experienced fear because their world got turned upside down and they didn't know why. They felt betrayed because the people they trusted failed to protect them. They endured in silence, but their eyes teemed with disillusion and dread.

*   *   *   *   *   *   *   *

In the summer of '85, when I brought Trixie home then kept her there through the fall and winter I began to comprehend many things. Whenever the home situation got bad, I left and went to be with Trixie. Now that she remained home, getting away became impossible.

I never understood how my Mother and brother ever endured staying home all the time. Where were their sanctuaries? As I watched my brother, I realized Ev found his haven in books. He went to his room, read, and became a part of the book. That way, he no longer resided in his room. Instead, he lived inside the book.

Mom escaped only infrequently. Sometimes she worked and got away from the house or Dad stayed out in the garage, laboring on some pet project. Mom played country music. Anne Murray, Ronnie Milsap, John Denver, Crystal Gayle, and Alabama filled the house with joyful sounds. Mom and I sang along as Ev playfully plugged his ears and made faces at us. The house brimmed with happiness and laughter until Dad came back.

I realized that the things I loved most about my father were his possibilities, but he never lived up to them. I loved his beautiful blue eyes, except they only truly sparkled when he screamed at us. I liked his intelligence, only he found it impossible to refrain from "lording" it over us. I respected his strength, although he never really put effort into his work. I admired so many things about him, and yet he never even seemed to consider his potential. When I looked at my father, I dreamed of all the achievements within his reach. He failed to see that dream or maybe he didn't care about it. He behaved just the way he wanted to and saw no reason to change.

On Dad's bad days, I still joined Trixie out in the lean-to, brushing her and talking to her. But I never really escaped, because I still heard Dad screaming in the house. Back then, I always felt guilty that I spent my time hiding in the barn. Mom couldn't run away and hide. Ev went up to his room and sometimes Dad followed him upstairs and yelled at him loud enough for me to clearly hear every word from outside the house.

I felt like a coward, always running. Yet I found it impossible to force myself to stay. When my father yelled at us, a horrible anger filled me, because he always lied. My mother's intellect allowed her to figure out the taxes for my father's business. No stupid person ever figured out taxes and my brother ranked as one of the top ten students in his class. I tested above normal at school as well, but according to Dad, we were all complete idiots in every way.

Now, at sixteen, I understand more, I realized that names existed for what Dad put us through, names like emotional and psychological abuse. My brother considered us lucky that Dad never physically abused us.

I doubted any such luck. I'd received many bad bruises, strains, and cuts over the years. When they healed, the pain went away. But with the injuries our father inflicted, the pain never left. No bruise showed. Sometimes, I wished them to be visible. Maybe then people would realize what sort of man he was. Whenever I spoke of my father to anyone, the preacher, the teacher, the boy next door- they always said how lucky I was to have such a smart father. I wondered, if I sported bruises would they have thought the same thing. But these bruises remained hidden where no one ever saw them.

Ev shook me awake. "Get up."

"Ugh…. Uh." I rubbed my eyes hard. "What?"

"Get up. Dad wants to cut down a tree."

I rolled over and stared at my clock on the night stand. The blurry red numbers glared ominously at me. "It's the middle of the night, 11:30, Ev."

"Since when has that mattered. Get up. Dad wants us to

help him." Ev threw over his shoulder as he left my room.

I slid out of bed, shook my head hard to clear it, and got dressed because Ev as usual, hit the nail on the head. To Dad, it never mattered that it happened to be the middle of the night. He never got up before eleven in the morning and we frequently saw him eating his breakfast when we got home from school at three in the afternoon. So to him, it failed to compute that Ev and I needed to go to school in the morning, or that the neighbors lay in their beds sleeping, or that cutting trees after dark invited disaster. He wanted to cut trees. So nobody and nothing stood a chance of dissuading him from doing it, right then, *because* he wanted to.

I stumbled downstairs. Mom handed me a flashlight. "He wants us outside."

I followed her out. Dad walked partway down the driveway dragging a rope behind him. He tied it to the back hitch of the pickup and waved Ev towards the driver's door. "When the tree starts to go over, you pull it down the driveway to make sure it misses the house."

I traced the rope back and up into the air with the flashlights beam. About fifteen feet off the ground, the rope looped the tree and knotted around itself.

"Dad, that pine looks heavy." Ev cocked his head to the side and looked Dad in the eye. They stood nearly the same height now that Ev shot up in another growth spurt. "Do you really think the trucks strong enough to pull it over?"

"I'll cut the tree to fall in that direction. You just need to tug it to start it going." Dad turned back towards the tree as Ev hesitated at the pickup door.

I tried to follow the trees height, but the flashlights beam faded into nothing long before I reached the trees top. "Dad, is the rope long enough?" I asked as I realized the tree stood far taller than the ropes length.

Dad failed to even glance at me or the trees height. "I know what I'm doing."

I looked over at Ev. I worried about the pine landing on the pickup and him. Ev's eyes met mine and his right hand reached out and patted the pickups roll-bar.

I nodded at him as I got the message. He thought the roll-bar held enough strength to keep the pine from crushing the cab on top of him.

"Pay attention." Dad screamed and I turned my eyes back to him. He pointed at me. "You watch the treetop. When it starts to go over, you wave Ev to start pulling it."

"The light doesn't reach the treetop. Wouldn't waiting for daylight be safer?"

"I want to do it, now. And watch the tree as far up as you can see." He turned to Mom.

"You shine your light on the trunk so I see clearly where to cut."

"Evans, maybe we should do this during the day?" She said as her shaking hand made the light beam dance around the tree trunk.

Dad's head went back and he screamed at full volume. "I know what I'm doing." His right hand shot up and grabbed his hard hat as it slid back, nearly falling off his head. His eyes squinted at us. His brow furrowed. He jabbed his finger into the air in front of Mom and me. "Do what I tell you to?"

Mom nodded and shined her flashlight on the chainsaw as Dad poured gas and oil into it. I walked around and looked at the mighty pine from the sides. It measured wider at its base than my arms span by a good couple of feet and it stood about twenty feet away from the house. Ten feet to its right, the electrical wire that carried juice from the house to the garage hung suspended fifteen feet off the ground. Behind the pine in the driveway turn-around stood Mom, me, and Dad and fifteen feet to the left the pickup idled as Ev waited for his signal to race down the driveway.

I rubbed my sleepy eyes and tried to think it through as Dad tugged the pull cord, jerking the chainsaw to life. Oily smoke tainted the air with a greasy stench as the chainsaw's growly, thundering roar shattered the night's peace.

Suddenly, my mind snapped into full wakefulness and I realized this night stood no chance of achieving a happy ending. The tree had absolutely no direction to fall in that wouldn't result in a disaster of some sort.

Dad sliced the chainsaw's blade into the tree. The smell of pine pitch mingled with the smoke. I stared at the tree as far up as possible. Dad pulled the chainsaw out and began another cut into the trunk.

The tree groaned as its branches shuddered. I turned towards the truck to holler and wave for Ev to go. But he'd already gunned it. The tires spit gravel up into the air as the truck lurched, bouncing full-speed ahead down the driveway.

The tree leaned towards the house. Dad screamed.

"Drive! Drive!"

I yelled back at him. "He's already driving."

The pickup raced away. The tree toppled closer and closer to the house. The rope stretched and stretched and then stretched some more. Dad dropped the chainsaw on the ground. He hopped from one foot to the other, waving his hard hat in the air.

"Drive! Drive!"

Mom moaned. "Oh, no. Oh, no." She clapped her hands to her mouth, nearly bashing her nose with the flashlight.

Pops, snaps, and cracks exploded into the air. The tree loomed over the house. Time slowed. I shook my head in resignation. Time stuttered and started back up. I muttered. "Bye-bye, house."

Ev ran out of driveway. The trucks tires skidded to a halt. The rope thrummed through the air, stretching even further. Dad swore.

"Fuck! Fuck! Fuck!"

The tree crashed down. The roof splintered as the tree sliced through it. A continuous reverberating volley of snaps and pops as loud as gunfire filled the air. The whole house shook on its foundation. The ground quaked under my feet. With a resounding groan, the tree shuddered to a stop. It quivered along its entire length as the double sill above Ev's bedroom window halted its descent. The house shuddered. The tree trembled. The world held still, frozen in the moment.

"God damn it!" Dad kicked the chainsaw with his iron-toed boot. It somersaulted over and over, clanking in protest. Dad strode down the driveway, screaming at Ev. "Why the fuck, didn't you drive? You idiot! This is all your fault!"

Ev leapt out of the truck, slammed the door, and hollered back. "I drove. The rope just kept stretching." He waved his arm at the road running horizontally in front of the pickups bumper. "I drove as far as possible."

Mom sniffled. I edged sideways and laid my arm over her shoulders. I shined my flashlight at the house. "It's not really that bad." I tried to reassure her.

Her watery eyes turned to stare at me.

"Well, I mean…. The tree stopped. The house still stands."

Mom sniffled again.

Dad stomped his way back up the driveway. "I'm going to call Carl to help clear up this mess." He headed towards the house.

Thoughts chased each other through my head in quick succession. Only my father, "the genius", behaved in such an idiotic fashion. Get real, cutting down a tree in the middle of the night. Only he possessed enough nerve to expect the neighbors to help him clean up after he ruined their night's sleep. How bad had he managed to mess up the house? I yawned mightily and wished that I could sleep in in the morning, but only Dad got to do that.

Carl refused to help Dad in the middle the night because "nobody with an ounce of sense operates a chainsaw in the dark."

The clock read 1:30 as I climbed back into bed. Dad's snores swelled and ebbed through the house. I lay in bed, shivering into wakefulness at every creak and groan of the roof over my head. Dad proclaimed the house to be safe. But the tree lay over Ev's bed, its branches poked into the roof over mine, and Dad's bed lay under a roof free of damage. He slept easy. We had no such luxury.

I struggled through classes the next day, barely able to stay awake. Most of the courses, I glided through without needing to concentrate. But I failed a test in Modern

History, too tired and befuddled to even understand the questions, let alone answer them. The test counted for thirty percent of my grade that semester, which meant I looked forward to getting a screaming fit from Dad about my bad grade in the report card.

I tried to find the humor in the situation. Dad refused to let us get a decent night's sleep. Every night since school started he banged, swore, and revved engines for more than half the night. He instigated the lack of sleep which caused me to get bad grades, and then claimed the bad grades to be proof of my idiocy. It was a sick paradox of his making. So sick, that even my best friends didn't understand why a parent behaved so. But honestly, I failed to comprehend the reasons too.

Finally, a near sleepless week later I couldn't stand it anymore, I convinced a friend at school into letting me go to her house. I wanted to run away. I wanted to get a normal night's sleep. After school I went to Jennifer's house and we talked till evening. She convinced me that my mother deserved to know where I went. She called my mother, told her the truth, and asked permission for me to spend the night. My mother knew I felt exhausted and overwhelmed. She let me stay. When I went home, she never asked me why. I think, she realized I needed that escape, that normal night with a friend.

The very next day, Dad spent the afternoon screaming at Mom as she put the groceries away.

"How many times do I need to tell you? You idiot! I refuse to eat this store brand crap. I want Del Monte canned string beans and B+M Baked beans. And where do you get off spending twenty-eight dollars and thirty-six cents on groceries? I told you, *under* twenty-five dollars a week."

I wanted to leave and never come back. Hearing Dad scream at full volume drove me to the edge of my psychological endurance. I feared that one day I'd snap and start yelling back. Because I so wanted to tell him what a horrible father and husband he was. I so wanted to make him feel remorseful for all the things he had done, for the names he called us, for the times he made my mother cry. I feared that if I stayed, I'd become him.

So that afternoon, as Dad paced downstairs screaming at Mom, I went into my brother's room. Retreated inside the book, Ev failed to detect that I grabbed his hiking backpack and took it into my room. I loaded up my clothes and the small amount of cash I possessed.

I went downstairs and walked right past Mom and Dad and out the door. Neither one of them noticed. My mother as she always did when being screamed at watched the floor. Screaming away at her intently, Dad ignored everything else around him.

I felt horrible about leaving Trixie behind. I wanted to take her with me, but how would I feed her? What about sheltering her in the winter, vet care, and having her hooves trimmed?

In the movies, it always looked great getting on a horse and just riding away. But was it fair to the horse? No open prairies grew here for her to graze on. I lived in New England where housing developments ruled. Yes, the sides of the road grew enough grass to feed her, but where would she bed down at night or find safety from cars and traffic? Plus, how could I hide her, so that people didn't wonder why I constantly led a horse southwards?

I planned to head south, somewhere with mild winters, so I need not worry about shelter. I figured if I got far enough south, maybe I could find work on a farm. Maybe, with no winter to worry about, I'd be all right.

I went out to the pasture to say goodbye to Trixie. I hugged her, kissed her on the nose, and stood there just patting her. I wanted to stay, but I needed to leave. I kissed her on the nose once more, turned, and walked away.

The moment I left the pasture Trixie started screaming. It was the scream of separation -- the scream a horse gives when you took away its herd mate. That scream caused a horse's whole body to shake with the effort put into the call. But I needed to leave, so, I kept walking. I guess Trixie wanted to go with me, so she kept screaming.

I only made it half a mile. I just couldn't leave her. Her safety required staying home. I turned around and went back. Trixie screamed until I got in the pasture with her. Her whole body shook and trembled. She put her head over my shoulder and her warm, earthy smell filled my lungs. The heat from her body warmed me. My hands glided over her slick, smooth hide until my fingers dove into her thick, luxuriant mane and I pulled my face tight against her, standing there in the shelter of her powerful neck, holding onto her with a desperation that rivaled my need for air.

She remained as my refuge, my anchor, and my wings. I told myself that I could stay home as long as some part of me remained free. That part of me was Trixie.

*　　*　　*　　*　　*　　*　　*　　*

In the summer of '86, I knew of no place to find pasture

for Trixie. I began to search the fall before when Julie informed me that both their stables and pasture spots already stood reserved for horses sent to them for training. The Browns sold the last of their horses in '85 and Woody had already taken down the pasture fence.

I asked around. Some of the stables I contacted cost way too much and others enforced way too many rules. For example, owners only got to see their horse at certain times and needed to ride at proscribed hours in pre-defined areas. Most of the established stable locations existed too far away for me, anyway, a distance too long for me to ride my bike back and forth. Mom couldn't give me rides all of the time, Dad would have a fit over such a waste of gas.

I called some of the local farms, the ones with fenced pastures. Most of them raised dairy cows. None wanted to have a horse as a boarder. So I kept asking around.

Finally, in the last week of May, I found a pasture for Trixie. A lady who went to my church bought a big house off the Waterhouse Road. She owned a thoroughbred mare and foal, and also a pony. She believed her pasture could support another horse. I think she mostly pitied Trixie and me.

I felt overjoyed to finally find a pasture. Trixie, of course, showed her emotion in typical horse fashion, rolling, running, and eating grass like she feared it might disappear if she so much as blinked.

In a couple more months, I'd be able to ride her once more. She hadn't favored either injured leg for four or five months, although the vet explained that re-injury presented the problem that I needed to worry about. We successfully gave her time to heal and now, those healings required more time to strengthen. I knew that if she got re-injured, healing again would likely become impossible.

I stood doubly glad that Trixie now ran with a thoroughbred mare and foal. She loved to compete. When they galloped, she raced them and held nothing back. Plus, a mare and foal wouldn't be provoked into constant racing by Trixie like a gelding might.

Andrea gave me permission to lunge Trixie in the driveway. I experienced profound gratitude for her consent because it allowed me to safely exercise my girl. I planned on working her at a trot, to build up her muscles and endurance.

*   *   *   *   *   *   *   *

In mid-summer of 1986, ten months after her injury, the vet said it was safe to ride Trixie again. I rode her bareback to spare her the saddle weight and myself the kicked-puppy-dog looks. I tried to mostly ride at a walk. She impatiently kept pulling at the bit, prancing, and acting like a kid on a sugar high. Each time I rode her a tug-of-war ensued. I pulled back, trying to take it easy and slow and Trixie pulled forward, ready to run. One Saturday, it all came to a head.

Her continued restlessness wore me down, so I decided to let her run. I gave her her head and told her to canter. She grabbed the bit in her teeth and raced off. I had no choice but to hold on and let her take control. As she galloped full speed along the side of the road, I enjoyed the wind whipping my hair back, the sun warming my shoulders, and watching my girl's graceful hooves churn the sand up into a cloud of dust that billowed out behind us. Then something spooked her and she skidded to a complete stop.

I lasted for four bounces. The first bounce slid me forward onto Trixie's withers, gripping as hard as possible with my legs. The second bounce landed me on her neck. A horse's neck measures way too thin to grip with your legs. But I *did* try. At the third bounce, I touched down in the middle of Trixie's neck. I knew then that I was dismounting the fast and painful way. The fourth bounce alighted me squarely on top of Trixie's ears. I flipped heels over head and ended up flat on my back with all the air driven out of me.

I lay there, gasping for breath, hurting all over, not sure if or when I wanted to try to move. A small thrill of pride went through me when I realized I still gripped the reins tightly in my hand, because as Jane always said "A true rider never lets go of the reins."

I opened my eyes to see Trixie's head directly above mine. She cocked her head and looked at me then turned to look at her back. When she looked at me again, I saw the question in her eyes, "How did you get down there?" Laughing hurt, my ribs rattled around shaking instead of holding secure. It felt like they had gotten jolted loose.

Trixie pulled back some and sneezed. I noticed sand covering her nose. She sneezed again and I covered my face.

"Thanks a lot," I muttered. "Up end me and then give me a shower." It dawned on me as she shook her head that I had landed on her ears and driven her nose into the sand. I rolled over and got to my knees.

"Great, I hurt all over and I probably gave you a concussion." She snorted and shook her head again. I managed to get to my feet. I wiped the sand off her nose and checked it out. Her cute nostrils flared wide, the insides sprinkled lightly with sand and her nose darkened to a pinkish-red, but it wasn't cut or bleeding.

I gripped the ends of the reins and circled her around me a couple of times. She walked along steady on her feet with no limping. "Whoa!" *How did you check a horse for a concussion?* I couldn't hold up my fingers and ask her how many she saw. I felt unsure about calling Jane Allen and asking her. I'd never live this one down.

*　*　*　*　*　*　*　*

In the summer of '86, I still worked for Miss Waterhouse and Charlotte Cole. Mr. Logan reduced my hours because he cut his business size down as he prepared to retire. He only needed my help a couple of hours, every two or three weeks.

I got a call from a guy named Peary in July. Gordon Cole leased his hay fields and equipment to this man, who told me Gordon gave him my name and number. He needed a haying crew. So I worked on a haying crew again that summer and got a lot more hours with Mr. Peary Merrifield than with Gordon, because Peary just baled hay and never put up any silage.

I first met Peary over to the farm while I worked for Charlotte Cole. I answered the phone for her one day.

"Hello."

"May I speak with Peary please?"

"Who?"

"Peary Merrifield."

"I'm sorry. You must have the wrong number."

"This is Cole Farm Dairy, isn't it?"

"Yes."

"Peary bought up the left over hay. He's supposed to be loading his truck out in the barn. Can you get him for me?"

"Ah…. sure. I'll go check in the barn for him." I ran out to the barn. As I entered the open main door, I saw the big white flatbed Chevy backed up to the loft. A movement in the corner of my eye made me glance up. Halfway up the ladder to the top of the hay pile a man climbed.

"Hey!" I hollered and he twisted with his left arm hanging loose to look down at me.

"Yeah!"

"Are you Peary?"

"Yep!"

"You've got a phone call in the house."

"Who is it?"

I raised both my hands and shrugged. "I don't know, a woman."

He shook his head and his long brown hair waved back and forth under the barn lights showing off both red and blonde highlights. "Why do phone calls always come when you're as far away from the phone as possible?" He asked as he began backing down the ladder.

"I guess maybe for the same reason why the dogs always start barking after you just fell asleep?"

A loud laugh boomed out of him and echoed around inside the barn. "Ayuh, that sounds about right." His boots clomped loudly and quickly down the stairs.

As we walked towards the house I realized he stood over six foot tall and looked nearly round because his chest depth almost equaled its width. His tan face was creased with weathered wrinkles.

I delivered phone messages to him half a dozen times since that first call. He laughed often and never seemed to frown. I thought it might be interesting working for someone with such a cheerful outlook on life.

Mom and Dad bought twenty-seven acres from Irene Harris. It stood as the highest piece of land in Dayton. On a clear day, Mount Washington perched as a grey peak on the horizon. A nice mix of oak, maple, aspen, birch, pine, and spruce trees covered the hill that had a stream running along the bottom of it. In the winter, the run-off from the hill froze on the granite cliffs that made up the front of it, making huge frozen waterfalls that sparkled like glass in the sunlight. Dad cleared six acres on the top and back side of the hill. Ev worked real hard, saving up money for college. Dad paid him to help drill wells and work on the new property.

Dad wanted me to work for him for free. I suppose he believed his daughter's labor belonged to him, but I argued right back that I already held many jobs. He needed to pay me the same rate as my other employers before I agreed to work for him. I also informed him that he resided at the bottom of my work lists because I'd made commitments to my other employers, and I believed in filling my work responsibilities.

Dad ranted and raved. But I refused to back down. Working for my father rivaled living with him on the totally-sucks scale. I always rejected working for him when any other option presented itself. Dad finally relented, grousing that while stupid, I at least possessed some business sense.

I did however, freely seed and fertilize inside Trixie's designated pasture area. I also bought some fence posts and Mom helped me put them up.

*　　*　　*　　*　　*　　*　　*　　*

I never understood how my brother achieved it. Living with Dad sucked; having to work with him equaled locking yourself in a closet with a rabid dog. No matter how hard you worked or how well you accomplished the job, he always screamed and swore at you.

He threw things a lot more when he worked, too. The stuff never flew or bounced in a predictable manner either. But then again, he tossed drills, chisels, hammers, saws, and pieces of lumber not cute little play balls.

My brother commanded the quickest reflexes I ever encountered in a human being. He once stepped into the paddock with Sheba and she tried to strike him. A horses strike moves so fast; it becomes a blur in your sight. Most people needed to jump out of the way the second that they saw the horse raise its hoof. Ev just stood there until Sheba's hoof started to come down. Then, almost quicker than I found possible, he jumped back out of the way. Sheba tried to strike Ev three or four times in a row and Ev just leapt back out of the way every time. He moved so quickly, it sent shivers up my spine.

My brother showed the same reactions on his track team. While he wasn't the fastest runner in the school, when required, he put on an awesome spurt of speed. He knew the exact limits of his endurance. I watched him run in a relay race one time where he ran both the first and the fourth lap. He pushed himself a second faster on the second lap than on his first.

After working for my father, I understood how Ev got those reflexes and learned his body's limits. Working for Dad, taught us to move quickly or we received some real nasty cuts and bruises. Dad usually refrained from throwing things directly at us on purpose. He just got mad and started chucking things without looking. In no time at all, the air filled with flying and bouncing objects. Sometimes, I wondered if his behavioral development somehow stopped at age three. Throwing, screaming, crying, spitting, whining, and everything always got blamed on someone else.

Most times, just going over to see Trixie or taking her for a gentle ride made me feel better after being around my father. But on occasions when Dad acted particularly nasty or after he made Mom cry, a gentle ride wasn't enough.

On those days, I rode Trixie to the flats over at Cole Farm. The long, level fields of timothy and alfalfa covered an area from the Gordon Road to the back of the Brown's property. I stopped her at one end and looked out over the expanse in front of us, patted her neck and waited. I think she sensed what I needed on those days. Her ears pointed forward, her breathing deepened, her heartbeat quickened.

I waited. I felt Trixie's ribcage swell, pushing my legs out with every mighty inhalation. Her pulsing heart reverberated through her ribs into my left calf. And when I felt her muscles quiver in excitement beneath me, I leaned forward and wished my heart to beat right along with hers, my lungs to fill with hers. Then I asked - I asked for all she had to give.

Her feet blurred in my vision, her mane whipped back against me, her powerful muscles flowed under me. The earth held still and I flew above it. Here, nothing could catch hold of me, the anger, the pain, the yelling voice, the name-calling, the flowing tears - none of it touched me here. I soared above the world, above it all. I simply leaned over and watched it glide away beneath me. I flew because Trixie gave me wings.

No weights hung on me. No heaviness pulled down my heart. No load held my soul captive. I rose up, lighter than air; as free as the breeze that made the timothy grass sway and dance, agile as the wind that blew through the leaves, powerful as the gale that pushed the water up into crests and waves. And I wasn't alone because Trixie flew with me, soaring, gliding, taking wing with me. She was my freedom, my strength, and my truest friend.

Chapter # 7   Changes

In the spring of 1987, I pastured Trixie out on my parent's new property. We slogged away building the house on the very highest spot. Dad went into rages more and more often working on the house. A huge post and beam construction, with six different levels and steps everywhere it overshadowed even the trees that grew on the lower slope.

Dad kept making excuses for himself. Stress frayed his meager patience. According to him my mom, my brother, the carpenters, and I, everyone surrounding him labored and thought at sub-par levels.

However, I now took a class in school called Psychology and Sociology, one article in the psychology book made me nearly jump up and scream, "This is Dad!" Every symptom and behavior pattern of manic-depressive (bipolar) disorder fit my father to a terrifying degree.

When I proudly went home and told Ev about my discovery. He simply looked up at me from his sprawled out position on his bed and said. "Yeah, I know." As usual, he figured things out so much quicker than me. Suspecting Dad suffered from a mental illness made it no easier to deal with him.

More and more often, I took my escapes on Trixie's back. No flat areas existed close by. This allowed me to discover that Trixie actually liked running on hills.

It felt amazing to experience riding Trixie as she ran uphill. I sensed all of her surging muscles. The raw power she poured out instilled awe and wonder in me. It also humbled me because of two things. One, I seemed so weak in comparison. And two, with a loving heart she gave all of her vast power to me.

Mostly, she loved to run downhill, a terrifying and exhilarating event for me. She barreled full speed downhill, her feet flying faster, and faster, and faster to keep up with her momentum. One part of me sat there, clinching her sides as tight as possible, praying she didn't stumble or trip.

The other part of me felt like a wild thing set free. Triumphant, powerful, living gloriously and totally in the moment! Riding Trixie full-out on the flat seemed like flying. Riding her full-out going downhill felt like a power dive from the highest cloud, plummeting towards the earth, reveling in the speed, wondering if your wings possessed enough strength to stop you.

*   *   *   *   *   *   *   *   *

We got two ponies to put out in the pasture with Trixie. The lady who owned them wanted to get rid of them. She wanted them to stay together, so we took them both. The smallest one, a mare named Gibbons acted really sweet-tempered and mild-mannered, a dark steel grey, so dark that in the evenings or in the shade, she looked black. Light grey hairs sparsely sprinkled throughout her coat became visible only in direct sunlight. She bore a white blaze, three white socks, and reached only forty-two inches tall. She stood on slender legs and carried a delicate, tapered-in face and muzzle like an Arabian.

She loved to talk. She neighed happily as Trixie and them ran and romped around the pasture and trumpeted loudly whenever she found herself alone. She nickered anxiously when it got close to grain time and whinnied joyfully as it landed in her bucket. She watched me brush Trixie and when she wanted a turn, she gave a series of half volume whickers and shouldered in between Trixie and me. Trixie liked her so much that she only retaliated with a nasty glare and a couple of swishing tail slaps.

Frisky, the gelding stood about fifty-four inches tall with a stocky build and a chest as wide as Trixie's. A bonnet and shield pinto colored mostly white with a brown bonnet that covered the top of his head, his ears, and stopped just above his eyes. A big brown splotch shaped like a roundish shield covered his chest and shoulders. He also wore a brown spot on his left nostril and muzzle, another big one on his rump, and a couple of hand-sized spots on his belly and sides. He always bit Trixie and Gibbons and he nipped at anyone who went near him.

The only time he stopped nipping happened to be when he got brushed. He turned into a perfect gentleman, the moment a brush touched his hide. His feet stayed perfectly still, but he twisted, stretched, and arched his neck and body until the brush hit one of his favorite spots. Then he leaned into the grooming, closed his eyes in ecstasy and gave out great, big sighs. The moment you stopped brushing him, he started nipping again. Bite marks always marked the hide of Trixie and Gibbons. My girl loved the company, though.

Watching Trixie out in the pasture relaxed me. She seemed so content with life, laying and rolling in the shade, taking sun-naps in the bright summer sun, her hide glistening like a copper penny. In the pasture, Trixie took life in at a slow, relaxed, stroll interspersed with gleeful bucking sprees, dust baths, and tag games with her pony friends. I wished life somehow remained that simple for me. But it wasn't, and I should have accepted its complexity by now. At least, I told myself that.

For as long as I remembered, living with Dad endangered our family. So why did I continue to get upset by it? Maybe because he appeared to be getting worse as time went by. Or maybe I was just getting fed up with it. Sometimes, I felt like yelling at him. "Grow up!"

Everything needed to revolve around him. He threw a fit, if someone or something else became the center of attention. I doubted if he cared about anybody but himself.

Today, when I came home from school, a note lay on the counter to call my Great Aunt Irene, handwritten by my Mom. I called up Aunt Irene and she told me earlier in the day she rushed Mom to the hospital. I got on my bike and rode up to the new property to tell Dad.

When I got there, he stood yelling at the carpenters. They built good construction and would likely improve if he left them alone. Quality workmanship proved to be very difficult to achieve when someone constantly screamed at you.

I interrupted him. "Aunt Irene took Mom to the hospital. I called and they don't know what's wrong with her yet. They just started running tests."

Dad nodded. "Irene drove her. Well, I didn't have the time to." He smiled. "So they don't know what ails her?"

"You knew she was sick?"

"Yeah, she's been bitching that her guts hurt all day. I've got important things to do instead of wasting my time chauffeuring her around."

"You asshole, the closest hospital is only fifteen minutes from here. Oh yeah, you need to stay here to scream at the carpenters. They don't know what's wrong with her; it could be something life-threatening. And you refused to take the time to bring her to the hospital?" I screamed as I walked away.

"Where are you going?"

"Mom needs a family member with her to show that we care. If no one wants to give me a ride, I'll ride my bike," I said as I got on my bike and pedaled off.

Dad yelled after me, "I'm not an asshole."

"Yes, you are!" I yelled back. I went home and called around. One of the neighbors gave me a ride in to see Mom.

Pain made her shift and twist on the bed as the Doctor's ran tests. They ruled out heart attack, appendicitis, and gall-bladder problems. Eventually, they figured it out: a ruptured ovarian cyst, very painful and likely to cause an infection, but not life-threatening.

When evening came, Mom told me to get a ride home because school ran the following day. The Doctors kept her overnight to adminster painkillers. She asked me to call my Great Aunt Irene and tell her everything was okay.

I called great Aunt Irene when I got home and gave her my Mom's message.

"I bet that pissed Evans off, good and proper. I never saw the man happier in my life than when I got there. Your Mom doubled up in pain, and he wanted to talk, showing me this and that. He wanted her to die. He's going through that mid-life crisis thing and wants a young, beautiful woman to adore him. He told me, "Oh, she just can't handle a bellyache." Yup, he wanted her to die, I felt it in my bones. He didn't want me to take her to the hospital where they'd save her. He isn't a good man. Your Mom needs to be careful with him around. I'm glad to hear that everything turned out okay. She deserves better than being tied to that man."

"Thanks for taking Mom to the hospital, I really appreciate it."

"No problem, my dear. I like to annoy Evans. People give him too much credit. He deserves to be irritated." She laughed before she hung up the phone.

I stood there holding the phone, thinking it through. My stomach churned queasily. The more I thought about it, the sicker I felt. I realized Irene hit it in the bull's eye. Dad acted like he hoped Mom would die. I disliked the fact that simple and irrevocable biology made such a slime-ball my father.

* * * * * * * *

Trixie's neck bore a bad bite barely scabbed over.

Gibbons, the little pony, carried two bad bites on her rump. Frisky needed to go. Mom agreed with me, so we called up the people that we got them from. They wanted them both back. We wanted to keep Gibbons. They declared that they wanted to take either both of them or neither of them. We did agree to keep them together, so we returned them both.

When they picked them up, I recommended a vet check for Frisky. Usually more playful than mares, geldings tended to be a handful, but an animal never constantly bit for no reason. The vet failed to find anything wrong with him when we first got them and he gave them their shots. But at that time, we remained unaware of how much Frisky bit. The vet needed to be informed of the problem to find the cause of it.

I was working for Miss Waterhouse when the telephone rang. All of a sudden, I got a bad feeling that something had gone wrong. I went out to the living room to check.

Miss Waterhouse looked up from hanging up the phone. "Your brother got hurt."

I stuffed my feet in my sneakers and grabbed for my coat.

"Call me later and tell me if he's all right," Miss Waterhouse said as I ran out the door. I raced home wondering to myself.

Ev, why did you come back? You got away to college; why agree to work for Dad in the summer and on your school breaks? Why? If I ever managed to escape Dad's grasp, I wouldn't willingly put myself back in it. But then again, Ev really had no choice. The scholarships he won helped with his college tuition, but Dad made too much money for Ev to qualify for financial aid. Ev needed Dad's help to pay for his education. And Dad refused to do that unless Ev agreed to come home and work for him during every school break.

When I ran into the yard, Mom sat in the already idling car. I jumped in. "Where is he? What happened?"

"Goodall Hospital in Sanford. Dad called. Somehow Ev got hurt on that well-drilling job in Springvale."

My mind churned with negative thoughts all the way to the hospital. For Dad to waste his time taking anybody to the Emergency Room, it had to be bad. Working with a well-rig ranked as dangerous labor especially working with Dad. He took shortcuts on safety - not his own safety, but other people's. Neither Mom nor I said anything else on the way to the hospital.

Ev had a broken left arm, straight through both bones, such a bad break the doctors needed to do emergency surgery. The bones failed to set. They needed to use plates and screws to bring the broken ends back together and hold them in place.

Mom went with Ev to pre-op, leaving me the task of keeping Dad company. Only we sat in the surgery waiting room. Its dead silence punctuated by Dad's muttering. His voice slowly rose up barely into the hearing range and then faded out again. His lips constantly moved. And his skin gleamed a pasty white under the bright hospital lights.

I watched him intently. He seemed to be in shock. I debated with myself, about getting a nurse? Dad would probably rant and rave, making the nurse and me miserable. I watched him again. Yup, he really had a bad case of shock. He'd never allow himself to sound so dumb just for an act. I started to stand up just as his voice rose up again.

"It was my fault, all my fault. I nearly killed him. Lucky, I didn't kill him," he muttered.

I sank back down in the chair. I looked at Dad. It felt sneaky to do it, but this offered me a chance to find out what really happened. If I got him talking while his mind swirled about too disoriented to make excuses or cover up, I'd find out what really happened. I kept my voice low, a gentle whisper. "What happened?"

His voice rose a little. "Distracted, I got distracted. I forgot to pay attention. My fault...." His voice faded again.

Anger swelled in me. How many times had I heard him scream at Ev. "Pay attention, you idiot!" How many times had he yelled it at me? I breathed in slowly, barely managing to restrain my temper. I wanted to know the whole story. I needed to hear the truth now, not a pack of lies later. I waited a couple of seconds. "What distracted you?"

"Thinking, I got distracted thinking. Ev's good to work with, knows what I want him to do." My jaw dropped. Dad admitting one of us was good at something, proved how much shock he suffered from. A lot of it!

"I like working with Shelly more. I like watching her while she works." Dad's eyes began to take on a certain glint. My jaw slammed shut.

I shook my head, got up, and walked off in disgust. Shelly worked helping Dad drill wells, when Ev needed to stay at college. She liked to wear tight clothes and she flirted outrageously. But geez, she took classes two years behind me in my school. Her reputation with the boys stood out more colorful and widely known than anyone else's, including the Seniors.

Shock or no shock, he deserved to suffer through it on his own. I stomped out of the room. He'd endangered my brother's life. Only Ev's seeing the chain coming at him and his quick reaction of blocking it with his arm had prevented it from breaking open his head or wrapping around his neck. And Dad failed to even notice the accident he caused until he lifted Ev up ten feet off the ground by the chain wrapped around his broken arm. All, because Dad spent his work hours fantasizing about a sixteen year old kid.

I knew what that glint in his eye meant. "What an asshole," I said to thin air. He came close to killing my brother, because he spent his time daydreaming about having sex with a teenage girl instead of watching the equipment he operated.

*   *   *   *   *   *   *   *

We got our senior pictures for the yearbook back. I disliked mine. It came out okay. But I really wanted to have it taken with Trixie. I called the photographer. It cost over three hundred dollars for a private shoot, too much for me to afford. So even though my picture came out good, even though Mom really liked it, I felt disappointed.

She bought me a class ring and a yearbook. I picked the smallest style boys ring. The girl's rings looked delicate. I thought I'd end up breaking or bending one of the girl's rings. A watch never lasted more than a month without my shattering it. The boys' rings carried bigger stones that seemed large enough to handle some knocks and bangs. Mom and the ring guy thought I made a strange choice. I guess they thought my decision seemed queer or something. I just wanted a ring that wouldn't break on me.

As for the yearbook, I didn't really want it. Mom thought I needed it for memories' sake. I accepted it not wanting to hurt her feelings, but I wanted to forget the whole school year. Shelly made my life at school pretty miserable. Every time we passed in the hall, she started in on me.

First, she ridiculed my "lack of style" and pathetic clothes. I wore hand-me-downs given to me by a neighbor. Dad never gave me money for school clothes and my cash went towards Trixie or saving for a car. Shelly wore and bragged about all the new clothes that her sugar-daddy, my Dad bought her.

Then it became about cars. I still rode the bus, unable to afford a car yet. Shelly's sugar-daddy bought her a used sports car for two thousand dollars. Then it turned into snide jokes about Dad's sexual preferences and then my graduation. Dad didn't want to waste his time going to a stupid graduation.

Why? Because Shelly's parents told her to straighten out her behavior or get out, so her sugar daddy busily searched for an apartment for her. I needed and wanted nothing for memories' sake from my senior year. I just wanted it to be over.

Most of my classmates oozed excitement over looking at colleges, filling out applications, and taking their SAT's. I knew since I became a freshman that that future never stood open for me. I wasn't smart enough, athletic enough, musically or artistically talented enough to qualify for a full scholarship and no way would Dad dish out money for me to go to college. Strangely enough, that inspired me to sign up for and take all college courses in high school. I knew my only opportunity to get a free education existed right then so I wanted to learn as much as possible.

In my sophomore year, I considered joining the Air Force. My Uncle Eli sent me packets of information and researched pay scales and the various fields that I qualified for. It had seemed like a possibility for me. It would mean not having Trixie with me for the first couple of years. But Jane had found good people to lease the horses of some of our 4-H group who headed off to college and offered to do the same for Trixie and me.

But then Dad started to get more and more out of control and I needed to make a decision. I came to realize that while the possibility of seeing and experiencing unique places sounded fun. I deemed Mom, Ev, and Trixie to be far more important than that nebulous future. And the only way to keep them safe required my staying with them.

I knew that staying in Southern Maine without a college education meant low paying jobs. Most of the work available to me involved manual labor. But I never minded that. I actually got a sort of perverse thrill out of doing physically demanding jobs because I proved that Dad's beliefs held no merit. Women weren't inherently weak. I easily worked as hard if not harder than most men.

Dad showed up at my graduation. He waited until everyone gathered around, then he walked up to me, pulled me into a hug, and announced. "I'm so proud of you."

I pushed him away. I refused to be a piece in his be an asshole at home and a doting father in public game anymore. In the past year, I'd learned that he held no respect for my mother's life or my brother's safety and his morals leaned beyond the questionable, close to the unlawful.

I couldn't change the facts that made him my father, but I controlled my decisions and reactions. I denied him the right to play games with me. I gave up on being a kicked spaniel, licking his hand, it had never earned his love in the past. Why continue the charade?

He could no longer mentally or emotionally kick me at home, pat me in public, and expect me to accept it adoringly. This dog knew better. This dog realized it had teeth at its disposal. I refused to become him and turn on those weaker than me. I choose to turn on the one who hurt me. Physically and mentally, he loomed bigger and stronger than me. None of it mattered I had reached the turning point and decided not to take anymore.

When I pushed Dad away, he looked in my eyes. He recognized my determination because he stepped back hastily. He turned to Ms. Waterhouse, Charlotte Cole, and Miss Gay. "Let me escort you ladies to your car."

After he left, Mom turned to me. "What did you do that for? He was trying to be nice."

"He had an audience, Mom. He never puts the effort into being nice unless someone stands there ready to clap and oh-ah, over his performance. "Oh, what a good father, such a polite man, etc." All lies, all of it complete lies. He complained for a month about wasting his time coming to my graduation. Then he does the loving, doting father act for the little old ladies."

"He is proud of you and he loves you in his way," She

said gently as she patted my shoulder.

I shook my head in frustration. "Don't you get it? His way is the wrong way. He doesn't love us. He controls, manipulates, and uses us." Mom just gave me an odd look. She always used humor, so I tried that.

"I'm not taking any more bull shit. My bull shit cup runneth over. If he keeps trying to dish it out to me, a real big mess awaits him."

Mom stared at me, frowning in confusion with worry lines creasing her forehead. I sighed. Ev and Mom never got my humor, which ran too sarcastic and cynical, too jaded for their tastes. Oh well, I had warned her. The shit and the fan now existed perilously close to one another.

*   *   *   *   *   *   *   *

The only good thing following my graduation came from Andrea, the lady in my church who let me pasture Trixie with her horses. She lent me her pony Cinnamon in the fall of '87 to keep Trixie company.

Trixie and Cinnamon became great buddies, when they'd pastured together. A Shetland pony, Cinnamon measured about forty-six inches tall. Her sturdily built bones scaled much bigger than Trixie's. When they stood near each other in the sunshine, they looked like metal statues, Trixie a brilliant red copper with silver socks and blaze, larger and more finely sculptured, elegantly posed next to Cinnamon who was a beautiful mottled mix of silver and pewter, as if the artist couldn't decide which to cast her in. They often stood beside each other motionless, glistening in the sunlight, truly works of art by an accomplished creator.

I'd never met a pony calmer than Cinnamon. Nothing startled her, not yelling, swearing, or screaming, not cars, trucks, or motorcycles, and not wind, thunderstorms, or blizzards. She remained perfectly composed through it all. She watched everything with bright, curious eyes. And I sometimes wondered if she acted so calm because she considered herself to be an observer, watching life flow around her. She also happened to be well-trained and good-natured and I felt grateful that Andrea lent her to me.

She requested that I pay for Cinnamon's bills, vet, farrier, hay, and grain. I accepted the deal gladly because I needed to see Trixie happy.

Dad and I fought almost nonstop. He constantly called me names; telling me how ungrateful and useless I was, worth less than the salt in me. At first, I remained ignorant about how much salt that meant. Dad educated me. He grabbed the Morton salt container out of the cupboard.

"This holds more salt than your whole body." He read the tag and smiled. "Wow! You're worth about sixty-nine cents."

I refused to cry for him. No matter what he did, I shed no tears for him. I decided not to let him hold that power over me any longer. I tried not to show any emotion. Sometimes it became too much, and I'd snap.

"You're an asshole, a total and complete asshole." The words burned up my throat and spewed out of my mouth. I poured all my anger into those words. Then I returned to a blank, no emotion showing, until the anger over-powered me again.

Mom called me heartless. Ev said I was becoming like

Dad. They failed to understand. If I gave Dad my emotions, I handed him the keys to me. If I gave my thoughts and emotions to Mom or Ev, Dad used them against Mom or Ev. I wanted my feelings to simply exist not be used to cause more pain. Our family already held too much pain. I gave my emotions to the only one who never abused them.

I went out to Trixie, brushed her and kissed her nose. When she put her head on my shoulder, I hugged her neck and cried everything out. She stood there as still as a statue, as strong as a mighty tree, and as warm as the sun shining down on me, cradling me between her head and body, unmoving, patiently waiting out my emotional storm.

*   *   *   *   *   *   *   *

In the late fall of 1988, my father gave up the pretext of a separation and left for good. Gladly, I watched him go. My mother became devastated when he filed for a divorce. All of those years of putting up with him and then he left her. She existed in a state of denial. It seemed inconceivable, impossible for her to comprehend that Dad acted so heartless and cruel.

I naively thought things would get better after he left. They only got worse, as Dad prepared for the coming divorce. He wanted to make sure Mom declined to ask for anything. He started an intimidation campaign.

He often showed up in the middle of the night, parked on the side of the road, and yelled obscenities and threats at us. He came over on our day off from work. He kicked down the door, threw furniture around in the house, threatened us, and left. He called Mom in the dead of the night and told her he was coming over to kill us.

Mom lived in terror. Ev, now 21, got a concealed weapons permit and began carrying a gun. I tried to fight back. I became what my brother called, "The Enforcer". I called the cops and filled out report after report.

When the door landed on the floor, I took my position in the entryway. If he wanted at Mom or Ev, he needed to go through me. I learned that lesson from Trixie when she protected me, at her own cost, from Stormy and Sheba. True love meant going up against something bigger and stronger than you to protect those you love, fighting to defend them even when you knew you couldn't win.

The year and a half of hiding my emotions from Dad gave me an edge. Even though, he terrified me sometimes, it seldom showed. Saying what you mean and meaning what you say, awarded me another advantage. It enabled me to tell Dad in an authoritative voice that I refused to let him do this or that, and he knew I meant it.

At first, my stance against Dad surprised him. It confused him that I appeared unafraid of his threats. But all too quickly, his anger at my refusal to bow to his will overcame everything else. He focused his attention on breaking me. If I broke, Mom and Ev stood defenseless. I vowed not to break. I needed to stand my ground. There was no way feasible for me to win. No possibility of triumph existed over someone as smart, nasty, and devious as Dad. Refusing to break achieved the biggest victory within my reach.

*   *   *   *   *   *   *   *

I brought Trixie home for the winter season of '88-'89 and reluctantly gave Cinnamon back to Andrea. I felt unsure about having enough money available to feed both Trixie and her.

Dad bragged about how he planned for the divorce ever since he bought the new property. The loan for the new house lay on the old house and property. Since the new house remained un-finished, and Ev and I still lived at home, Mom got the old house.

We became saddled with the mortgage, while Dad received twenty-seven acres and a post and beam house worth two hundred grand that only needed under thirty thousand dollars to finish it and no debts. Mom got under an acre and a half, a house literally falling down (part of the roof actually collapsed into the bathtub), and a mortgage. Plus, the town declined to take Mom's name off the new property, so since Dad refused to pay the property taxes, we got billed for both properties.

Mom never got a higher education, so no high paying job stood open for her or any of us. Ev had never returned to college after his arm got broke. Funds grew meager and I expected it to continue to be that way for quite a while.

So even though I wanted to keep her, I cut my expenses where necessary, and gave Cinnamon back. Plus, I needed to search for a pasture for Trixie next year. Andrea had sold her house and moved up state. I hoped to find some place.

*   *   *   *   *   *   *   *

I finally convinced Mom to file for a restraining order. The cops declined to do anything about Dad yet. Every time I filled out a report, they came up with an excuse. Parking on the side of the road in the middle of the night broke no laws. Yelling obscenities while rude, wasn't illegal. Threats only counted as scare tactics. Kicking down the door, throwing furniture? The divorce proceedings continued on, so technically he still owned the house.

"Without a restraining order, we can't do anything. But if you get a restraining order, arresting him becomes a possibility." They constantly repeated.

In the two weeks following Mom filling out the paperwork, Dad came over four times and kicked down the door twice. It looked like an accordion now. Repairing it became more difficult each time. First, I nailed it together, then screwed it, and finally, I put a plywood backing on it. But the damage far outweighed the restoration. Heck, a shove took it down now, usually in pieces.

Did the cops do anything? No, they refused to deliver the restraining order to Dad. They declined to invade his privacy and bring it to him. No, they waited in plain sight at the bottom of the road. When he got to the end of his driveway, he saw them, turned around, and drove out the road on the other side of the property.

Mom had wound herself so tight, she grew close to popping a vein. She thought Dad would flip when he got the restraining order. I agreed with her. But I'd have to face him when he eventually wigged out, so why worry about it before then.

The rain sheeted down outside making it a good day to lean back and read a book, so I set out to do just that. I sat in the recliner, leaned it all the way back, and dove into the book. I had learned from Ev. Immersing yourself in another world relieved stress beautifully. I loved science fiction.

I got thirty-four pages into the book before the door flew in, not just kicked in this time, but forcefully propelled. It came into the house a good six feet.

Shit! I tried to jump up, but the recliner refused to fold back up. By the time I got out of the dang chair, Dad held a lamp in his hand raised high above Mom's head. I tackled him.

The room became a blur. We bounced off walls and furniture. We tripped, stumbled, and whirled. He cursed at me and yelled in my ear. I refused to let go. If I let him get room to swing, he'd pulverize me.

Stronger, bigger, and more experienced, Dad managed to break free. He swung once, a right roundhouse. I zigged out of the way. Out of the corner of my eye, I saw my softball bat leaning against the closet wall. I stood no chance, bare-fisted against him. Time to even the odds; my hand clasped the bat and began swinging it before I finished the thought. I backed Dad up, swing by swing, until he hit the wall.

The tight quarters made it hard to find room to swing. If you handled it right, a bat worked well just as a poking instrument. Dad hugged the wall. Mom screamed. I held the bat ready. If he came at me again, I planned to let my Louisville slugger get personal with his face.

"No!" Mom jumped between us.

Dad smiled, reached over beside her, pulled the phone out of the wall, and threw it on the floor. Shit, how could I call the cops now? Dad laid his head on Mom's shoulder and started bawling like a baby.

"My own daughter, what did I do to deserve this?"

Great, she always fell for his tears.

"Mom, get away from him." She looked at me, her eyes wide and teary. "Mom."

Mom shook her head slowly, gently patting Dad's hair. "Go to Miss Waterhouse's, if you want to call the cops. I'll be fine. Go quick."

I doubted the validity of her being fine. Dad could go back to being violent the moment I left. But I knew that tilt of Mom's head. She stubbornly refused to budge when she looked like that. Even if I somehow got her to move away from Dad, she'd still stand between me and him.

Halfway to Miss Waterhouse's house, I realized I still carried the bat in my hand. I barged into Miss Waterhouse's house without knocking. I ran to the phone and dialed the cops. Miss Waterhouse started to stand. I stuttered and stammered, gasping for air.

"Dad kicked...door down...Mom alone...with him. Cops...need cops!" Miss Waterhouse walked over and held me in her arms as I talked to the dispatcher.

When I hung up, I stood there in the shelter of her arms, sobbing. She spoke to me as I cried.

"I need to wear a hearing aid for normal conversations. My phone requires a special ringer so I can hear it. Yet over the years your father's voice remained loud to me, yelling, yelling, always yelling. He overflows with anger." She patted my back.

"When your mother brought you home from the hospital, I made a baby pillow for you. The first night I heard your father screaming, I knew that pillow would soak up numerous tears. I prayed for you over the years because I knew this day grew closer and closer." Miss Waterhouse patted my back again, and then she pulled away and looked me in the eye. "You can't protect those who don't want to be saved."

I swallowed hard and took a deep breath. "I need to try."

Miss Waterhouse smiled and nodded. "Trying is a big part of you. Tell your mother, I'm praying for her, you, and your brother."

"Thank you," I said and ran before I started crying again. Finally, someone understood. I needed to fight Dad. If I stopped, if I gave in or gave up, it meant giving up on my mother and my brother. Fighting Dad took a huge emotional toll on me. But I did it to give Mom and Ev time, time to realize that they need not put up with Dad. Like the time escaping to Trixie had given me.

As I ran, words came into my mind and with them came a memory of my Aunt Connie. I didn't remember if she said the words, read them to me, or gave me a book with them in it. But I remembered her and the words at the same time: "Life will get me no lower than my knees, even when fate and time weigh and bend me down. I may trip, stumble, and fall to my knees. But on my knees, I'll pray and gather strength. When I stand again, I'll stand strong, straight, and tall. Life will never get me lower than my knees."

Another memory of Aunt Connie swiftly followed the first. She called last week and spoke to me before she talked to Mom. She wanted to know the truth about the situation with Dad. She knew Mom toned it down, so that she wouldn't be tempted to drive up and "teach Evans some manners."

I told her about the kicked in door, the threats, and the

temper-tantrums that Dad threw. I mentioned that I hoped he'd calm down soon, and that filling out police reports became easier with experience and that Mom had finally got a Restraining Order.

"Well, if Evans refuses to calm down or if you feel beyond your ability to handle it anymore, you give me a call. I know some guys who love to give out real good thrashings. They work at a cheap price too."

I had laughed and laughed and laughed. Finally, I managed to sputter out. "Well, we have no money, so we'll have to let that offer pass by."

Aunt Connie chuckled. "Oh, don't worry about the money Kim-Sue. I know the rest of the family wants to chip in. Plus, once these guys hear what an asshole Evans is, they might even beat him up for free."

My ribs began to ache as I struggled to hold in my laughter. "Nah, tempting as the offer sounds, I think we'll have to pass. Dad continues to be too stubborn for a beating to straighten him out. He'd just use it as an excuse to be a bigger jerk. And between Murphy's Law and our luck, the guys would get caught and we'd all be in trouble."

"All right, if you positively mean it. Just remember if you change your mind, I know some guys." Good ol' Aunt Connie, a tough lady on the outside and a sweetheart on the inside.

As I turned my running feet up our driveway, I made a promise to myself: Dad would never drive me lower than my knees. And when I needed to laugh, I need only remember that Aunt Connie knew "some guys".

Dad got arrested and brought down to the police station, but he got let go with a warning because he failed to understand what a restraining order was. Yeah, right! He just happened to be smart enough to play dumb.

Amazingly enough, after that time, he always told the police that he stood on public property when he yelled at us from the side of the road. His car just happened to always break down right in front of our house and who didn't swear at a broke down car. When he came over and kicked down the door he never stuck around long enough for the cops to catch him. I filled out reports with the cops after every incident. But it came down to my word against his and he sounded more convincing telling lies than I sounded telling the truth. Mom remained too scared to fill out a report. My brother wanted to stay neutral in the whole affair. Plus, my wanting to nail Dad to the wall counted as nothing because the restraining order got granted to Mom. Stalemate!

*   *   *   *   *   *   *   *   *

The first two weeks of July 1989 came and went and I still hadn't found a pasture for Trixie. I worked over at Cole farm full-time on the haying crew. We delivered hay out-of-state in the winter. When I went home for lunch today, Trixie surprised me by being out of her pasture. I cut grass every day and brought it home. I feed her three times daily and she seemed pretty content with that.

A blazing hot, humid spell raged on week after week. The heavy, moist air smelt kind of moldy. Probably because everywhere you looked, pools of scummy water gathered heating and vaporizing in the sun. Every day started the same, by ten in the morning my clothes stuck to me and the heat and humidity sucked all my energy away until I just wanted to find a cool place to lie down.

Every afternoon, the thundershowers rolled in. Boom-**Boom-BOOM,** the downpour started up and for the first couple of seconds I felt grateful. But then the wind gusts hit, the rain sheeted down so hard visibility cut down to a couple of feet. It quickly soaked me to the skin. My sneakers squelching water out with every step. My socks got saturated. And my underwear clung to me, dribbling rivulets of water down my legs, causing me to shiver in disgust. Staying out in the rain for more than a couple of minutes caused even the money *inside* of my wallet to get soaked.

At least, Trixie had deep shade under the trees at home and she truly seemed to appreciate it. At the first thunderous boom, she darted into the lean-to and turned to stare out at the gathering gloom. When the downpour started, she dashed outside and stood in the pouring rain until her hide turned dark brown with only her belly showing her normal fiery red shine, then she sprinted back under cover and shook her neck and shoulders. Her thick mane whipped back and forth violently showering the shed walls with a spattering of thick raindrops. She stayed there waiting for the clouds to power off as they raced across the landscape in their fury. Then she returned outside to stand in the sunlight and steam rose from her back and sides as the light baked the moisture away.

But on that day in late July, Trixie wasn't content. She was out and seemed upset. She ran up to me and huddled her head in close to me. I realized this meant she needed comforting. I stood there patting and talking to her until she calmed down. Then I headed out to the paddock, knowing without looking that Trixie would follow right behind me. Partnered together for nine years now, she knew that she'd get a treat for following me without a lead rope.

But she fell behind so I turned to check on her. She limped along on her right foreleg, just a little. When I checked it, I found a scrape on her knee, small with just a little swelling around it. I inspected her all over. I discovered a small cut on her left foreleg, way down near her hoof, and another one on her right rear leg, again down near the hoof. Neither one penetrated that deep and Trixie favored neither of those legs. Her knee seemed to cause her the most pain. I walked slowly and Trixie followed me to her paddock.

Shaped like a triangle with an electrified wire on two sides, the paddock's third side consisted of chicken wire and needed no electricity. A drop-off lay on that side, about four feet at a seventy degree angle, then a little granite shelf about eighteen inches wide, then a seven foot drop-off. Trixie knew better than to go out on that side. But how did she get out today? The electric fence remained up.

Sometimes when Trixie got bored, she played with the hook gate. If she tinkered with it long enough, she often managed to get out, but today the gate remained closed. I opened it and Trixie followed me in. I went to the van and got her an apple as a treat. I grabbed the bag balm and put some on her scrape and cuts.

I tried to figure out how she got out. She could jump the fence, if she wanted to. But she more commonly ran through the fence. I looked around the paddock searching for deep hoof marks that signified a jump. A reflection caught my eye. I walked over and picked up a glass Welch's grape soda bottle. I found two more and some rocks.

Dad drank Welch's grape soda. I doubted coincidences. Yesterday no bottles had littered my girls pasture. From the churned dirt and fresh hoof marks all around, I surmised that they got thrown at her today.

But it made no sense. If Dad spooked Trixie on purpose, how did the fence remain up? I looked around again. Then I spotted the bent chicken wire. I went over and examined it. Yup, deep hoof marks inside the paddock, and sliding tracks down the incline. Trixie had jumped here, but why? Even if Dad pelted her with bottles, she'd want to go out the sides of the paddock, not this end.

How had Dad got her to spook out that end, where he knew, she'd get hurt? Luckily, she avoided a serious injury. A horse could easily break a leg or its neck, jumping down onto a slope like that. I walked out of the paddock, shaking my head and stepped right over the answer to my mystery, tire tracks.

"What an asshole," I stated for probably the millionth time in my life. The son of a gun had parked his car between the van and the barn, so Trixie couldn't run out the side. Then he'd stood on the other side and pelted her with bottles and rocks, eliminating all escape routes except over the end.

Infuriated, I tried to think of names foul enough for the man and failed.

"I'll take care of this, beautiful." I gave Trixie a pat and a kiss on the nose. I went inside to call the cops.

On the first call to the cops, they informed me that I

needed to call the Humane Society. The first call to the Humane Society, they explained that since a non-owner perpetuated the abuse, it became a criminal matter for the police to handle. The second call to the cops, they once again instructed me to call the Humane Society. Nothing involving animals concerned them. The second call to the Humane Society had me telling the receptionist what the dispatcher told me. That upset the receptionist, almost as much as it frustrated me. "Please give me your number and I'll get back to you within ten minutes."

I read my number off to her. I hated talking on the phone. People brushed you off so easily when they never met or saw you. The Humane Society receptionist called me back and provided me with the number to a police detective.

"They now realize it's their responsibility. Officer Johnson will handle your case."

I thanked the receptionist, called the officer, and explained the situation. He honestly said they'd invest little effort on such a low priority item. Proving and prosecuting such a case rarely got done. He also told me, that if Trixie got killed, priority-wise an assault case mattered more. They'd try to get to it. But they believed it to be a waste of effort to investigate; after all, monetarily a horse's value rated less than an automobile's or even some brands of electronics.

Discouraged, I hung up the phone, Dad had evidently done some researching and discovered what meant next to nothing to the cops and everything to me. I sat down in the chair and cried. How could I protect Trixie?

I managed to hide my anger from Dad the next time he

put in an appearance. Acting ignorant gave my girl more protection than confronting him offered. I told Mom and Ev that Trixie escaped the paddock but not how it occurred. If Dad thought I assumed she got out on her own, maybe he'd leave her alone. I think it worked. She only got chased out once more in September. I again acted ignorant to the cause.

On an early October day, I came home to find Dad breaking into the garage. I called the cops when I saw his car, then I went out to confront him. He slammed the trunk shut when he saw me. I knew he'd stolen something. "Hey, I guess I need to give the cops a call and fill out another report."

Dad laughed. "Don't you get tired of wasting your time? You know, they never believed you. I told them how you've been unstable your whole life. You put such a stress on our marriage; you drove your mother and me apart."

I shrugged. I figured Dad had come up with a story that made him the victim. I couldn't even really blame the cops for falling for his story. When he wanted to, Dad could convince an Eskimo to buy an air conditioner. It usually took people quite a while to figure out that he only sounded nice. And typically, that happened after Dad got everything that he wanted from them and no longer considered them worth keeping up his act for. And as for pitiful, Dad play-acted a great victim. He put on kicked-puppy-dog-eyes, better than Trixie. Well, maybe if I stalled him long enough, the cops would arrive.

"You know the story about the camel and the straw? I figure with cops, its paperwork. So I keep piling it up. Sooner or later, one of their backs will break. When they look at the paperwork that broke their back, they'll find your name on every piece."

Dad cocked his head. "Your name shows up on all that paper, too. They could go after you."

I smiled and nodded. "Yes, but to go after anyone, they actually need to collect evidence and prove who broke the law. We both know who the evidence is going to convict."

Dad's eyes roamed in a circle looking at the woods beside the house, behind the house, behind the garage, and beside the garage. Then his eyes looked down to Trixie, standing in her paddock in the middle of the property.

Dad got into his car and rolled down his window. His eyes glittered brightly. His voice turned cold.

"You better watch out. Hunting season starts soon. A brown horse in the woods looks a lot like a brown deer. Hunting accidents happen so easily," he smiled as he drove off.

I managed to stay on my feet until his car disappeared, then I sank to the ground. He'd shoot Trixie and get away with it simply because he wanted to break me. The cops would do nothing to help protect her and probably simply blame her death on a hunting accident and not even bother to investigate.

I sat on the ground and wondered, why couldn't I just run way? Find a job up-state, or out-of-state, take Trixie and leave. I sighed. Leaving Mom and Ev at Dad's mercy would be an act of cowardice. Plus, if Dad drove me into leaving that meant he still controlled me, by making me run. I refused to allow him that. But what could I do? Hunting season loomed on the horizon less than a month away. Where would Trixie be safe?

Twice, I thought I found a place for Trixie. But when they asked why I needed to move her before hunting season, I honestly told them the truth. I thought Dad wouldn't cause problems on other people's property. But I knew nothing for sure. Both times, the people thought about it and changed their minds.

I wanted to but couldn't blame them. Standing up to Dad took a lot of courage and edged towards dangerous territory. He always balanced on the knife's edge, just one stumble or step away from outright physical brutality. I believed that he wanted to avoid violence simply because he got his thrill from terrorizing and bullying people. But I often worried that just the tiniest nudge might make him lose control completely. Therefore, if given a choice, I'd avoid having anything to do with Dad, too.

With time running out and hunting season less than two weeks away, I had to do the hardest thing in my life. I gave Trixie away.

Chapter # 8   Lonely Days

In October of 1989, I handed Trixie over to a girl named Alicia, who lived forty minutes away. She lived way out on this road that went nowhere. My girl would be safe there far from Dad's sight.

I gave Trixie to Alicia on two conditions. One, if she ever wanted to sell Trixie, she needed to offer her sale to me first. Two, if I ever wanted to buy Trixie back, she must let me purchase her. At first, Alicia argued about the second condition. Then she realized she made money on the deal. She received Trixie for free. I'd have to buy her back.

Trixie declined to go in the trailer for Alicia and my spirits buoyed up. But I squished my emotions down before Trixie sensed them. Learning to adjust to a new owner would prove to be difficult enough for her without my mucking things up. If I let my emotions leak through she might associate Alicia with my being upset and hold it against her.

The situation necessitated that I act like today just

happened to involve a trailer. I needed to introduce Alicia as a friend and forget that I balanced only moments away from curling into a ball and crying my heart out.

But even with my act, Trixie simply remained unwilling to trust Alicia that took time. Alicia got frustrated and asked me to put her in the trailer. My girl went right in for me.

"What am I going to do with a horse that refuses to obey me?"

I tried to reassure her and myself. Life would continue on, allowing Trixie to adjust, and hopefully, causing Dad to eventually calm down, permitting me to buy my girl back. "Alicia, she followed you around perfectly. Trixie's first trailer ride happened to be to the Vet's to get stitches. That trip resulted in a lot of pain for her and because of that she fears trailers. She neither fought you nor acted mean. She just refused to go in the trailer. You need to win her trust, just like you need to with any animal you get. Spend time with her, talk to her, brush her, let her get to know and trust you."

"It makes no sense. A trained horse should obey anyone."

"Up to a point, she does. But when it comes to something that represents pain to her or that she fears strongly, she won't do it until she trusts you. The only person ever successfully able to load Trixie into a trailer after her first experience with one is me. A painful first memory of something new becomes nearly impossible to train out of a horse. They happen to be very pain sensitive. Therefore, painful memories linger the longest. Only deep trust allows them to overcome or overlook painful experiences."

"What else invokes fear in her?"

I thought about it. "She dislikes running water of any kind. Trying to ride her across running water where she can't see the bottom scares her. And never try to ride her right beside a river or stream-bank."

Alicia turned and stared at me. "She refuses to cross water?"

"No, she crosses water. But you need to lead her across the first couple of times, so that she knows where the safe path lies. A bad experience taught Trixie that river banks and stream beds produce dangerous footing, capable of shifting and collapsing under a horse's weight. Her survival instincts persist sharper and stronger than yours, pay attention to what she tries to tell you."

"I'm smarter than a horse and I refuse to lead her across a stream or ride around one just because she scares easily. If I want to cross a stream, I'm riding her across it."

"If you try to force her across a stream without her trusting you or being able to see the path, she'll try to throw you." I believed Alicia might learn some painful lessons from Trixie, but I declined to force the issue, because no other place stood ready to take my girl and protect her.

"She won't throw me." Alicia's chin tilted up and her eyes flashed. "I ride Cherokee most of the time and she barely takes a saddle. I won't have a problem with Trixie."

I smiled to myself and tried to think graciously, possibly Alicia rode better than me. I knew Trixie could throw me, if she wanted to. She just never wanted to throw me. A couple of times, she shifted her balance to help me stay on, something highly unusual for a horse to do. Then again, not many horses trusted their riders enough to scratch their ears with their rear hoof while being ridden. I felt that Alicia underestimated Trixie because of her small size and gentle personality. Time would tell.

After the trailer drove out of my sight, I went into the lean-to, propped myself against the back wall, and cried until no more tears came. I stayed there until after dark, avoiding Mom and Ev, because I was supposed to be the strong one, the "Enforcer", indestructible, not this broken-hearted child weeping from her soul.

*   *   *   *   *   *   *   *   *

I missed Trixie horribly and it showed. I tried hiking, kayaking, and reading. While I liked those things, none of them relaxed me and made me feel good like being around Trixie. I became nervous and short tempered. Mom kept telling me to go check on Trixie.

I feared three things. One, what if Dad realized where I planned to go and found Trixie? That totally irrational fear lingered, I gave her up to keep her safe. I wanted there to be no chance for him to ever find her. Two, I in no way wanted to confuse her. I guessed she must feel pretty bewildered just adjusting to life with Alicia. I yearned to make it easier on her. Three, I feared I'd break down and bawl like a baby.

Alicia called three weeks after she got Trixie. She needed help. Trixie refused to let her get in the saddle.

"Well, sometimes she starts off walking before I get totally settled. Is that what you mean?"

"No, she refuses to let me mount at all. I get my foot in

the stirrup, start to swing up, and she sidesteps right out from under me. I get left hopping along on one foot, trying to keep up."

I managed to change my laugh into a cough. "Trixie never acted like that before. Is this the first time you tried to ride her?"

"No, I've ridden her every day except I took the last three days off. She threw me four days ago and I got a little bruised."

"What caused her to throw you?"

"I tried to ride her across a stream where she couldn't see the bottom. Is she holding a grudge?"

"I don't know. I usually backed off before she got that upset. Sometimes she got frustrated with me, because she failed to understand what I wanted her to do or feared doing it. Every time I came off her, something spooked her and she reacted quicker than me."

"She moves a lot faster than I thought possible. Can you come up and help me figure out how to get on her?"

"Sure." I figured it out before I got there. "How did you catch her?" I asked Alicia as I patted Trixie's neck and scratched behind her ears.

"I call her. She takes her time, but she comes. I give her a piece of apple or carrot every time I take her out."

"Can you show me what she is doing?"

Alicia nodded. I backed away.

She put her foot in the stirrup and tried to swing up. Trixie sidestepped away from her. She also walked, backed, and turned in circles with Alicia hopping along beside her. Then Alicia managed to get her foot out of the stirrup.

I burst out laughing. "I apologize. I never saw anything like that before. She gives you no chance at all. She just keeps dancing around." I shook my head and wiped my eyes.

Alicia's lips cocked up on the right and her left eyebrow hitched up. "I imagine it looks funny. How about you try? I kind of want to see what it looks like."

"Are you sure?"

"Go for it." Alicia handed me the reins and backed off.

Trixie stood absolutely still as I swung into the saddle. I shook my head and shrugged. "I guess this proves that she can hold a grudge. I came up with an idea on the way here." I gave her neck a pat and dismounted. I led her over to the corner, where the barn joined the house and walked her forward until her right side rubbed against the barn wall and her nose touched the house.

"You can mount here."

"Good idea. Why didn't I think of that?"

"I trained Trixie to sidestep, by putting her face up against the barn and rewarding every time she shifted sideways so I've used something like this before. Would you mind if I came up once in a while and looked in on Trixie? Gave her some treats, maybe?"

"That sounds fine to me. Can I call you if I encounter more problems?"

"I look forward to hearing from you, whether problems arise or not."

We put Trixie back out in the pasture. She trotted off to the greenest, richest section. Cherokee lifted her head and made a passing snap at Trixie, who turned and went to another spot. When we went into the barn to put away the tack, I looked into the open stall, sized about sixteen by eighteen feet.

"They both go in here?"

Alicia nodded.

"You put their grain in these pails?"

"Yeah, I just got Trixie's hung today. I got tired of it getting kicked around."

Oh well, I might as well just spit it out. "The pails hang too close together."

"Meaning what?"

"Have you ever seen Trixie actually eat her grain?"

"No, I usually put it in and then go in the house. Why?"

"I think Cherokee probably drives Trixie off and eats both buckets."

"How can you tell?"

"Well, Cherokee seems to still be asserting her dominance, which after three weeks proves her to be exceedingly aggressive. They usually settle down in a couple of days. Those pails measure about eight feet apart, which happens to be too close for an assertive horse to resist the temptation to steal both buckets. When do you grain them?"

"Usually about now, let's watch and see."

Trixie got about one mouthful of grain before Cherokee turned and drove her off by nipping at her. She ran out into the pasture, wheeled, and peered in the door, looking at me. I waited until Cherokee moved back to her bucket, then I reached in and grabbed Trixie's off the hook. I carried it out to her.

"I didn't realize."

"You'd have noticed eventually. I've been with Trixie a

long time and know how she reacts to other horses. She avoids fighting. When she pastures with other horses, she usually feels more comfortable being the submissive horse, especially when dealing with aggressive horses like Cherokee. Okay, if I use your tools?" I asked, pointing at the small tool chest.

Alicia nodded. When Trixie finished her grain, I mounted her pail hook on the outside of the stall. If Cherokee never saw Trixie getting grain, she wouldn't be tempted to take it. Even once Cherokee figured it out, the buckets hung far enough apart. Trixie stood a chance of sneaking in and eating out of Cherokee's bucket if she got driven away from her own.

*   *   *   *   *   *   *   *

As the weeks turned into months, I got more and more frustrated with Dad. The cops never helped. They still fell for Dad's sob stories. I strongly believed in respecting the police. But I was beginning to get frustrated by their naiveté.

We held a Restraining Order against Dad and he managed to convince the cops to violate it. They brought him to the house and accompanied him as he surveyed every room and floor of the garage and house. The two State Policemen walked a couple of steps behind Dad on the whole tour, looking and acting like his bodyguards. Dad's face spread into a wide grin as they entered the house. He had convinced the police to break the Restraining Order that they were supposed to enforce by telling them he owned the property solely and feared we might damage it.

It managed to backfire on Dad though. With the cops there to keep Dad under control, Mom surprised us all by asking.

"When will you take me on my protected tour of the property where he lives? I want to look for the bulldozer, metal lathe, and Corvette that disappeared from the garage." Mom asked them as she pointed up the hill to the now almost completely empty garage. Dad had systematically stole stuff for months and the cops always arrived too late to do anything about it.

The policemen stood speechless for a few moments. Then the taller one cleared his throat and spoke.

"We can't violate Mr. McLaughlin's privacy. He owns that property along with this one."

I opened my mouth. But Mom beat me to it.

"You are misinformed. My husband and I jointly own both properties. And I have a Restraining Order in place barring him from coming within five hundred feet of this property." Mom started to shake. "He comes here, kicks down the door, breaks and throws things, and threatens to kill us. I get a Restraining Order for protection and then *you* bring him here. *You* are supposed to be protecting us." Mom's shaking got worse, her face flushed, and she started to cry.

Both of the policemen's eyes swiveled from Dad's smug face to Mom's quaking body to me standing protectively in front of her. I saw the light dawning in their eyes. They began to look very uncomfortable.

"I think that we need to leave now, Mr. McLaughlin." The older policemen's voice calmly said. But one look at his stern face had Dad shrugging and turning to leave without a word.

Mom remained so worked up that even the tranquilizer that her Doctor gave her for her angina attacks failed to calm her down. She totally blew my mind by actually calling the Chief of Police and complaining about the officers breaking the Restraining Order. They talked for nearly half an hour and somehow the Chief not only apologized to Mom and helped calm her down, but he managed to encourage her.

After that, Mom began to stand up for herself on a regular basis. She didn't dare face down Dad yet. But if anyone else tried to intimidate her even a little, she turned into a civilized grizzly bear; she verbally ripped them to shreds.

Ev continued to remain neutral. At home, no matter what happened he exuded this aura of complete calmness. He personified a cool placid lake, fathomless, clear and undisturbed.

I, on the other hand, got so cranky my mother and brother avoided me. I felt like wringing Dad's neck every time he came over and gave us crap. But even though the cops never caught Dad, I knew they'd throw me in the lockup if I touched him in anything but self-defense. But, oh, I so wanted to hurt him! Because of him I had to get rid of Trixie and that hurt me bad. I wanted him to pay for that.

All of the joy got sucked out of my life by Dad. Work toiled on. Home life continued to be what I thought of as "The Enforcer Torture," constantly on guard, waiting for the next threat.

When the frustrations got to be too much, I went over to

the back pole barn at Cole farm. I wrapped some old coats around one of the support posts and stapled them in place. I punched, elbowed, and kicked that makeshift punching bag until the loose metal roofing rattled an echoing staccato beat to my hits.

After that, I walked through the woods and fields out to the Saco River and watched the water flow by. For some reason, the knowledge that the river's glass-smooth surface deceptively hid the deep eddies, sharp rocks, and treacherous, sometimes deadly currents calmed me almost as much as being with Trixie.

As winter came, my patience shortened as Trixie lost weight. I'd never seen her lose weight before in the winter. Alicia only put out two piles of hay. Cherokee devoured them both. Trixie put up with constant harassment when she tried to eat. She carried bite marks all over her shoulders and neck.

I mentioned it to Alicia. She said Trixie needed to learn to fight for her food. I explained that asking Trixie to fight a mare six inches taller than her and built heavier than her, who constantly bit, just to get food wasn't right. Simply spreading the hay out into three piles, would give Trixie an opportunity to eat.

Alicia got mad and said I had spoiled Trixie. She need not waste her time and energy doing the same. I never thought of it as spoiling an animal, but as proper care. However, Trixie no longer belonged to me and I could do nothing to change how Alicia thought.

I bought some hay myself of better quality than Alicia's. Every time I went to see Trixie, I took up half a bale. I stood by the fence and feed Trixie by hand. She always hungrily gobbled up two or three leaves of hay. Cherokee learned the hard way that my girl refused to share my attention or the food I handed out. Usually, mild tempered, Trixie turned vicious when pushed to it. Cherokee tried to drive her away from me only once and my girl put up such a fight Cherokee decided the effort outweighed the benefit.

After Trixie finished eating, I spread the leftover hay on the tussocks in the swampy side of the pasture. She possessed this part of the pasture because Cherokee refused to share the good section of the field with her. Now, it worked to Trixie's advantage. Snow and ice covered the ground. Cherokee knew not where the paths lay in the swampy area, so when she tried to steal the hay I left for Trixie, she headed in a straight line and broke through the ice ending up knee deep in freezing cold slush.

Trixie knew the paths and easily defended them from her rival. She simply stood her ground. I got a perverse joy from watching the bigger mare try to circle around her and end up in the slush pools. Trixie acted merciless. She nipped the slush splattered bay repeatedly, as she floundered around in the icy mix. By the time, everything froze solid Cherokee no longer tried to steal from my girl.

I tried to go see and feed Trixie once every week or ten days. I felt terribly guilty about not going more often. But during the winter, money got sucked up by plowing and heating bills. I couldn't afford the gas it took to go see her more frequently.

Even with the extra food I gave her, Trixie greeted spring skinnier than I'd ever seen her before. I ran my hand along her side and felt her ribs. Some horse people considered that the optimum weight to have a horse, lean.

But Jane Allen often told me, and I agreed with her that it seemed wiser to have an extra fifty to seventy-five pounds on a horse.

Horses sometimes lost weight for a variety of reasons. A dry year with poor pasture quality, a minor sickness, an over-abundance of flies so that a horse fidgeted a lot, lameness so that a horse failed to travel to the best part of the pasture, any one of these could cause a horse to drop weight. A lean horse to begin with lost muscle weight. Then it took time to get the horse back into condition. I considered it much better to have the security of some extra weight on a horse just in case.

Trixie carried no extra weight now and this worried me. I wondered if she could manage to gain some weight over the summer. She got the poorest pickings in the pasture. Plus, Alicia rode her three or four times a week, for three or four hours at a time. How would she get through next winter, if she failed to regain some weight? Another thing worried me badly, Alicia never got a farrier to trim Trixie's hooves. They stood in very bad shape and could easily lame her. I asked Alicia about Trixie's hooves.

"Wild horses never get their hooves trimmed and they get along fine. Why should I have to pay a farrier for Trixie's?"

When I recovered from my shock, I tried to explain it to Alicia. "Domestic horses get more nutrients from their grain and from having a steady source of food all year round, so their hoofs grow tougher and faster than Mustangs. Plus, mustangs run over areas that have a lot of shale rock. Shale rock abrades their hooves and helps keep them in shape. Domestic horses are kept in pastures or paddocks and ridden on trails or the side of the road. They get less abrasive wearing down of the hoof. These two reasons combined together make it so; you need to trim domestic horse's hoofs."

Alicia refused to believe me. Trixie went lame. Alicia tried to keep riding her to toughen her up. In a way, it worked. Trixie never let Alicia ride for more than a hundred feet before she bucked her off. When Alicia still kept trying to ride her, she started biting and kicking when she tried to saddle her. Alicia relented and called the farrier. Three weeks later, Trixie allowed Alicia to saddle her again.

I got more and more irritable. Trixie by my way of thinking wasn't being treated right. Yet, I couldn't buy her back, because Dad still acted erratically and posed a danger to her. I visited her as often as possible. I always brought her grass I cut from somewhere, usually two or three trash bags at a time. I dumped the grass in her swampy area. Cherokee now disliked the area enough to stay away from it. I left fly spray in my car and always gave her a spraying when I saw her.

By the fall of 1990, Trixie managed to regain some of her weight, but not all of it. I worried about the coming winter. Alicia called me and asked me how much Peary charged for hay. The bales cost more than she wanted to pay. I thought little of it. A lot of people, bought hay from small local farmers who sold hay cheaper than Peary's. Usually the bales from small farmers weighed less and held less alfalfa and clover in them. But generally speaking, it passed as good hay. The hay Alicia had bought last year registered on the low end of the quality scale. I assumed she wanted to find some better hay at a fair price.

I continued on like I had the winter before. I brought hay up and fed Trixie whenever I got a chance. Alicia called me in the middle of the winter. She needed more hay to last till spring. Could I get her some more? I told her honestly, most of Peary's hay was already reserved. The available product cost a lot. In the middle of the winter, the prices went up dramatically.

"But I have no money." Alicia cried. "My Dad only gave me two hundred dollars to buy the horses hay. I spent all of the money already and that farrier keeps showing up every ten weeks. He threatened to call the Humane Society on me if I fail to keep the horses hooves trimmed. If I run out of hay, I know he plans to call them. He mentioned how low my hay pile was last time he showed up."

I smiled to myself. I didn't know the farrier, but I liked him. Thank goodness, he somehow put the fear of God in Alicia, because she sounded near hysterical. "Alicia, I can't afford to buy hay for you. But I can try to help you."

"I've seen you bring hay to Trixie."

"I only own eleven bales Alicia. That wouldn't do you long. I need to call my boss and ask him for a couple of favors. I'll see what I can do and call you back in an hour or so, okay?"

"Yes."

I didn't really need to talk to Peary. I knew he'd agree because he was a goodhearted fellow. Also, what I planned to ask of him only counted as a small favor. I intended to make it seem like a huge favor to Alicia. I needed to use this to Trixie's benefit. Peary agreed to the favor and I called Alicia back up.

"Okay, I can help you some."

"How?"

"Well, you know how you always end up with a little loose hay on the barn floor. When you deal with twenty to forty thousand bales of hay a year, you end up with a lot of loose hay on the floor. Since right now, hay sells for three fifty to four dollars a bale, Peary generally re-bales the loose stuff. But I called in my favors. If I do it on my own time, I can put that loose hay in bags and get it for free."

"Thank you. Thank you."

I broke her bubble real quick. "If I invest my time to bag that hay and my gas to haul it up to you, conditions will apply."

"What conditions?"

"I plan to still stop and give Trixie treats, that's not going to change. I want you to give the horses their hay in a different manner. You need to give Trixie her hay down in the swampy area."

"I'm not trudging through the snow to bring hay down there."

I still found it hard to believe that someone who claimed to love horses complained so much about getting wet or dirty. "You need not trudge through the snow. Your pasture runs right beside the road. You simply walk down the side of the road, climb up on the snow bank, and throw the hay into the pasture. Your feet won't get wet. If I spend my time and my gas getting you hay, half of that hay needs to go to Trixie. Either you give Trixie her hay where Cherokee can't steal it or I refuse to bring you hay. If the Humane Society takes the horses from you, I stand a chance of getting Trixie back. The Humane Society might even keep her until I can safely bring her home. I have nothing to lose Alicia."

"Okay, but I only agree to do it with your hay."

"That's fine." So we arranged everything. I agreed to bring up as much hay as I could, every time I went to visit Trixie. I always stopped and gave her a couple of bags full first. Then I put the rest in the barn. Alicia fed the hay I brought in the morning and some of hers in the evening.

Trixie managed to hold most of her weight through the winter. Her condition remained the same as the year before. I felt riddled with guilt. She always gave me the kicked-puppy-dog look when I said goodbye and left her. I usually needed to stop on the way home to cry.

*   *   *   *   *   *   *   *

I lay reclined back in the chair, enjoying a good book, when with a mighty crack the bottom of the door came flying in. With a series of thuds and snaps, the left half cartwheeled end over end across the living room and landed with a ka-thud against the couch, while the right half slid across the floor, pulling itself apart, leaving a trail of wood from the doorway to ten feet inside the house. Amazingly enough, the top half of the door remained closed.

I had installed a screen door latch on it to hold it secure because the door had become extremely dilapidated from repeated repairs. The top half barely stayed attached to the bottom anymore. It leaned away from the doorframe whenever you closed it. Now, the flimsy latch held the upper half of the door shut while only a dangling bottom hinge remained of the lower half.

The first thought that crossed my mind was this feels so familiar. Yes, half the door remaining closed added a new twist, but the kicked in part of this drama seemed *so old*. Usually at this point, I leapt out of the chair to stand between Dad and Mom or Ev, but today with no one at home to protect, all I wanted to do was read my book in peace.

A grunt drifted in from outside, then the sound of a hand hitting wood. With a pop the latch ripped free, the remaining portion of the door banged open. The hinge shrieked in protest. Then with a shudder the top half of the door fell to the floor and cracked into pieces. Dad stood in the doorway backlit by the afternoon sun, smiling widely. His eyes swept the living room before landing on me. He cocked his head and looked up the stairway.

A second thought popped into my mind as I looked at Dad, I got my horrible fashion sense from him. He looked ridiculous, pathetically ridiculous, the Panama Jack floppy-rimmed hat and the tan slacks kind of matched. The denim sheepskin lined vest clashed with the tan, long-sleeved, pin striped shirt. His fuzzy white Albert Einstein hairdo helped him portray, the "maniac" look. Add on the high laced work boots and the whole ensemble declared, my mother dressed me for years and I failed to adjust to life without her.

"Get out," I said, without bothering to get up. I no longer held enough patience to put up with the bull shit any longer. A third thought dawned in my mind and my temper flared into the hot zone; that destroyed it. Six totally separate pieces. I knew it. The door was totaled. And now, we would need to come up with the money to buy a new door, preferably steel, so at least maybe he might break a toe. He only wore those dang boots to protect his toes while he kicked things around.

Dad just stood in the doorway, staring at me. "Get out."

"Is that any way to talk to your father?" He whined. "I come over to talk to you, and you yell at me to get out. What kind of daughter are you?"

"The kind that refuses to fall for any of your bull shit. So get out. Now."

He switched tactics, like someone changing channels on a TV. "I'm tired of you being so mouthy. You better learn to watch your tone with me." I watched him make a big production out of flipping the vest back to reveal the gun he always carried.

"That does it!" I screamed and jumped out of the chair. "Who do you think you are? John flipping, Wayne? You're not; you are just a selfish asshole."

Dad backed up as I approached. I kept screaming.

"This has gone on for way too long! I refuse to waste my life on this crap any longer. This ends today."

I stuck my face right in his. His eyes widened with shock as I leaned in until I nearly kissed him and yelled at full volume. "Pull the gun!" He flinched and stepped back so I followed him. "Pull it. Pull it, you asshole."

Dad started walking backwards, stumbling as he went. I kept following him, screaming. "This ends today. This is it. Pull the gun. You hear me. Pull the gun or leave and never come back. Those are your only choices. This ends today. Pull the gun!"

As I followed, Dad moved backward faster and faster

until he reached his car. He fumbled with the door latch behind his back. I kept right on screaming. "You will not give us any more shit. It ends today. Do you hear me? It ends today." I leant in so close; Dad barely managed to get the car door open. He squeezed into the seat like a snake sliding down a hole. I pounded on the car door with my fist.

"No more bull shit, no more. Do you hear me? No more giving us shit."

As he drove down the driveway, I picked up some rocks and threw them at the car. Lucky for Dad, my aim sucked. I only hit it once. I continued to scream. "No more. No more. It ends today." I kept screaming until the car disappeared.

My legs started shaking. My teeth chattered. My throat hurt. My knuckles on both hands seeped blood. I probably scraped them on the car. I walked back to the house, collapsed down onto the doorstep, and sat there shivering. I felt cold, all of a sudden. What had happened?

My mind tried to sort out the events. I came to the only logical conclusion. I had lost my mind. But that made no sense. If I lost my mind, could I come up with a logical conclusion? Maybe I had just reached my limit.

I nodded to myself. I had been fighting Dad, since my graduation in '87 and the spring of '91 now bloomed outside. I had known in '87, that my bull shit cup held too much. But Dad had continued to pound away, cramming more shit in that cup day after day. Today, that cup and I exploded in his face.

He would return, oh yeah, he always returned. But I knew with every fiber in me that he'd never come back with a gun or kick down the door again. He'd try whining, crying, begging, and pleading now, poor, poor Evans, wah, wah, wah. I smiled to myself. Even that would fail to work for him now, because Mom no longer fell for it. Even Ev's patience ran thin these days. Maybe Dad had learned something today. I knew I had.

There came a point when living no longer mattered. It didn't matter, if you lived or died, just as long as the torment ended. I knew I had stood on that edge, and if Dad had refused to back off, one of us would have gone over it. I cared not which one of us went over, just as long as it ended. Maybe Dad cared; I think he feared death. I didn't. I knew that now, and so did he. I held the power now. I knew what he feared.

I leaned back against the door frame and sighed. Things would get better now. It would be a pain in the ass, hearing Dad whine and cry, but that was all he would do now.

"Yes." I jumped up and threw my arms up to the sky. "Yes, I'm getting Trixie back." I yelled. I could protect her now. "Trixie, I'm going to get you back!"

I stood there with my face tilted back to capture the shafts of sunlight that stabbed through the pine trees, and my whole body felt warm. My face split into a wide grin. My eyes began to tear. At first, I failed to recognize the feeling; so much time had passed since it filled every crevice of my being. I doubled over giddy, light- hearted, overflowing with joy. "Trixie, I'm getting you back." I closed my eyes and let the tears flow.

*   *   *   *   *   *   *   *   *

I called around and found out that Phyllis Gay had room

in her pasture for another horse. She offered pasture and a stall at night and during bad weather. I just needed to pay for hay and grain, and a modest fee. I felt like Phyllis had handed me a winning megabucks ticket.

I started trying to figure out when I could buy Trixie back. It all depended on how much Alicia charged for her.

Alicia scared me by calling unexpectedly. Had something happened to Trixie, now that I could get her back? I picked up the phone, said hello, and went into verbal paralysis at the sound of Alicia's voice.

"Hello. Kim. Kim, hello. Kim, it's Alicia, hello."

I swallowed hard. "Oh, hi." I said the first plausible thing that came to my mind. "Sorry, I almost dropped the phone."

"I hoped you might come up."

Fear clutched me. "What happened?"

"Trixie refuses to come to me even for grain."

"I'll head right up." I drove way above the speed limit. Trixie always came for grain. Her refusing it just never happened. Could she have colic?

When I turned onto Alicia's road, I saw Trixie in the swampy area of the pasture. I pulled the car over and ran up to the fence. Trixie trotted over. She moved freely with no lameness, belly kicking, or any other signs of colic. I patted her and kissed her nose. I went to the car and got the partial bag of grass from the trunk.

"Sorry girl, I only brought a little. I didn't expect to come up today." She started eating. I gave her another pat and headed back to the car.

Sitting on her side lawn, holding a bridle and a coffee can, Alicia sat in the shade pouting. As soon as I got out of the car, she jumped up. "What did you do that for?" Alicia pointed down to Trixie. "You knew I wanted to catch her. Why bother to feed her?"

I held up my hands. "Alicia, one, I checked her over some. She neither acts lame or colicky. Two, if she wants to come to you, grass won't keep her away. You called me, because she refused to come for grain. I thought she might be sick, so I checked that first." I sat down on the grass and stretched out. "This feels like nice day, not too hot, not too cool."

Alicia sighed. "I wanted to go for a ride."

"I understand that. It seems like a good day for it. She failed to come for grain. I've never heard of Trixie not coming for grain. She loves grain." I sniffed at the coffee can. "I smell it over here, so we know she smells it. Did she come in, even part of the way?"

Alicia shook her head. "Not even one step. She looked up, watched me for a minute, and then went back to eating. Today makes the fourth day."

"She has ignored grain for four days." Alicia nodded her curly black hair bouncing and twisting in the light breeze. "That means she must be pissed at you for some reason. What happened?"

Alicia shrugged. "I haven't ridden her for a week. She threw me last time I rode her." I looked at Alicia.

"No, I didn't make her cross a stream. I only made it half a mile, before she dumped me."

I grimaced in sympathy. "That sounds bad."

"That stands as an understatement. I own a horse who refuses to come to me even for grain. Will you catch her for me?"

I thought about it. "No, I don't think that would be wise. If she refuses to come to you, I think she'll just throw you again. How about you think it over and decide how much you want for her and sell her back to me?."

"I might as well get rid of her. I can't do a thing with her. You spoiled her so much; she refuses to work with anyone else."

I shrugged and got up. "Maybe I spoiled her in some ways, I don't know. I just like spending time with her, and she likes spending time with me. I guess maybe, we became partners along the way. Neither of us behaves very well when you split us up." I said with a chuckle.

Alicia called out behind me. "Six hundred and seventy-five dollars cash."

I turned and looked at her. She paid less than that to feed both horses through two winters. But Trixie's value easily reached that amount and Alicia had kept her safe. She failed to always treat her good, but she had managed to keep her safe. "It'll take me till Tuesday to get the money. I need to call around and line someone up to trailer her. How about I call you Monday evening and tell you what time?"

"Okay."

I stopped and spent some more time with Trixie, before I went home. Tuesday felt very far away.

I called Peary right off when I got home. This past winter and spring he replaced and rebuilt a lot of the farm equipment and slowly fell behind in my pay. I never worried about it because I knew when we started baling new hay he'd be flush with money. Plus, the barn still held about a thousand bales of hay. I rejoiced about that now, because he owed me eight hundred dollars. Enough to buy

Trixie back, pay to have her trailered home and purchase her first month's board.

"Peary, hi. I need the back pay you owe me."

"Is something wrong?"

"No. I can safely buy Trixie back now and Alicia wants to get rid of her."

"Okay. I need to call around and schedule some deliveries. I left the truck parked over at the barn. Load it up. How about we leave tomorrow at eight?"

"All right, thanks."

By Saturday, the money resided in my wallet and Jane agreed to haul Trixie home. I called up Alicia to see if we could set-up an earlier pick up date.

"No. You need to wait till Tuesday. Three in the afternoon is the earliest time possible for me. I want my cash before you load her and you have to catch her."

"None of that poses a problem, Alicia. See you then."

I worried and fretted all weekend. I kept dreading that something would go wrong; Alicia changing her mind, Trixie getting hurt, or Jane's truck breaking down. I just found it hard to believe that everything in my life could go from bad to good so quickly.

Nothing went wrong and on Tuesday afternoon I stood in front of Alicia's barn counting money into her hand.

Jane stayed beside the trailer, because she felt angry that Alicia dared to charge me so much to get Trixie back. "Not that she isn't worth it." Jane explained on the trip up. "But she got free use of a well-trained, sweet-tempered horse for a year. If you'd had more time before you got rid of her, I could have found someone willing to pay you to lease Trixie."

Alicia folded the money into her pocket and held out the lead rope with a grin. "She refuses to even come up out of the pasture for her evening grain. Have fun catching her."

I chuckled as my face cracked open into a wide grin.

"Watch this!" I walked over to the pasture gate and ducked through it. Trixie stood about five hundred yards away, out in her swampy domain, over half hidden behind some blackberry bushes.

"Trixie girl! Come on beautiful!"

Trixie's head shot up so fast that she reared up. She trumpeted a loud nicker and sprinted forward. She nimbly weaved around and through the brambles and in moments she thundered across solid ground. Her neck stretched out, her muscles surged, her tail flew in a banner behind her.

She skidded to a halt in front of me, gently nudged me in the chest with her nose, whickered softly, and started prancing circles around me. I threw back my head and laughed. I had my girl back. Anything and everything was possible again. Alicia stood beside the fence staring at us in shock.

Cherokee started to trot up, curious about the commotion. Trixie caught sight of her and squealed angrily. She charged straight at Cherokee with her teeth bared and her ears pinned back. She wheeled at the last second and her back hooves lashed out. Cherokee's shrill whinny immediately followed the loud thud. Trixie's head swiveled around and as she glared at Cherokee, she jumped her hindquarters up, threatening to kick again. Cherokee turned and trotted back out into the pasture.

Trixie trotted back to me with her hooves flashing high, her neck arched, and her tail swishing gracefully behind her.

"That's my silly filly!" I said proudly and rubbed her neck. She nuzzled me affectionately and then lipped at the lead rope as she stopped by my right side.

"Ready to go, girl?" I asked. She nudged my hand with her nose and lipped at the lead rope again.

"She acts like a totally different horse!" Alicia exclaimed.

I snapped the lead onto Trixie's halter. "We're both happier and stronger when we stay together." I explained. Alicia's forehead wrinkled, her eyes widened, and then with a violent shake of her head she opened the gate.

Trixie walked up into the trailer without a fuss. But as we started down the driveway, she started kicking in the trailer. Jane stopped the truck.

"This trailer hasn't got front windows or vents. She can't see or smell you. She needs you to be in the trailer with her to keep her calm." I jumped out of the truck with a wide smile. "Stay in the opposite stall in case, she losses her balance." Jane hollered out her window.

I nodded and climbed in the trailer side door. Trixie nickered in my ear as I ducked under her neck into the other stall. I stood up and she leaned her head over the partition, stretching her nose out in the way that signaled she wanted a kiss. I chuckled, kissed her nose, and rubbed her neck. She sighed, closed her eyes, and we both leaned into the partition wall separating us.

I inhaled the scents of clover and fresh grass with her every exhalation. Her breath blowing over my shoulder and drifting around me made all my muscles relax with its familiar warmth. Her mane and my hair tangled together with every bump in the road. And by the time we reached our destination, I felt like my life had been handed back to me.

Chapter # 9   One of a Kind

Life felt good. The grass in the pasture grew tender, rich, and succulent. Cool, fresh water tinkled over the rocks in the streambed. Sun-warmed clover and alfalfa perfumed the air with their scents. The wide-branched, tall and sturdy oaks and maples bordering the edges of the field offered shelter and deep shade against the sun's heat. And the warm breeze blew constantly keeping the flies away. I leant back against the barn's faded boards and watched Trixie grazing. Life was good.

Trixie had pastured here at Phyllis's since I got her back in the late spring of '91. It only took her about six weeks, to gain back her lost weight. It took her longer to regain her trust of other horses. Cherokee left an impression on Trixie. She no longer acted laid-back around other horses like she used to be.

The natural course of horse relationships, especially between mares usually settled quickly. Within a couple hours or a day or two, the dominant mare became mutually agreed upon. After that, little changes. Years often passed in total friendship between horses without any change in herd dynamics.

It became obvious on the first day that Phyllis's mare, Star would end up being the dominant mare. Not just because of age or size, but she possessed the needed social skills and experience. Trixie had only become the dominant horse when she pastured with ponies. Other than one brief afternoon, when she believed herself to be super-horse, she had never held the dominant position in a herd of horses. She lacked the needed social skills and experience to be the dominant mare.

After her experiences with Cherokee, Trixie refused to let any horse hold dominance over her. She'd pastured with Star for over two months now and she still failed to concede to defeat. Her challenges on Star's leadership slowly receded to about once a week now.

Luckily, Phyllis held a natural affinity for animals. She knew Trixie acted up out of fear, and she willing gave her the time she needed to overcome her fear. Even more luckily, Star remained good-natured and fairly laid-back. Sometimes, Trixie challenged Star so fiercely that she backed off in shock. Most of the time, she just stood her ground and waited for Trixie to calm back down.

The one thing that always set me to laughing happened after it ended and they calmed down again. Star always turned and looked at Trixie. Horses' faces, once you got used to them, expressed so many things; fear, pain, happiness, curiosity, contentment. Star's expression as she looked at Trixie, stood out as obvious to me as white clouds against a brilliant blue sky. It simply asked. "What did you do that for?"

It always got me laughing and wondering. How could people think that an animal's emotions and intelligence only developed as a means of survival, both as a species and an individual? I dared anyone to watch Star look at Trixie and not believe otherwise. If only survival mattered, Star should act angry or frustrated with my girl. Instead, she behaved in a bewildered and curious fashion to Trixie's odd behavior.

Our separation and reunion seemed to change Trixie's and my relationship. We both seemed to be more content and easy with each other. We no longer needed to run, escape, or go anywhere in particular. We happily wandered. We often headed out on a ride and only ended up going a couple of miles. We usually stayed out riding for hours. We spent most of our time, just stopping and watching things together, the river flowing by, cows in a pasture, a fox hunting mice in a freshly mowed field. We often stopped and listened to birds singing or the babbling of a brook. Life felt good and we enjoyed it together.

*   *   *   *   *   *   *   *

I took a job working with Mom in Cape Porpoise for two reasons. One, it gave me forty hours a week year round, instead of eighty hours a week in the summer and ten hours a week for the rest of the year like the farm. And two, I no longer needed to check up on the house during the day, because Dad had calmed down a lot.

In lots of ways, Trixie and I went back in time. John Gay's farm where she pastured stood right next door to the Browns'. It also lay beside the road Mom and I traveled to work. Once again, I found myself staring out of a vehicle window every morning, desperately hoping for a glance of Trixie. Not usually a morning person. Mom learned the one way to get me moving in a near or above normal rate in the morning. She simply needed to mention that if we had time, we'd stop and see my beautiful girl. I not only moved faster, I became very helpful in getting ready to go. The downfall appeared if I finished getting ready before Mom, then I became impatient.

"Hurry, come on hurry!" Every second lost reduced the time I had to spend with Trixie.

She got used to us stopping by in the early morning. She ran to the fence, whickered, and waited for her treat. She knew she always got a morning treat of some sort, a carrot, and apple, or molasses on white bread. It took till the end of the summer, before she allowed Star to eat anything from my hand. If it came from my hand, Trixie owned it. After Cherokee, it took a long time to let another horse eat something that so obviously belonged to her. Even when she started sharing strict limits applied. Trixie only allowed Star to get one treat compared to her two.

Phyllis planned on buying another horse so I needed to find a different pasture for my girl next year. Phyllis also talked about having Star bred. That got me thinking. I'd dearly love to have a foal out of Trixie.

*　*　*　*　*　*　*　*

I brought Trixie home for the winter. As always, she acted like a yearling after the first big snowfall. She bucked, kicked, and twirled. She spun, rolled, and pawed.

She tossed her head, pranced around with high flying hooves, and snorted. She basically acted like she'd never seen snow before.

She behaved this way every year and I finally decided to try to take some pictures of it. Mom said and thought that I was wasting film because neither the scenery nor Trixie looked pretty in the typical fashion or way during the winter.

Trixie's winter coat darkened to a dull brown with no hint of the red highlights that shined so brilliantly in the summer. The hair looked coarse and thick, puffing out instead of lying down sleekly against Trixie's hide.

Plus, the half-rusted out cube van and the ramshackle lean-to bordered the paddock on one side and an old doghouse and a couple of junk cars made the background on the other side. None of it looked picture worthy, except to me. By my perspective, Trixie always looked beautiful. No matter what the background held.

I took the pictures and I dearly loved some of them. They showed Trixie's power, speed, and playfulness. They captured her inner strength instead of her outer beauty.

*   *   *   *   *   *   *

Trixie pastured at Cole Farm in the summer of 1992. Valerie Cole kept her horses over there. She was Andy Cole's wife and stood about five and a half feet tall with a wiry build, a pixie-shaped face, dark, brown curly hair, and a spontaneous, bubbling laugh. She happened to be the most meticulous horsewoman I ever met.

After watching her take care of her horses one evening,

it became apparent to me that she not only loved her horses as much as I loved Trixie, but that she also knew how to care for them well. She had a routine, after the horses occupied their stalls for the night and happily began to eat their grain, she went into each stall and cleaned and checked their hooves. While she did that she looked for any cuts or burrs the horse picked up during the day, then she checked whatever problem area that horse had before moving onto the next stall. It only took about five minutes for each horse, but it allowed her to spot issues *before* they become problems and it ensured that the horse's hooves remain healthy.

I'd read a lot of books about horses and took a couple of riding lessons, but mostly I learned how to take care of Trixie as I went along. Valerie's way seemed much more sensible and I tried to emulate her when possible.

In the mornings, Andy or Valerie put the horses out. We took turns cleaning the stalls. And Andy or Valerie kindly brought Trixie in if I got held up or needed to work late. Sometimes when they wanted a weekend off, I took care of the horses for them.

The vet came out and administered all of the horse's spring shots. Having them done together saved us money. I asked the vet if he thought, it'd be okay to breed Trixie? He said that if I wanted to have her bred, I needed to do it within the next year or two. Trixie would turn thirteen in June and luckily, she bore no health issues that would prevent a pregnancy.

Our area held some excellent stallions. I knew the qualities I wanted. My choice came down to three main contenders, Jane Allen's Fjord workhorse stallion, a black

Tennessee Walker in Alfred, and a Palomino Tennessee Walker who lived a little further away.

Although, I knew and trusted Jane Allen the most, her stallion got eliminated first. I didn't need the strength of a workhorse. I wanted Trixie's foal to be a riding horse and I wanted to be positive that her smooth gaits and comfortable riding size bred through. Work horses felt fun to ride on occasion, but not for more than half an hour, if you wanted to walk the following day. Their rib cages splayed out too barrel-chested to ride comfortably.

That left the two Tennessee Walkers. I felt certain that with either of them Trixie's smooth gaits would carry through. After all, Trixie inherited her smooth gaits from her Tennessee Walker sire. After observation, I knew that both of the stallions possessed good personalities and nice dispositions.

The final choice came down to my vanity. I wanted Trixie's coloring and markings to breed through. But even if her beautiful bay coat failed to carry through, I wanted her markings to. I found her blaze and socks to be exceedingly beautiful. They would stand out and look astonishing on any colored horse. The Palomino Tennessee Walker carried the exact same white markings, so he became the top choice. I entered into a contract for the following year to have Trixie bred.

Near the end of the summer Valerie informed me they planned to move their stables to the Waterhouse road the following year. Because they needed to renovate the barn to accommodate horses, no room stood open for Trixie. Originally, designed and built as a heifer and hay storage barn such a project might take years to accomplish.

So once again I started the process of looking for a pasture. By the time, I brought Trixie home for the winter I had found one. The place came with benefits and drawbacks. The main benefit being it cost next to nothing. It possessed numerous drawbacks, but none loomed large enough to dissuade me, probably because I found no other pasture available.

The barn stood leaning, ramshackle, and unsafe. Barbed wire fencing surrounded the pasture which hadn't seen an animal or mower for about five years. For shelter, I designed a canvas lean-to between the biggest trees and the barn. I bought half a dozen rolls of fluorescent surveyor's tape to mark the fence line. I planned on weeding the pasture in the spring.

I hoped to find a better arrangement before the following year and the foal's birth. I trusted Trixie not to have a problem with poor fencing. She had gotten to the point where all I needed to do to keep her in was lead her around and show her the fence line.

In the early spring, I tied a rope around trees and she mowed my mother's lawn. She could easily get out, if she wanted to. As long as I walked her around the fence line before letting her go, Trixie stayed in it. But a rambunctious foal needed a well-marked and sturdily built real fence. A barbed wire fence became too dangerous to have around a foal.

*   *   *   *   *   *   *   *

When spring arrived and the snow melted in the March of '93, I built the lean-to, marked the fence, and weeded the pasture. Trixie seemed to like it, well enough. When she came into heat I paid to have her trailered over to the breeder's. I disliked the fact that the breeder's wanted owners to stay away. Trixie's scheduled stay called for six days at the breeders. I missed her and worried about her.

I kept calling and asking about her. Trixie behaved fine and the breeders encountered no problems handling her whatsoever. They called me one evening because Trixie stood in the corner of her stall facing the wall, apparently hiding. I asked them if anybody had yelled in the barn. They said yes, an argument took place there.

I explained to them ever since Dad first led her home and hit her she hid when she heard yelling voices. If they wanted her to come out of the corner, they needed to go talk to her calmly. They found this to be highly amusing. They adored her gentle, sweet, and mild-mannered temperament.

Three days later, they relented and gave me permission to come over and visit her in the late evenings. They explained that they wanted most owners to stay away because some horses became difficult for them to handle when they got bred. But Trixie remained so easy-going and timid that they wanted me to stop by to reassure both her and me.

I drove over, parked my car, got out, and called Trixie's name. When she answered me, I knew which barn she stabled in. The second time she got bred, we thought the breeding took, but when the vet checked her, she carried no foal. Even though the timing now ran a little late in the season, I decided to have her bred one more time. After all, Trixie's birth happened on June 1. If she conceived this time, the foal would be born in early May.

I once again went to the breeders to visit my girl. I got out of the car and called her name. I received no answer. I knew then that something bad had happened so I walked through the barns, calling her name over and over. Still, I got no answer. On my third walk-through, I started looking into every single stall. When I found her, she lay flat on her side on the floor of the stall, breathing hard and not moving. No one answered the breeder's house door. I needed to go to their renters' apartment to use the phone. The breeders lived out of my vet's service area, so I needed to call their vet.

He diagnosed Trixie as colicky. He treated her and the breeders trailered her to the pasture in the morning, but I still thought something was wrong. Trixie refused to eat and she barely moved around at all. Finally, in the afternoon, I called my vet. I explained that another vet examined and treated her the previous evening, but I thought that something still ailed her.

The vet arrived and checked her. He discovered that the breeding had gone badly and ripped her open on the inside. He said she needed to be hauled to the veterinary clinic right away. I called up Valerie in tears. Could she trailer Trixie?

Valerie arrived in less than an hour. She carried her baby Matthew with her in a backpack that held him secured with him peeking over her shoulder. At the clinic, they ran various tests on Trixie. Within a half hour, they knew that she had peritonitis, an infection in the abdominal cavity. The internal injury allowed an infection to set in. Her chance of survival looked bleak. One of the vet assistants, gave her odds of one in a hundred, another said it actually stood more like one in a thousand.

When I got back home, I called the breeders, livid about Trixie's injury. They admitted that she dripped blood and kicked at the stud after the last breeding. But they assumed because she immediately went back to being sweet-natured that nothing serious could be wrong so they neglected to check her for an injury. Horrified to hear that she contracted such a life-threatening infection under their care, they immediately sent me a check returning the breeding fee. They kept insisting that Trixie had received excellent handling in their custody. I believed that to be untrue but none of that mattered at the moment. I decided to concentrate on what happened to be really important; getting Trixie better.

She stayed at the clinic for a couple of days. Valerie trailered her back to Cole Farm and passed on Gordon's permission to keep her there until she recovered. The setup of the barn gave her a better chance of survival. The stall Trixie went in measured about fifteen by sixteen feet. I spread out a bed of second crop hay against the back wall and set my sleeping bag up on top of it.

I kept taking her temperature and hosing her off when it spiked. If I failed to keep her cool, she'd get brain damage. Jane Allen's Morgan Silkie took ill with a fever and the horse acted like a different animal when it recovered, unable to remember most of its training. It seemed to have lost its spunk for life. I never wanted that to happen to Trixie. I kept an alarm clock in the barn that woke me every couple of hours to check her temperature at night.

She got used to the routine of me getting up, turning on

the lights, and checking on her. She remained unmoving, lying down like a dog, curled up with her head resting on her folded forelegs. Sometimes she woke up enough to lift her head and watch me stagger about half-asleep. Her eyes drooped lower and lower and her head slowly dropped down until her nose got buried in the shavings. Her every exhalation caused two miniature blizzards of sawdust to swirl out in opposite directions away from her face. Then her head started to sway back and forth as it balanced on her nose and her right ear twitched in time with each wobble until finally, with a muted thud her head fell over into the cushioning bedding.

By the time morning arrived, I wanted to stay inside my warm sleeping bag cocoon and not move. But as soon as the sun came up, Trixie started shifting her hooves about and rocking her weight back and forth. She wanted to get up but her sickness knocked her sense of balance out of whack and she couldn't stand unaided, so I crawled out of my warm nest and walked around to her outstretched head. I stood in front of her, grasped her halter on each side, widened my stance, and pulled up and back as she struggled to her feet, helping to steady her balance in the direction she wanted to go.

Together, we staggered across the stall. Trixie lifted her head over the half door and I propped my arms up on it. Leaning there side-by-side, we watched the barn swallows swoop down out of the loft, dart through the shafts of light streaming in the front door, and fly out into the world.

The vet came over twice a day, tubing water with dissolved confectionary sugar in it into Trixie's stomach. Over the years, he came to know us fairly well, and I believed he really liked my girl because he waived his normal barn call fees and got us a discount on the clinic bill.

Trixie's sickness persisted and she failed to drink enough water. The sugar gave her some calories. I cut fresh grass for her daily, but she hardly touched it. Twice at the clinic, and once at Cole farm, the vet asked me if I wanted her put down. He even offered to give me one of his horses as a replacement. I said no. Trixie acted uncomfortable at this point. She never exhibited any pain symptoms and she continued to get up for me. Horse's often lay down when they got sick and refused to get back up.

I found that just being with her provided a big comfort, not just to me, but to her. When I left the barn to go get something to eat and then came back, she acted restless and fidgety. As soon as I got out of the car, I heard her turning circles in her stall. We established a routine. The moment she saw me, she stopped and stared and I put down whatever I carried or did, and went to pat her.

She pushed her whole face flat up against me, like she wanted to hide from the world. I talked to her, rubbed her ears, and patted her neck. I cuddled her until she let out a big sigh. After the sigh, Trixie slowly pulled away from me.

"Brave girl, Momma loves ya. You know that, don't ya beautiful." Trixie's ears came forward. "Yes, I'm talking about you. You are beautiful and you know it."

As I spent all that time in the barn, I began to wonder. How did you pass so much time enclosed by four walls without going nuts with boredom? No wonder so many horses got stall sour, resentful of long enclosures in the barn.

I discovered that we shared another interest, reading. Well, I enjoyed the reading and she enjoyed listening to me read. I introduced her to some of my favorite authors like Anne McCaffrey, Mercedes Lackey, and Brian Jacques. My voice got raspy, my throat sore. But if I stopped reading out loud, she pawed the floor and shook her head. So I spoiled her, so what. As long as no one else started reading a book to her, they'd never know.

As long as Trixie refused to give up, I wouldn't either. Slowly, she improved. Within two weeks, she no longer needed water tubed into her; she drank enough by herself. In the third week, I started bringing her out to eat grass for a couple of hours in the early morning.

Trixie stayed on antibiotics for over three months before she finally got declared free of infection. I slept in the barn for the first six weeks, while she fought fevers. Valerie and Andy Cole allowed me to keep her at the farm through the whole time. Plus, they said next year I could board her at their farm. That news gave me great comfort. I trusted Andy and Valerie with my life. I knew if they even suspected Trixie felt ill, they'd tell me.

Trixie received a lot of adhesions in her intestinal tract which became the only lasting effect of the peritonitis. The vet informed me that she'd always colic easily. I needed to be careful not to let her get dehydrated. He said breeding her still existed as a possibility, but carrying a foal to term and giving birth posed a great danger to her because of all of her internal scarring.

The only reason I ever wanted a foal was because as Trixie aged, I found it hard to bear the thought of someday losing her. I thought that if she birthed a foal I'd always have part of her to hold on to. But even though I easily pictured the foal and longed to see it prancing by Trixie's side, pregnancy posed too great of a danger for my girl now. I nearly lost the most beautiful horse in the whole world. I refused to endanger her health again.

*   *   *   *   *   *   *   *

Winter passed quickly. Spring flew by. The snow melted. The days gradually got longer. Grass sprouted and turned a healthy, rich dark green. The mud holes dried up. And then the time came to ride Trixie over to Valerie's and Andy's for the summer of '94. As always, she seemed to know when the time to go out to summer pasture arrived. As usual, she instinctively wanted to go to the Brown's. Through the years, she always considered that her summer home.

That day when we reached the intersection with Waterhouse Road, Trixie yearned to continue on straight to the Brown's. I turned her towards Valerie's, but she twisted her neck and tried to side-step on down the Buzzell Road.

She behaved like a car sliding on ice, travelling diagonally to the direction she faced. And as I tried to urge her through the intersection her motion forward decreased and her slide sideways became more pronounced. We ended up stopped with Trixie's nose beside the stop sign and further forward motion blocked. She wanted to turn right and head to the Brown's. I needed her to turn left and travel up Waterhouse road to reach the Cole's. I barely won our contest of wills. Trixie proceeded up the knoll on

Waterhouse road dragging her hooves with every step.

Once we reached the top of the hill and the road to the Brown's passed out of our sight, she picked up her pace. She seemed to decide that getting to that pasture grass in a hurry sounded like a very good idea.

Once again, it felt like going back in time. I still tried to take our rides slow and easy. I retained a fear, left over from her long illness. I never wanted her to ever get injured or sick again. The last time, I'd nearly lost her. So I held her back even though she pulled forward. We played the old tug-of-war again. With a laugh, I gave her her head. She knew her limits and I needed to trust her judgment.

Trixie's long illness also affected our riding relationship in another way. I didn't know if the long spell of time I spent with her in the barn caused it or if all my reading to her began it. But we seemed to understand each other's reactions better. I rarely needed to use word commands or rein signals. She just seemed to know what I wanted her to do and I read her reactions better. A slight turn of her head warned me that some movement caught her attention and she needed to stop and figure it out. A tensing of her muscles, a flickering of an ear, a hesitation in her step, they all carried a meaning that I understood now.

I thought this happened to be a very small accomplishment for me. Some people had a natural ability to read horses from birth. Jane Allen and Valerie Cole possessed that gift. I wasn't born with it. I failed to understand most horses but I knew how to read Trixie, maybe because she finally succeeded in training me.

Trixie being able to read me without verbal or sensory signals was a big accomplishment. Few horses and riders stayed together long enough or developed a relationship deep enough for the horse to read the human. Layer upon layer of contradictions, humans sometimes failed to even know for sure what they wanted themselves. A horse being able to successfully see through those layers was a rare and beautiful thing. I cherished this new connection with Trixie.

*   *   *   *   *   *   *   *

Trixie loved to flirt. No way around it, she acted like a tease. Valerie's two geldings pastured next to her, she constantly teased them. Two things existed that Trixie loved to do in that pasture, one of them happened to be flirting with the geldings. Trixie whickered at them and sidled up to the fence. She pranced and danced until she captured the gelding's complete attention. They came over to the fence, strutting their stuff, necks arched, high-stepping show-offs. When the three of them crowded around the fence together it became apparent how truly different their coloring and body conformation looked.

The stockiest of them, Reylen carried heavy bones and bulging muscles. He exuded power even when he stood still. Jordie looked taller, long-backed, long-legged, and sleek, he seemed like a speed machine. The smallest of them, Trixie stood a good six inches shorter than both of them. With her finer boning and delicate features, she appeared fragile in comparison.

But most strikingly evident when these three group together was their coloring. For while they all technically counted as bays, they showed the diversity within that coat color. Jordie carried the darkest hide of them, a deep rich brown like wet fresh-tilled dirt. He bore no white markings but his muzzle shaded to a darker brown with a dusting of delicate long lighter hairs sprinkled across his nose, begging you to pat it. Reylen looked like that same dirt left out to dry in the sun, bleached light brown on the surface with darker shades beneath revealed with every breath and movement accentuated by a white blaze and one white sock. Trixie truly shined beside these two because her coat held as much red as brown with golden highlights that reflected the summer sun.

She gleamed, shimmied, and sparkled as she coaxed the geldings to her side. And when she got their sole, undivided attention, she changed her tune. She squealed at them, turned, and sauntered off. She acted like a teenage diva and I couldn't help but laugh.

The poor geldings stood frozen in place, all bewildered. Their confusion showed up markedly on their faces'. They seemed to be asking themselves. "What did I do wrong? I thought she liked me." They lingered there, hopeful, then finally gave up and wandered off.

Trixie allowed the geldings about half an hour of peace and then she started all over. Luckily, Valerie had an excellent sense of humor and the geldings thought Trixie walked on water. I failed to understand how she managed it. To me flirting existed as a foreign language, totally beyond my realm of comprehension, confusing, and governed by rules that I lacked understanding of. My idea of getting dressed up consisted of wearing a pair of jeans with no holes in them that happened to be in a color other than the standard blue with a T-shirt that bore no brand names or advertising logos on it.

The men who become attracted to me liked strong, independent women. Unfortunately, they seemed to fall in one of three categories. The first of which contained the mommas' boys. They struggled to handle anything on their own, their jobs if they existed, their cooking, their laundry, and their bills, all appeared to be too much for them to handle. And they made me want to scream. "I encounter enough problems in my own life. I don't need or want to take care of yours too!"

Next.....

Category number two held the intellectuals. They assumed that physical strength never answered any of lives problems. They thought things through. They used brains not brawn, which worked fine as long as nothing went wrong like the flat tire my truck got on one evening and my date chivalrously *tried* to change it.

"The mechanic must have put these lug nuts on with an air ratchet. They refuse to come off." And after watching the poor fellow strain, grunt, and gasp I took his place and changed the tire, because I put the lug nuts on the same way I removed them with a four-way tire iron.

Next....

And the last, but definitely not least category accommodated the macho men. They liked strong, independent women because they behaved like extreme alpha males who failed to fear anything. These guys thought that sky-diving and bungee-jumping qualified as relaxing hobbies. Generally, truly nice guys I wished, really wished I happened to be that brave.

Next....

I failed to find the next. I remained uncertain of Mr.

Right's existence. I often found myself avoiding the dating scene. After all, I never needed a man to take care of me; I just wanted; someone to share life's ups and downs with, someone to lean on who never acted ashamed to occasionally lean on me, someone who brought out the best in me. But most people my age didn't understand what I wanted, so why bother to keep looking for it.

Trixie though, perfectly understood the horse version of the rules, to her flirting/dating was a walk in the grass.

The second thing Trixie loved to do in the pasture was to roll in the mud or dust hole. She rolled so often in one spot that she managed to kill the grass. When it rained, she rolled in the mud. When the mud dried out, she rolled in the dust. I came near to wearing my brushes out, trying to keep her clean. Every time, I went to get her out of that pasture, she looked horrible.

She appeared dirty and unkempt a total stranger to brushes. I cleaned her up, went for a ride, and put her back in the pasture. Murphy's Law, the first thing she did.

Roll, roll, and roll until she covered herself with dirt. Lucky for her, love really was blind.

*   *   *   *   *   *   *   *

I decided that Trixie deserved better than a lean-to. I planned to build her a real one stall barn. Actually, it measured closer in size to a shed, but it would hold the heat in and the weather out better than that old lean-to. I designed two sheds, one with her stall and space for five or six bales of hay. The other destined to hold the remainder of her hay, and her tack and brushes.

Getting them built before I brought her home presented a problem. Mom had a really nice boyfriend, Clyde who helped us all summer long. We needed to put a new roof on the house and replace or splice about half of the wall joists. The house was a modified A-frame Dad built with green wood and never installed ventilation in, it had proceeded to rot all the way down to the sill in some spots.

The sheds needed to wait until we finished working on the house. I purchased the lumber, the windows, and the roof shingles. Gordon Cole let me borrow his pickup to haul the lumber home. I just needed to concentrate on one building project at a time.

Finally, we finished working on the house and I moved on to Trixie's sheds. Over the years, I helped and worked on enough carpentry jobs to be able to do this project. But like most jobs being competent achieved only the first step. Some tricks to the trade, you needed to either be taught or learn yourself, the hard way.

I experienced one such lesson that imprinted itself forever in my memory while building the sheds. I finished the shed floors and walls, then nailed the roof rafters in place. Next, I needed to put the plywood on the roof. But how could I get it up there by myself?

I thought I was being intelligent when I pushed the plywood up the ladder in front of me. I even felt proud when I shoved it off the top of the ladder and it plunked down onto the roof rafters. Then I realized that a big problem existed. The plywood with gravity's help, slid back until it reached the ladder. Only my weight on the ladder kept the plywood from knocking it over completely. If I climbed down the ladder, it'd tip over on me. If I stepped off the ladder onto the plywood, a very interesting, but abrupt ride to the ground awaited me. And since I foolishly placed the ladder between the roof rafters, I couldn't just nail the plywood down because it lay a foot in from the edge of the roof.

I came up with what I thought was a brilliant plan. I'd push the plywood forward, so that I could step off the ladder onto the top of the stall partition wall, then I'd lift the plywood over my head, let it push the ladder back until it reached the correct spot, and then nail it down. Stepping off onto the stall wall proved to be easy, turning around while holding a sheet of plywood and balancing on top of a two by four wasn't. It took more body contortions than a game of Twister.

The plywood slid down the rafters pushing the ladder back. The problem then became that it wanted to continue off the edge of the roof. I balanced on my right leg while using my left knee and elbow to exert enough downward pressure to hold the plywood in place. I failed to hit the nail in that contorted position. But my thumb offered a much bigger target. The resultant "Oh-ah-oh!" yelling and hand waving caused me to lose my grip on the plywood.

It careened off the roof, flipping the ladder over and landing on it with a crash audible to the whole neighborhood. Now, I stood stranded on the roof with two options, jumping down into the stall or waiting fifteen minutes for Ev to finish his shower and yell for help. I figured that the safest option involved screaming for mercy.

Ev rescued me from the roof and asked how the plywood ended up on top of the ladder. I explained the dilemma.

Ev chuckled. "You need to be smarter than it is, Kim. You'll figure it out."

For a while, I remained unsure if my brainpower exceeded that of a sheet of plywood. But with the help of some scrap lumber to make stops at the end of the rafters and placing the ladder in a different position, I finished the sheds without any more mishaps.

I finished hanging the split stall door on the 29th of October in 1994. I brought Trixie home for the winter on the 30th. I only got a coat of primer on the sheds but if the weather warmed up in the near future, I'd put on the topcoat and do the trim.

Trixie seemed to like the new shed quite a lot. She used the rough cut wood of the built-in manger as a scratching spot for her head and neck and the split door when latched stood at the perfect height for rump-rubbing. But she absolutely hated the ramp up into the barn. It lay even and solid. When I built it, I took off the top board and filled it with concrete. But evidently the concrete either settled a lot, or bubbles formed in it, because when Trixie first walked on it, an echoing, hollow sound came from the ramp, sort of like a bass drum. She refused to set a hoof on it after that.

She acted like Pegasus. From the outside, she got a running start, leapt over the ramp, landed in the shed, and slid all the way across her stall. From the inside, she stood on the very edge of the shed. She twitched. She quivered. She swung her head back and forth. When she succeeded in agitating herself enough, she partially reared up and launched herself out of the shed.

It made me very glad; I never tried to jump her. She

cleared the ramp. But well, I might as well put on a tutu and try to pirouette. It wasn't graceful. If she still refused to walk on that ramp when the snow flew, I planned to borrow a video camera from someone. It may not be graceful, but it sure was funny.

* * * * * * * *

Andy renovated a shed at Cole Farm and put up a fence to make a pasture for Trixie over there. It made good sense. Valerie needed to use her stables for people who wanted lessons and to train in her arena. Plus, having us at the farm meant the poor geldings avoided torture by teasing.

Trixie just needed pasture and shelter. We never used an arena anymore. I only bothered to use a saddle when I gave someone else their first ride on a horse. Especially good with children, Trixie gave numerous rides over the years first to schoolmates and cousins, and then to the children of relatives, co-workers, friends, and neighbors. I never kept count of how many rides she gave out. But I guessed it to be well over a hundred.

Amazingly, the pasture bloomed with a profusion of buttercups. Trixie looked so beautiful in them. I kept trying to get a good picture of her surrounded by them. First it rained, and then it got hazy. Every time I tried, something came up.

Finally, I just started snapping pictures. In most of them, Trixie stood way too close. But in a couple, she grazed on the other side of the pasture. I held hopes for those pictures, and then I got them back. I thought the buttercups looked beautiful and wanted to capture an image of my girl in them. And there Trixie was walking through them with her mouth hanging open, looking like she couldn't decide whether to eat the flowers or sneeze on them.

*   *   *   *   *   *   *   *

Trixie came back home for the winter of '95-'96, and if anyone asked me at that time if we spoiled her, I'd honestly have to answer, oh yeah, definitely. She succeeded in wrapping the whole family around her little hoof.

For weeks, I tried to figure out where her hay disappeared to. I opened a bale and fed her one leaf in the morning. When I went out in the evening to feed her, over half the bale had vanished.

Finally, one morning when I went back in the house, I asked Clyde if he thought Trixie could somehow be reaching the hay on her own.

"No, I don't think so. She always stands outside when I feed her."

"You've been feeding Trixie in the morning?"

Clyde nodded. Mom and Ev walked into the kitchen and said at the same time. "Yes."

I held up my hands. "Everybody has been feeding Trixie breakfast." We all looked at each other. "Why have you all been feeding her? You know I feed her."

Ev shrugged. "Well, when I go out to go to work the stall door stands closed, and Trixie acts very hungry, I just figured she got locked out and the hay remained inside. I don't have the time to go in and open the door, so I just throw a leaf of hay into the pasture."

"I've been doing that too." Mom said as she packed her

lunch bag.

Clyde raised his cup of coffee and nodded. "Me too."

"Trixie managed to trick four breakfasts out of us every morning. I've got the day off. I want to watch from the window. Don't feed her again. She'll turn into a butterball turkey, if we let her pull this stunt all winter long." Everyone nodded. I headed for the window.

I had given Trixie her hay indoors. She must have sucked it up like a vacuum cleaner, because she ran outside within ten minutes. She raced once around the paddock and then she trotted over to her stall door. She put her nose behind the door and with a swing of her head, slammed the door shut.

When Clyde went out to get in his truck, she went into full parade. She pranced up and down the fence line, nickering. She ran back and forth to the stall door, tossing her head. She stopped and gave Clyde the kicked-puppy-dog look. Clyde kept walking. She nickered in desperation and pawed the ground. She let out one last frantic nicker as Clyde drove away.

Mom went next. I opened the window and heard her talking to Trixie. I only got to hear part of it, because Trixie whinnied up a storm, darting from the fence to the stall door, tossing her head and rearing.

"Oh, you poor starved... wasting right away... so skinny. Poor...." Trixie stopped and snorted. She ran up to the stall door and pushed on it. She turned to Mom and whinnied frantically. Mom laughed and kept going.

By the time, Ev went out. Trixie acted furious. She reared. She twirled. She nickered. She ran to her stall door. She shook her head, pawed the ground, and backed up all at the same time. She trumpeted and wheeled. She charged up to the fence. I saw Ev flinch as she trumpeted again.

I pictured the neighbors rolling over and putting their pillows over their heads. A barking dog sounded like a gentle breeze compared to the racket Trixie made. She reared up and trumpeted again as Ev drove off.

Trixie spoiled? Oh no, whatever gave you that idea?

*   *   *   *   *   *   *   *

In May of 1996, Trixie had been out to pasture at Cole farm for a couple of weeks. Her behavior worried me a little. She acted sore, achy, and exhausted. Not lame, she just moved around real slow, like she hurt all over. I planned to check on her again at noontime.

When I went over to check on her, she was lying down in the pasture, in the middle of the day, in bright sunlight. If she wanted to take a nap, she either stood and sunbathed, or she went to the shade and lay down. She very infrequently lay down in the full glare of the sun. She failed to get up, when I called her and when I approached her. I grabbed her halter and asked her. "Come on, girl. Can you get up? I want to check and make sure you haven't got colic."

She staggered to her feet. I put my ear to her side, back near her hip. I heard rumbles, burbs, and gurgles. Her belly made good active sounds. I tried to get her to walk. She took a couple of halting steps. She acted like everything hurt.

"I'll come right back girl. I need to call the vet." I patted her neck, gave her a kiss on the nose, and ran for the main house.

Charlotte let me use the phone to call the vet. When I got back out to the pasture, Trixie was already lying down again. She moved no closer to the shade. She just laid back down right where I left her.

Since she showed no signs of colic, I decided to let her remain lying down. I went over and sat beside her neck. I patted her and talked to her until the vet showed up.

He asked me get her up and walk her. He took some blood. He said a lot of older horses start having problems with their thyroids, which caused symptoms like this. He hoped that it turned out to be her thyroid because medicine easily treated the problem.

At the age of nearly seventeen, blood tests diagnosed Trixie with thyroid disease. We put her on a powdered medicine that went in her grain. Within a couple of weeks, she returned to normal. She needed to stay on the medicine for the rest of her life. But other than that, thank goodness, she remained healthy.

*   *   *   *   *   *   *   *

In early October, I brought Trixie home riding past numerous Presidential campaign posters for Dole/Kemp and Clinton/Gore. A chilly fall so far, heavy frosts in the morning made the leaves brittle. They snapped and crunched under my feet as I headed out to the shed. Almost every morning Trixie's water bucket held a film of ice in it, really thin in the center and about half an inch at the edge of the bucket. This winter, I started bringing out water, hot from the tap to melt the ice.

Trixie enjoyed that hot water as much as some people liked their morning coffee. I kept thinking it would burn her mouth. She'd drink it straight up if I let her. I needed to block her with my body, hugging the water pail as I poured in the steaming water. She hovered over me, snorting impatiently in my ear as I checked it with a fingertip.

It usually still felt hot on my finger as she started crowding me, inching her hooves forward, and gently bumping my ear with her nose. Her moist breath fluffed my hair and slid down inside my shirt collar bringing a moment of warmth before the chill morning air replaced it, making me shiver. Through glasses fogged by the rising steam I saw a pink blob wiggling furiously over my right shoulder. Centimeter by centimeter it crept forward, slowly angling over in front of me as she pressed her left cheek against my ear and nudged, nudged, nudged me aside. The moment I got out of the way, she guzzled up that still steaming water before it even finished melting the ice. It took two or sometimes three trips with jugs of water before she left the hot water alone long enough to melt all the ice.

Then one night the first snow came and it ended up being about four inches of heavy snow with a crust on top, I knew Trixie would act like a silly yearling. I held the camera loaded and ready, when I swung open the stall door. She didn't disappoint me.

She bucked. She reared. She pawed. She rolled. She tossed her head. She kicked up her heels. She rolled again. I took a whole roll of film.

When I got it developed, I decided to have Christmas cards made out of one of the pictures. Prancing and tossing her head with her mane flying amongst softly falling snowflakes; it captured Trixie's playful nature.

To me, the pictures personified Trixie. Free, wild, strong, and beautiful! Dancing, prancing, through life's storms. Not unaffected by them, but refusing to be bound, trapped, or held down by them. To me, Trixie embodied a never ending lesson about dancing in the rain, prancing in the snow, rolling in the mud, and enjoying every moment of it.

*   *   *   *   *   *   *

I tried to get some pictures of Trixie in the buttercups again in '97. I failed. I got some of her waiting by the gate. I tried sneaking up on her. No go, she heard the car. I tried riding my bike over, she saw me coming. Then a freak thunderstorm hit and the buttercups lost their petals or got flattened.

But I received a pleasant, unexpected surprise. Alden Cole came up to visit his parents and brother this summer. I talked to him some. He seemed like a real nice fellow, interesting, funny. He took some pictures of Trixie and me. I didn't think much of it.

He sent copies of the pictures up to Clark and asked him to give them to me. My goodness, those pictures came out awesome. Somehow, Alden managed to capture the connection between Trixie and me in those pictures. I respected his skill with a camera and thought it an extremely kind thing to do. Especially to have them sent to me. I cherish those pictures.

*   *   *   *   *   *   *   *

What a winter, this season of '97-'98 turned out to be. The snow and the cold didn't have me wishing for spring, but the neighbor's dog did. Trixie loved that dog. Personally, I think I hated the darn thing. It looked cute, but cute only went so far. That dog proved to be a major pain in my rear.

The problem lay in the fact that the neighbor let the dog run lose all the time. The dog liked Trixie. When it got bored, it crawled under the wire into Trixie's paddock and played with her. But then, when the neighbor called it home or it heard one of us and decided it better go home, it forgot to crawl under the wire. It ran through the bottom wire, got a shock, yelped, and raced for home. Trixie saw her playmate running off, and the fence half down. She was smart enough to realize that she received no shock after the fence wire lay on the ground so she ran through the top wire and followed her doggie friend home.

Now, seeing a golden retriever dashing down the side of the road with a halter-less bay horse in a blue blanket right on its heels caused a unique reaction, which went something like this. The person's jaw dropped and bounced off their breastbone, then the jaw slowly rose back into position, and the person soundlessly mouthed, "What the heck?" followed lastly, by an unstoppable grin that spread across the person's face. After all, if you saw a horse apparently chasing a dog down the side of the road rider-less you had seen everything.

My unique reaction devolved into an intense dislike of the aforementioned dog, after about the sixth occurrence in three weeks. The dog's owner, who stood out in his yard feeding Trixie dry dog food from a coffee can, and announced at my arrival "I caught your horse", failed to inspire friendly emotions in me too. I quickly became tired of repairing the fence. And Trixie could get hurt running down the side of the road.

Then on a bitterly cold afternoon, the sound of hoof-beats on tar roused me out of the house. By the time, I got to the neighbors; I was shivering inside my jacket and grinding my teeth to keep my anger at bay. Why couldn't he keep his dog tied? It was the law.

The neighbor greeted me. "You know, I like being neighborly and catching your horse. But it isn't safe for her to be out and she likes the dog food. I'm afraid; she'll always come here when she gets loose."

"Of course, she always comes here. She follows your dog." I nearly screamed. "Haven't you ever wondered, why the only time you see this horse loose happens to be when she comes trotting in the yard following your dog?" My neighbor shook his head.

"Well, I'm going to tell you why. Your constantly loose dog goes up to my house. He crawls under the electric wire into the horse paddock. He plays with the horse, and gets her all excited, and then he decides to go home. But instead of crawling under the wire to leave, he runs through it. Trixie sees the fence down and her friend leaving, so she follows him." I took a deep breath. "If you want to do the neighborly thing, please keep your dog tied up from now on."

He rubbed his right hand through his short beard and blew out a puff of air. "Well, I never realized he caused the horse to get out. I'll keep him tied from now on."

I shivered once more, then reached and placed my hand gently on Trixie's jaw. "Come on you silly horse, let's go home."

As good as his word, the neighbor tied up his dog after that. It never came to see Trixie again. She stayed in her paddock and the people of rural Southern Maine lost their opportunity to see a horse chasing a dog down the side of the road.

    *   *   *   *   *   *   *   *

I planned to get a good picture of Trixie in those buttercups this summer, one way or another. My scheme involved a preteen brother and sister, about three pounds of apples and three pounds of carrot's cut up into sections, and my sneaking skills. I figured it stood around a twenty percent chance of success. I was trying it. After all, my grandfather used to say, "Fate favors the foolish."

I parked the car at the bottom end of the pasture. I gave Ashley and Dennis precise instructions. "Feed Trixie the treats one at a time, take turns feeding her. Stay out of the pasture."

I waited until they stood at the fence line doling out treats which caught Trixie's complete attention, then I headed out walking. I circled around Richard's house, went through the field, and up the backside of the hill.

I ended up right at the top of the pasture. I climbed through the gate. I got the camera in focus and then I called her. She whirled and came galloping through the buttercups to me. I snapped pictures as fast as possible.

It worked. In the summer of '98, I finally got a good

picture of Trixie in the buttercups. Carrots and apples proved to be a very cheap price for that picture. Plus, of course, the ice cream the kids and I went out and got to celebrate. Still even though, it took four years to get that picture. It was worth the failures, the planning, and the waiting.

*   *   *   *   *   *   *   *

The autumn leaves have withered to dark, brown parchment and been tossed to and fro by the wind until they carpet the ground. They scent the air with a dry, musty smell, like a flooded library that had its books re-dried and shelved.

Sometimes, I found a whole undamaged leave with its edges turned up into a shallow bowl that become the home of a spider and on cold mornings its web looked like glass lace with the frost outlining and freezing it in place.

But fall fled in front of winter's fury. It blew away quickly with the flying days. Winter pushed in. Snow-storms buffeted the land covering both nature and civilization with blankets of fresh snow. Either crisp and sharp, protesting every step with crunches and groans, or soft and moist, muffling footsteps and sticking to boots, layer upon layer until they weighed wet and heavy with moisture, creeping its way into boots and through gloves until toes and fingers turned bright red and went numb. The snow continued on relentless and just like winter, an oft complained about visitor who stayed longer than they were welcome and added work and turmoil to every task.

This year, I noticed something a little odd about Trixie.

Although, she still played like a yearling in the first snowfall, she no longer cut a lot of paths through the snow. She made one around the perimeter of her paddock, one that bisects it, and one to her favorite rolling spot. That was it, three paths altogether. She used to keep the whole paddock packed down. She acted neither lame or achy. She just stayed out of the the deep snow now. If less than three inches fell she didn't seem to mind. Once it reached above six inches, she avoided it.

I found nothing wrong. But I called and set up an appointment with the vet anyways. I felt better being safe rather than sorry.

The vet diagnosed Trixie with the beginnings of arthritis in her hocks. Her knees still seemed okay. He said it didn't seem bad for her age and he thought it wouldn't prove to be detrimental enough to warrant any treatment.

I needed to avoid riding Trixie in the snow and I shouldn't worry, when she dodged it. If she got to the point of lameness or seemed to have a hard time standing up or lying down, I'd need to get her rechecked.

After he left, I stood there pondering what he said. "For her age," now in the year of '98, Trixie's age reached nineteen years. That wasn't old, my mind argued. I walked into the paddock and up to her. I ran my hands lovingly over her head. I traced the white hairs above her eyes. So her coat carried some gray hairs that meant nothing. I probably had gray hairs.

I leaned my head against her neck. I breathed with her and admitted to myself that she had aged. Yes, she was getting older, but old, no. To me, Trixie would never be old. She acted too alive to ever be old.

*   *   *   *   *   *   *   *

I got a new job working at the bakery and it kept me busy. It paid well and had great benefits. The hours were extremely weird though, especially in the summer. Once the summer roll shift started up, I never knew when my work day would end. When I got some seniority, it'd improve. But at that time, I stood at the bottom of the seniority list. If no one wanted overtime, I got it whether I wanted it or not.

I hardly got to go riding at all in the summer of '99. I hadn't totally got used to working at night. Plus, I still worked on call. Even when I took Trixie for a ride, I needed to wear a beeper. We never went far, because if I got called, I only had an hour to get to the bakery.

It didn't really matter. We explored the fields and went back to the river. It all looked so different on Trixie compared to a tractor or on foot.

She always noticed the little things, a male Ring-necked Pheasant walking through the grass at the edge of the field. It's brown body with iridescent bronze highlights showing up vividly against the dark green of the shin-tall timothy grass. It's crisp white neckband allowing its purplish-green head feathers to be shown off to their full glory. He walked along un-disturbed by Trixie's presence until he disappeared among the juniper bushes that border the forest.

A female snapping turtle laboring up the bank of the gravel-pit, the track behind her a clear trail to the sandy hollow where she laid her eggs. Her eyes and attention focused ahead, across the field to the river that called to her in a low rumble.

A garden snake stretched out on a granite ledge, begging the sun to re-warm its night-chilled body. Trixie stopped and stared at these creatures. And I needed to figure out what caught her interest, so I noticed them too.

Scheduled to get out of work at eleven in the morning, I planned to go for a ride on that Wednesday in August. But the clock read nine fifty-three P.M. when I got into my car. Night had fallen. The air held a heavy fog. And I needed to put Trixie in for the night.

I forgot my flashlight at home. I pointed the car headlights to shine into the shed. I liked the old set up better. But Andy now used that shed and pasture for space for his business. His store had taken off and I liked seeing it flourish.

The old silo shed that Trixie stayed in nightly roomed large enough for three or four horses. The pasture lay only a short walk away. Shade trees bordered it and more grass grew in it than Trixie needed even on the driest of years. A nice breeze springing up from the river blew through the pasture, so the flies posed no big issue.

The only problem arose on nights when I arrived late to put Trixie in. I found my way out to the pasture, recognizing the path by the feel of the ground under my feet and the telltale swish of grass against my knees when I strayed from it. Trixie saw well in the dark, so coming back never caused a problem. But Richard Cole's house stood right below her pasture. Sound amplified and carried in a fog. I couldn't go calling her at ten at night in the fog.

I rattle the gate a little. "Trixie."

I waited and listened for a couple of minutes. Then I

tried it again. On the third try, a snort sounded out. "Beautiful, it's just me. You need to come in girl. Come on, Trixie."

I heard a few hesitant hoof steps. I didn't call out the magic words. I just said them. "Trixie, girl. Come on, beautiful."

Hoof beats in the mist; I couldn't tell which part of the pasture they reported from. But I knew she came towards me. The sound didn't tell me this, I just knew it. I peered out into the damp, heavy, darkness. Fog shrouded everything in white floating clouds of moist air that clung to the grass, the fence gate, and settled wetly, gently on to whatever moved; clothing, skin, the lead rope waiting to be snapped onto a halter. The hoof beats sounded like thunder, echoing off the hill, bouncing off the ground, reverberating through the grass, the Earth, the moisture filled air.

Then I saw it, a streak of white coming at me. If I knew not what made it, terror would cause me to run away screaming. But I'd seen this before on dark nights, by moonlight and starlight. The white came from Trixie's blaze; it glowed as a shining stripe that floated eerily at shoulder height towards you. It was the first thing you saw when she came at you after dark. The darkness hid her body. But that white blaze stood out and then I saw the glint of her eyes. Trixie ran up to me and nudged me.

"Beautiful. You're such a good girl. Now, you get to lead me to the shed."

Her steps landed strong and sure on the path. I let her lead me through the night, no longer fearful of a wrong step though my eyes still only perceived shadows, layered one on top of another, darkness over grey with blackness behind it all. For now, Trixie saw for me and I had confidence in her. It seemed as though, I'd followed her through most of my life. The jobs I had and the people I met shared a connection through her. I followed her without fear or worry. She never led me astray.

*   *   *   *   *   *   *   *

We experienced a nice February thaw in 2000 and the snow melted some. On a warm afternoon, I took Trixie for a ride. I headed up towards Harris Farm. I only went as far as the side of the road laid clear. Because even a couple inches of snow on the side of the road posed a hazard. I refused to risk Trixie slipping and getting hurt.

I owned a leather jacket, I wore when I rode in the winter. Given to me by a school friend, it measured thigh-length, bore a sheepskin lining with the wool still attached, and carried a real rough surface. For some reason, Trixie liked to rub her nose on it. The jacket kept me nice and warm. It weighed at least twenty pounds. I needed to climb on my pickup's bumper to mount my girl while wearing that coat.

The snow reflected the afternoon sun, making the drifts sparkle as if sprinkled with diamonds. An infrequent and not too cold breeze blew. I saw turkey tracks on the side of the road. I heard the stream running high with snowmelt from quite a distance away. A bubbling, gurgling song full of energy accompanied by the twisting, rubbing clicks, snaps, and rasps of leaf bare branches bouncing off each other, dancing to the rhythm of the blowing air.

Trixie and I learned to compromise over the past couple

of years. The tug-of-wars became more of a game than a battle. Trixie had passed beyond the prime of her life and I only let her do so much. But she still held enough fire to want to pretend she was young, so we compromised. When we came to level flat areas, I let her run. The rest of the time she walked, well sort of. She arched her neck, tucked her head in close to her chest, and pranced. She sidestepped. She tossed her head. She generally acted that way for the first half of the ride or until I let her run. Then she settled down and really walked with only an occasional sidestep, or head toss thrown in. We made it up to Harris farm. The side of the road remained clear the whole way. Trixie got to run a little. It ended up being a very nice ride.

The next morning Trixie lamed up, not real bad, just favoring her right foreleg a little bit. I could only surmise that the ride caused her lameness. We hadn't done anything unusual, but she possibly tweaked something a little. I kept an eye on it.

Trixie continued to get lame about half of the time, after we went for rides, never real seriously, just a little limp, usually on one of her forelegs. The limp stuck with her for three or four days though. Once it took a week, for it to go away.

I knew she wanted to continue with our rides so I made them shorter. I called and asked the vet. He told me it sounded like swelling in the joints that flared up when she was ridden. He said it became a normal occurrence in older horses.

I kept thinking of the books I read as a child. When a horse became old and aged past its usefulness, it got put out to pasture, retired to a life of green grass and warm sun.

The problem was Trixie enjoyed our rides as much as I. She acted heart-broken when I didn't take her out and give her attention.

And now, after all these years together, she expected that care to include a ride, even if we mostly walked and watched nature's show unfolding around us. If I put her back in the pasture without riding her, she got upset because to her it seemed as if I had cut our time together off short. I decided to ride her less often. I tried to take her for walks instead, leading her around and watching what we found interesting. She accepted that as a substitute sometimes. I only actually rode her in the summer because I thought the cold exasperated the problem.

*   *   *   *   *   *   *   *

I went over to put Trixie in and Andy came out to talk to me. A lady came running into his store today yelling. "The horse out in the pasture just fell over dead. It just fell over, bang, onto its side." Andy ran out of the store, across the yard, down the hill, out to the pasture, and leapt over the gate.

Andy stood beside me shaking his head. "She didn't move at all. I couldn't see her breathing. She lay stretched out, flat on her side. All I thought was, "How am I going to tell Kim, that her horse is dead?" I walk over to get a closer look. She opened her eye and winked at me. I saw the, "I got you." glint shining in her eye. I found it to be highly irritating." Andy shook his head slowly and cracked a lopsided grin.

I broke out laughing and it took a couple of moments for

me to be able to talk. "I know exactly what you mean. The first time she pulled it to me, I felt like throttling her."

"She has done it before?"

I chuckled. "Oh, yeah, once to my Mom and twice to me. She scared me half to death, both times. The lady wasn't joking Andy, she goes right over. She'll be standing there sunbathing. Then no warning, no bending of the knees, no swaying, nothing, just BAM! It must hurt. This huge cloud of dust puffs up when she hits. She just lays there. No twitching, leg or head movement, she really looks dead. Just when you get so that you lean over her and think, "She is dead, really dead." she opens her eye, and winks at you." I raised my right hand and shaded my eyes to reduce the sun's glare.

"I have no clue why she does it." I shrugged at Andy and lowered my arms, hands out in supplication and apology. "Maybe she likes living up to her name."

"She certainly tricked me." Andy chuckled and with a wave walked off.

I went down and put Trixie in. I ran my hands all over her rib cage and sides, trying to find any sore spots. The second time I saw her do the "BIG FLOP", she landed on granite with only a couple of inches of dirt covering it. I had thought for sure that she hurt herself. But just as it seemed to be now, I found no injuries, bruises, or sore spots. I shook my head in wonder. I patted her and kissed her nose. "Maybe they should have named you Magic."

Chapter # 10   A Home for Two

In the fall of 2000, I started looking for a house. I wanted to buy a place in the country, a safe place for Trixie and me to be together year-round; a place where I said who was welcome and who wasn't, somewhere to make a sanctuary for us, for always.

At the age of thirty-one, I decided to give up on the search for Mr. Right. We had finished the addition to Mom's house and paid off her mortgage. I could now make a home for myself. I looked at four or five houses in a single weekend, only taking the time to look at places zoned for horses. None of them felt right. Two of them needed extensive repairs. One place had no barn and heavily forested acreage. Another stood way out of my price range.

The real estate agent found another hopeful though. When we went to go look at it we found it to be rural zoned on a private road with a barn. The paperwork made no sense, because every sheet had something different written on it. One set of paperwork stated the lot size as three point two, another said four point two, and the last called it seven point two acres. The real estate agent arranged for us to go to the town hall. We planned to find out there, how much land really existed on the lot and get help sorting through the paperwork.

I liked the place. It needed work. The house needed new carpets and paint inside and out. I spent a lot of time checking out the barn. The setup looked nice, but it lay directly on dirt. Even in the summer, lying on dirt made Trixie's arthritis act up. She needed either rubber mats on concrete or a wood floor.

The pasture held numerous half-grown bushes and small saplings. I guessed it to be about ten years, since a horse grazed in it. Another clearing with a half grown in access road going to it stood beside the pasture. Its placement looked perfect for a summer pasture. But we couldn't tell, if it lay on the property or not. We needed to discover and authenticate the correct set of paperwork.

The people at the town hall generously helped us. The lot proved to be seven point two acres and the clearing stood on the property. I put in an offer for the property. They came back with a counteroffer for less money. Both the real estate agent and I asked that their offer be confirmed. We thought they'd made a typing mistake. No mistake, the house went through foreclosure twice previously, and they wanted to make sure to really get rid of it this time.

I bought the house on October 1, 2000. I started working on the barn on that same day. I planned to dig it out eight inches down, support the barn on cement blocks, put down three inches of crushed rock and a five inch concrete slab.

The first problem, I encountered lay in the fact that the main hall measured three and a half inches too narrow for even the smallest bucket loader. I needed to dig it all out by hand. The second problem turned out to be that the dirt in the stalls had gotten saturated with urine and solidified into a smelly rock-like mass. I needed to use a pickax to break it up.

As I dug down, I discovered six inch beams under the dirt. The barn's beams lay below ground level. I dug out the beams to block and support them and found six concrete pilings below the beams. By the time I dug down deep enough, so that the slab lay under the beams, the average depth dug out came to fourteen inches. About twenty yards of dirt ended up being moved with a shovel and wheelbarrow. I had eaten, worked, worked on the barn, and slept in that order. I became very exhausted and cranky by the time I finished.

I also worried about bringing Trixie home. Woods completely surrounded the pasture. Hunting season began soon and no horse had lived in the area for a long time. A very nice lady where I worked made Trixie a fluorescent orange blanket, so no hunter could mistake her for a deer: it stood out in my memory as one of those rare, kind, spontaneous things, that makes you really like the human race.

Andy trailered Trixie to the property on November 3. Trixie ran around the pasture, snorting and kicking up her heels. Suddenly, I knew this was truly our home.

* * * * * * * *

Trixie developed a new habit in the winter of 2000. I let her out in the morning and gave her a leaf of hay. I went back out at about two in the afternoon when I woke up, and fed her another leaf of hay. Then at about seven in the evening, I put her in for the night and dish out her grain and last leaf of hay.

The electric wire went across the middle of the hall. Trixie had gotten in the habit of unhooking it. After her afternoon feeding when I headed out to put her in at night, I could see her from halfway out to the barn. She stood with her nose pressed up against the plexi-glass in the front barn door. She stayed right there waiting for me. It made me smile every time I saw it; my beautiful girl, getting as close as possible to me, patiently waiting for me to come the rest of the way.

*　*　*　*　*　*　*　*

In the summer of 2001, the war of the lawnmowers took place on my property. Admittedly, the fault lay with me. I took the lazy way out whenever possible. For instance, my lawn held about a sixty to forty mix of weeds, clover, wild strawberries, and grass. Pathetic as it sounds, the weed portion made up the sixty percent.

I roped off my lawn and showed Trixie the borders. When the grass needed to be mowed, I tied a rope gate across the bottom of the driveway, opened the front barn door, and let Trixie loose. While I lay inside sleeping, she mowed the lawn for me. Unfortunately, she drew the limit at eating weeds.

So when the weeds grew knee high to an NBA player, I

dragged out the gas mower. The war started, when I decided to mow all of the weeds, the ones on the lawn and the ones in the pasture. Trixie only gave the lawnmower a passing glare or two, when it mowed the lawn. As soon as I started in on the pasture weeds though, she galloped into battle. This wasn't a happy; I'm coming to see you gallop. This was a get-out-of-my-way-or-else assault by a nine hundred pound pissed-off, horse.

My jaw dropped as Trixie charged towards me and the lawnmower. Trixie squealed and struck at the lawnmower as she ran by. Then she performed a loop and headed straight at it again.

"Trixie, no!" I screamed. She wheeled, kicked out with a back hoof that missed the carburetor by about two inches and trotted off snorting. I hit the kill switch and rolled the lawnmower out of the pasture.

From then on, the lawnmower never came out of the garage, unless I locked Trixie in her stall. I prepared by giving her an extra portion of grain, closing the stall and barn doors, and then mowed the weeds. After the lawnmower got placed back in the garage, I released her back out. She always paced off an inspection of her pasture to see what damage her nemesis managed to do. Then she stood beside the pasture gate, glaring at the garage.

I always made sure the garage door firmly latched, before I let Trixie out to mow the lawn. I easily pictured her kicking the lawnmower to pieces. I felt sure that she'd thoroughly enjoy doing it.

Trixie fervently claimed the pasture as her home. She defended it against known grass stealers. That grass belonged to her and no one and nothing else possessed rights to it. Deer and lawnmowers continued to be her main antagonists. In a way, it gave me a fierce surge of pride. She had never so thoroughly claimed a pasture before. To me it felt as if she declared to the world.

"I pick this home too!"

*　　*　　*　　*　　*　　*　　*　　*

In 2001, I decided that snow blowing didn't count as one of those winter pastimes that I enjoyed. The wind constantly blew snow back into my face. My toes always become miniature ice cubes. And darn it all, the paths only lasted until the next storm. That was of course, if luck stayed on my side and the wind failed to fill them in before then.

I made the decision about my dislike of snow blowing an hour and a half into my cleanup after the fifth snow storm of the winter. I had cleared the paths to the front door of the barn, through the gate to the back door of the barn, the one to Trixie's sunning spot, her rolling spot, and about three quarters of her perimeter. I still needed to do the paths to the back door and front door of the house.

Last year, I underestimated how much added snow lake effect would cause us to receive. Most of the snowfalls dropped above six inches at a shot. Trixie hardly cut any paths at all, because of her arthritis.

By the time spring arrived, only an eight by twelve foot section of packed down snow stood open for her to exercise in. Everything else lay covered in drifts deeper than her belly and grew impassable for her. She acted downright miserable, by the time the snow finally melted. So I decided in the fall of 2001 that I needed to buy a snow-blower for the coming winter to keep her paths open.

The salesman made snow blowing sound fun. I imagine he made a good living at his job. He spit up his coffee and laughed until he turned red, when I told him why I wanted a snow-blower.

"You need it to cut paths for your horse?"

I nodded at him, wondering why that surprised him. It seemed perfectly normal to me.

"Really?"

I quirked my eyebrow up and he composed himself.

"I apologize. I've never had a customer buy a snow-blower for that reason before."

I thought about taking my business elsewhere. But the salesmen apologized again and gave me a discount for being so unprofessional and laughing at a customer. By the time I left, he'd also thrown in a free delivery.

I realized from the way everyone watched me head for the door, that they wanted to be let in on the joke. I also guessed from the way the salesman hurried across the room to join his co-workers that he looked forward to sharing it with them. Oh well, a discount was a discount.

The first two snowstorms came and went and I agreed with the salesman. Snow blowing was fun, sort of. The third and fourth storm hit and snow blowing began to pale. The fifth storm helped me to officially make up my mind. I definitely disliked snow blowing. But when I did it, at least I got my priorities right.

*   *   *   *   *   *   *

Trixie escaped about twice a year since we moved here

to our new home. She met the neighbors up and down our dirt road. Most of them, she introduced herself to while grazing on their lawns. The neighbor's reactions varied from, "Wow, a horse!" and "Oh, that is Trixie, we need to call Kim." to "What the heck is that?"

I generally answered the phone and got told that Trixie had gone out visiting. It was a very laid-back neighborhood with so little traffic on our private road that the cats growled whenever a car drove by my house. So I never got worried about Trixie having gone to visit the neighbors. After all, she loved being around people.

Only once, did she go more than six houses away. Because the seventh house put in a new lawn and Trixie seemed to think that it smelled too tempting to resist. Even with that adventure, she failed to reach the main road which actually only counted as a back country road.

Usually when I got a call about Trixie's visiting, I simply took the portable phone to the door, opened it and hollered for Trixie, then asked the neighbor if she had headed home. Over three quarters of the time, she headed for home when I called her. The rest of the time, I needed to go to the bottom of the driveway and call so she heard me. The only time she went beyond hearing range occurred with the new lawn that she considered to be irresistible. New grass, just sprouting from the seed always stood out as a favorite with my girl.

On one momentous occasion though, things worked out a little differently. I got a call from my neighbor who lived at the dead end of the road. She sounded upset about Trixie being out. She and her kids sat and waited in their car as she called me from her cell phone. She didn't dare get out of the car.

"Why? You know Trixie always acts friendly."

"But she chased us home."

"She what? Why? What happened?"

"We were driving home. My son saw Trixie grazing on Al's lawn. I thought that was too close to the road, so I stopped and rolled down the window. I said."

"Trixie, girl, what are you doing, beautiful?" She came running at the car. I rolled up the window and drove for home. I felt worried that she headed straight for the car. Then my son says."

"Mommy, the horse is following us."

"Sure enough, she raced along behind us down the road. Now, we've reached home and she's standing right in front of the car, staring at me. What is wrong with her?"

I failed to restrain my chuckles. "I'm sorry. Nothing is wrong. I always call Trixie in from the pasture with, "Trixie, girl! Come on, beautiful!" She heard you say Trixie, girl and beautiful. So she thought she was supposed to go to you. When you drove off, she thought that meant you wanted her to follow you. And now, since she followed you, she expects to be rewarded with a treat for being so good."

"Oh, thank goodness. Only I don't have any horse treats."

"That's okay. I'll give her one, when she gets home. Give me a minute, to go to the end of the driveway and call her." So I went out and called Trixie. She came running up the road. She raced past me to the barn. She turned and looked at me. I knew the meaning of that look. It happened to be the 'Where is my treat?' look.

I gave Trixie her treat and put her back in the pasture. I found where she'd unhooked the gate and put it back up. I turned and shook a finger at her.

"No more chasing the neighbor's home. You know, you don't have them trained like me. They sometimes forget that you're a big harmless beggar, who will do about anything for a treat." I went over and rubbed under her mane in the itchy spot. She tilted her head until I scratched the other spot. Yep, she had me trained well.

*   *   *   *   *   *   *   *

On a quiet day in November of 2002 I peacefully slept off a hard nights work until a noise woke me up. It sounded scratchy, high-pitched, and repetitive. I realized I'd heard it on and off all summer. I'd thought the birds walking around on the tops of the windowsills caused it. But most of the birds left weeks ago so what really made that noise.

I needed to figure it out before I could sleep through it. I slid out of bed and tiptoed barefoot around the house until I located the noise. It came from outside of the mudroom door. I looked out the kitchen window.

Trixie stood at the door. Well, I had let her out to mow the lawn. Come to think of it, every time I'd heard that noise, Trixie was mowing the lawn. What was she doing? Her head lined up right above the doorknob. She couldn't be, could she? She opened the wire gate, by biting the handle and unhooking it. I walked out into the mud room. Trixie's head flew up and she stared at me through the window.

I opened the door. Sure enough, wet, gooey Trixie

slobber covered the doorknob. I shook my head.

"Trixie, you know you won't fit through the door." She stuck her head in the house and gave me a little nudge. "I can't let you in girl. You'd crash right through the floor. Houses aren't built like barns, girl. Wait a minute; I'll get you a treat." I pushed her head back out, grabbed a couple of apples and put on my sneakers. She waited until I opened the door.

"Here you go." I fed her an apple. "Now go on out to the barn, and I'll give you the other one." She backed up, took one last look in the door window, and then with a sigh she turned and trotted off to the barn. I followed her and gave her the apple. I brushed her and talked to her until she wandered back out into the pasture to graze.

I walked back to the house and washed off the doorknob. I smiled widely as I climbed back into bed.

I'd have to remember to lock the doors from now on. Better to hear a horse trying to turn a doorknob, than a horse crashing through the house floor.

*   *   *   *   *   *   *   *

In the summer of 2003, the biting flies gathered thick and ferocious during the day. Allergic to regular fly spray, Trixie breaks out in hives that itch far worse than fly bites if I use it on her. Instead, I resort to Avon Skin-So-Soft but it only works for a couple of hours at a time so she spent a lot of time hiding in the barn where I sprayed the regular stuff. Since she failed to get much pasture time because of this, I let her stay out in the pasture at night when I went to work.

Then one morning in August, I came home and found

the rope gate tied up across the driveway blocking my way. I let Trixie stay out in the pasture at night, not mow the lawn. When I got out to un-tie the gate, I discovered a carrot in the middle of the road. So I had two mysteries to answer; how did she get out of her pasture, and where did the carrot come from?

A couple of weeks later, I got the answers. I met up with Scott and Deb Brook on our private road. They lived one house beyond me and loved being out in the country. A stream ran through their property and they often watched wildlife from the comfort of their home.

"The other evening the motion-sensor floodlights started coming on out in the yard and I thought some deer grazed out there. So I called Deb over to the patio door and turned on the porch lights and there stood Trixie looking in the window at us." Scott tipped back his head and laughed.

Deb folded her hands over her heart and leaned back against Scott's shoulder. "There she stood the dream-horse I envisioned during my youth, but could never have. And I said to Scott that must be Trixie."

Scott's face broke into a wide grin and he wrapped his right arm around Deb. "And I asked do we have any carrots? And Deb got them out of the fridge and we went out and patted her."

"She acted so sweet. She followed us up the road as gentle as a pet dog. We'd stop and feed her a carrot and then go along a little further with her walking along behind us." Deb's cheeks dimpled in her pixie-shaped face, making it glow with joy as her curly white hair spread out over Scott's shirtfront.

"We tied the rope across your driveway and put some

carrots on the ground for her," he leaned down and kissed the top of Deb's head.

Deb closed her eyes and whispered, "And there she stood watching us walk away, the dream-horse of my youth."

After talking with them, I resumed locking Trixie in the barn at night. She might not always get so lucky in who she met after dark and I didn't want to risk her encountering and terrifying somebody lost or in a hurry.

But I couldn't help but wonder if she somehow got guided by a higher power in her wanderings; because she answered all my childhood dreams and somehow in the middle of the night she managed to grant my neighbor with a vision of the dream-horse of her youth, Trixie the equine embodiment of childhood dreams.

$$*\quad*\quad*\quad*\quad*\quad*$$

Summer came and went again and the fall that followed turned out to be a nice one. The breeze wafted the scent of wildflowers, timothy, and blackberry brambles into my nostrils, the sun shined strongly on shoulders, warming them and loosening muscles into total relaxation. I still let Trixie out to mow the lawn.

She woke me up one morning in early September by nickering at my bedroom window. I rushed out in my bare feet thinking something had gone wrong. She wasn't hurt; she wanted me to spend some time with her, to give her some pats and scratches.

Actually she wanted more than just attention; she seemed to be in a playful mood. She wanted to go out. She kept running around me, down the driveway, then back to me, until I got the message.

"Okay, let me go get dressed." I knew from the way Trixie acted that she wanted to go for a ride. I both looked forward to and dreaded it. Riding Trixie felt wonderful. Her gaits glided along as smooth as butter and she completely understood me. To me, it seemed like the most beautiful thing in the world.

But I dreaded the day after a ride. The worrying, would Trixie lame up this time? I had only ridden her about twice a year, since I bought the house.

The last time I rode her early in the summer. We only went a round trip of about a mile and a half. She pulled up lame for six days afterwards. And in the spring, Trixie had played around like a yearling for a couple of hours, running, bucking, and spinning. She never reared up any more. Still, she'd lamed herself for two days. I so hated seeing her limp, knowing she suffered through pain. As a genuinely gentle, loving spirit Trixie shouldn't have to endure pain.

But on that September day as I brushed her, I realized how excited she acted. When I took off her halter and reached for the bridle, she shoved her head into it, before I even got it lined up for her. I laughed as I untwisted the head stall and slipped it over her ears. I would worry about tomorrow, tomorrow. I decided to simply enjoy the day with my girl.

It happened to be a perfect day, blue sky, warm sun, cool breeze. Trixie managed to pick a good one. Amazingly enough, she settled down once I got on her. She looked alert, watching everything. But she waived her normal prancing or head tossing. She startled once when a Bush/Cheney campaign poster with one end ripped free began flapping against the Kerry/Edwards poster beside it, even in the country politics papered the roadside. She sidestepped until my voice reassured her.

We only went a round trip of about a mile and a quarter. We stayed at a walk the whole time. We went real slowly on the way back. We stopped and watched a dog running in a field, a cat sitting on a rock wall, and a flag flapping in the breeze.

I took care of Trixie when we got home. I brushed her again, combed her mane and tail, and lavished her with attention. She basked in it, falling asleep in the sunlight as I cared for her. I said goodbye and kissed her on the nose when I finished. She slowly opened one eye and winked at me.

I smiled to myself as I got back into bed. I got to enjoy a great ride on a beautiful day, I couldn't envision asking for more. I fell asleep and dreamt of the summers when Trixie and I spent our youths together.

Back then, a day became rated by how much time; I got to spend with her. A bad day meant I failed to see her at all. It was a horrible thing to endure. A good day allowed me to occupy hours or half a day with her. An excellent day happened when I got to pass the whole day with Trixie. I'd while away the day watching her, brushing her, talking to her. I often put a lead rope on her, climbed on her back, and just sat there on her as she grazed. I became the riding flyswatter, stretching down to get the ones on her neck, twisting to get the ones on her sides.

I dreamt of only excellent days.

*　*　*　*　*　*　*

I got hurt at work in the fall of '04 and needed to take physical therapy. I became unable to use the snow blower all winter. I utilized my snowshoes using them to get to the barn.

I employed the snowshoes in Trixie's pasture, walking around stomping as hard as possible, trying to pack the snow down for her. In some places, it seemed to work. In others spots it failed to.

We received a lot of snow throughout the winter. Trixie dealt with it in her own way. She walked on top of the packed down snow. She stepped over the fence, which only stood about six inches above the snow. Then she trudged out to the driveway cleared of snow by plowing and stood in the one spot where the sunlight shined brightly through the tree cover.

She didn't leave the driveway or wake me up. I just got up, went out to take care of her, and found her standing in the driveway. She always followed me back to the barn. I opened the door and she trotted in. I gave her some hay and told her how silly she acted. When I went out to feed her before going to work, there she stood in the driveway again.

She caused no harm and I resigned myself to having a horse in the driveway until the snow melted. She looked better than any lawn ornament, I ever saw. Plus, she behaved like a nine hundred pound guard horse.

If anybody turned into our driveway, Trixie woke me up by snorting. She nearly scared the CMP meter reader half to death in February.

By the time I got dressed and went to investigate Trixie's snorting, she stood nose to nose with his pick-up, every exhalation sending a cloud of steam rolling over the hood. Her ears lay pinned back and she stared at the meter man through the windshield. He stared back, wide-eyed and unmoving. He stayed in the truck until after I led her to the barn and locked her in. He jumped back in the pickup and headed down the driveway before I even got halfway back to the house. I could just imagine the story his co-workers would hear.

"A steam-snorting, crazy horse in a blue blanket faced off my truck and acted like she wanted to attack me."

*   *   *   *   *   *   *   *

On March 31, 2005, I went out to put Trixie in for the night. She stood with her nose pressed up against the plexiglass waiting for me. When I opened the barn door, I saw her twisted blanket. When I reached over to straighten it, I knew something had gone wrong. The blanket felt soaked. It hadn't rained at all that day. I reached under the blanket. Moisture saturated Trixie's hide and her breathing labored in and out heavier than normal.

I took off the blanket and checked Trixie over. I found no injuries on her. It made no sense; she'd been fine when I came out earlier. Why was she so wet? The answer came into my mind with frightening clarity. Trixie had been rolling on the ground, rolling for so long, she got soaked through by the snow.

Only two reasons existed for why a horse would roll for

that long. Either they cast themselves and couldn't get back up or they came down with colic. Trixie didn't kick at her belly, the most common sign of colic. But she worked hard to breath. I went into the house and called the vet.

I led Trixie out to the driveway. I tried to dry her off with some towels. Then I started walking her up and down the driveway. If a horse came down with colic, walking helped them. If she didn't have colic, walking would help warm her up and dry her off.

The vet said she'd head over as quickly as possible. She needed to answer another call first. She planned to call the other patient and see if they minded if she came and saw Trixie first. I felt unsure if Trixie had colic or something else. But I easily sensed how off my girl seemed to be. She wasn't lame, but she hesitated as she walked. I desperately hoped that it turned out to be something other than colic. She hadn't contracted colic since she'd survived her bout of peritonitis. She'd only ate her normal hay today. If she got colic on her normal food, it meant her intestines were in very poor working order.

The vet came and confirmed the worst. Trixie had colic. Her belly made barely any sounds at all. The vet performed a thorough exam. She became alarmed by the amount of adhesions, Trixie bore in her bowels. I told her about the peritonitis my girl experienced thirteen years previously.

"That explains it. Two options stand open for Trixie, surgery which generally carries a fifty-fifty chance of success." The vet cocked her head, blinked, hesitated, and then began speaking again.

"The amount of adhesions your girl has and her age mean lower chances than normal for her. Plus, the surgery causes adhesions, which would add to her pre-existing ones. Your other option is to wait out the night. I've seen three horses spontaneously, recover from this. They were all younger than yours, but she has a chance. If she fails to recover, you'll know it quickly. If her intestines don't start working again, she'll be rolling and kicking down walls within an hour from the pain."

"I don't want her to be in pain."

"I'll leave you something if you decide to wait it out, a shot for the pain, strong enough to hold her over till I get here. But if she gets in that much pain, the only humane option is to put her down. If she fails to recover by morning, her intestines will start to die. Surgery success rates get lower as time passes."

I thought of how trailers still terrified Trixie. I remembered how scared she got when I needed to leave her in the clinic for a few days. I remembered the fear, I saw in the eyes of the horses that went through surgery. All that fear, for under a fifty percent chance of survival.

And even if she made it through the surgery, she'd end up with more adhesions. She had got colic on her normal feed. I already fed her second crop hay and very little grain to prevent the chances of colic. What would I be able to feed her, when she got even more adhesions?

I took a deep breath. "Trixie has beaten the odds before. I don't want her to have to endure surgery. We'll wait and see how she gets through the night."

"If she doesn't improve, you'll be calling me back within the hour. Let's raise her chances as much as possible." She gave Trixie a shot of antibiotics, another shot for inflammation of the intestines, and she put a tube down into Trixie's stomach. The tube allowed her to throw up or burb. Something a horse couldn't do normally. The vet tubed some water into Trixie.

She also left me a pump, making it possible for me to tube water into Trixie.

"Try to keep her hydrated. Water might get her intestines started up again. Tube a couple of gallons into her every other hour. The shots will drop her body temperature, so you'll want to put a blanket on her. I'm leaving you this paste, which contains a mild, slow working sedative. Use it if she gets just a little pain. It isn't strong enough to work, if she gets a lot of pain. In case she gets really bad, I'm leaving you this." She handed me a syringe.

"It holds a one and a half size dose of a very strong sedative. It works quickly. You don't have to worry about whether or not you get it in a vein. It works no matter where you inject it. Use this, if you need to call me back to put her down. Use this if she experiences severe pain."

I took the needle with a strong sense of unease. To me that little needle represented the point of no return. That little needle symbolized the worst case scenario, I didn't know if I'd have the courage to give that shot to Trixie. That shot meant admitting that I'd given up on saving my girl.

When the vet left, I tied Trixie to my car by opening the door, throwing the lead rope in the car, and closing the door. I'd never try it with any other horse. But I trusted her not to damage the car, at least not on purpose. I ran inside and got her orange blanket. It lacked the thickness of her winter blanket, but dry and thin seemed to be a better option than thick and wet. I grabbed the portable phone on the way back out.

I put the blanket on her and called over to Mom's house. She worked the night shift, but Ev was home. I asked him to call her at work, and tell her Trixie was really sick. Could she come over, when she got out of work, please? Ev said he'd get a hold of her for me. When Ev said something, it meant it'd get done so I went back to concentrating on Trixie. She started to shiver and she still swayed where she stood from the medicine so I dared not lead back to the barn yet.

I remembered Jane Allen telling me how to make a horse blanket warmer by lining it with an old blanket. I'd donated my old blankets to the homeless shelter, but my new ones would work just as well. I performed the car door trick again and put two more blankets on Trixie. I used clothespins to close the front. One closed right in front of her chest, the other went halfway up Trixie's neck.

Finally, Trixie's shivering slowed, but by then I felt the cold. I hadn't been dressed to stay outdoors, when I went out to feed her tonight. I didn't want to leave her alone long enough to go change. I huddled in close to her to share warmth. She started to perk up. Soon, I'd be able to lead her back to the barn. We'd both feel better once we got in out of the breeze.

I knew she'd became fully alert, when she pushed her face up flat against me and hid from the world. I talked to her and rubbed her neck. It must be so confusing to be shot up with meds and not know why everything seemed out of balance. I wouldn't want to go to the doctors and end up drugged. To be all groggy and not really capable of understanding what went on.

I rubbed her neck for a long time, before she pulled her head away and looked around.

"It's okay, beautiful. We gave you some medicine to help you feel better. It's all up to you, beautiful. I won't let them take you away or operate on you. I know how scared you'd get and it might not make you better. So we'll just see what happens, you're quite an odds beater." I leaned in and hugged her neck. "I love you, beautiful. Do you want to go back to the barn?" She slowly followed me to the barn one hesitant step after another.

I took her water bucket out of her stall. She could choke, if she tried to drink with the tube still in her stomach. I headed to the house to change clothes and Mom showed up. We went out to the barn together. Trixie greeted Mom with a soft whicker and leaned forward so she'd pat her.

Mom stayed with her while I went in and changed. I brought a chair for Mom, a lantern, a timer, and a couple more blankets out to the barn. Mom and I took turns patting Trixie and talking to her. Whenever we stopped she nudged us, or stuck her head out at us, until we started patting her again.

Every other hour, I pumped a couple of gallons of water down the tube into her stomach. Most of it came right back out with a nasty silage smell to it. But I figured she kept down about half a gallon every time. Plus, she seemed to be in no pain, she just couldn't relax. It reminded me of when I just got over the flu. Not really still sick, but unable to get comfortable, no matter what I did. Trixie just needed to have someone keep her company until she felt better.

Mom got tired and went into the house to take a nap. I put the chair in the stall and sat beside Trixie's neck wrapped in a blanket. She kept huddling in closer and closer to me as I patted her. I kissed her on the nose, and she stepped back a little. Then she slowly inched in again. It became a routine, pat and talk to her for ten minutes, kiss her on the nose, pat her and talk to her for ten more minutes, kiss her on the nose.

At about quarter of five, I put water down her tube. Every time I carried out the task. She seemed to settle down a little more afterwards. I began to hope that the fresh water had relieved her bellyache by jump starting her intestines.

Then at about five thirty in the morning, she kicked her belly once. I cringed. *No, please no, she was getting better. Please God, please!* A couple of minutes passed. She kicked her belly twice. I kissed her nose and ran to get Mom.

Trixie's head leaned out the stall door when I got back. I walked up to her and she hid her face against me. I cried as I talked to her. My voice sounded raspy and uneven. She didn't seem to mind, as long as I kept talking and patting her. Mom came out and rubbed my back, as I rubbed Trixie's neck. *Please God, please she's my beautiful girl, please!*

Trixie kicked her belly twice, then twice again. Mom patted her as I ran in and called the vet. The vet said to give her the shot. If she was making a recovery, she wouldn't be kicking her belly. She said she'd be over in less than an hour.

I ran back out to the barn. Trixie stood fidgeting as Mom patted her. "Has she kicked her belly?"

Tears streamed down Mom's face, as she turned to me and nodded. "Yes, a couple of times."

I picked up the needle in one hand and the paste in the other. "I refuse to give up on her; maybe the last of the colic just needs a little more time to work its way out." I looked at Mom. She gave me a little half smile, half frown. I knew the same expression covered my face. False hope still qualified as hope in a desperate twisted form.

Trixie never liked taking pastes. This time proved to be no exception. She made faces and rubbed up against me, acting like she wanted me to take it back.

"Sorry girl. Hopefully, this'll make you feel better."

It failed to work. She started to fidget more.

"Maybe if you walk her?"

I took her out of the stall. She pulled me outside. On the way out, she swung to the side and knocked over the lantern. I heard shattering glass. Only Mom, quickly righting and extinguishing the lantern prevented a fire. Trixie began turning circles, pulling me in first one direction then the other.

"I've got no control. The lead rope feels all slick from her throwing up water on it. It slips right through my hands." I grabbed the halter itself. I used my body to herd her in the direction, I wanted to go. Only the fact that she wouldn't hurt me on purpose allowed it to work. She let me corral her back into the stall. I couldn't risk her getting loose in this condition.

I snapped the lead rope into the eye bolt in her stall.

"Get out!" Mom cried, as Trixie spun and rammed her body sideways into the stall wall. By the time I got out the door, she switched back and forth between kicking, pawing the floor frantically, jerking against her lead rope, and bouncing her body off one wall, then the other.

I grabbed the needle off the shelf with shaky hands. I barely managed to see through the fog of my tears. I turned back into the stall with the needle cover still on. I needed to make sure; I got it into her not me. I body slammed into Trixie's side, she chose not to push back at all. She let me shove her up against the wall. I pulled off the needle cover and injected her with the medicine.

"I'm sorry Trixie. I'm sorry." I knew not what I apologized for, waiting to give her the shot or giving it to her at all. Maybe it was both.

She started bouncing off the walls again, as I left the stall. I put the empty syringe, back on the shelf. Mom stood between me and the stall.

"Don't go back in. She feels too much pain right now."

I nodded as the walls shook from the punishment, Trixie inflicted on them. Mom stood beside me at the stall door.

"Easy girl, easy! Come on you stupid medicine work. I must have missed the vein. It'll take longer to work in the muscle. Work, work!"

I slid open the stall door about a foot and a half. Mom grabbed my shoulders. I waited until Trixie swung against the door. I laid my hand on her side.

"Easy, beautiful easy! Don't hurt yourself more, easy now. It'll work, girl. I promise it will work. Give it a minute. Just give it a minute, beautiful."

Trixie stood quivering against my hand, kicking her belly and the stall wall.

"Easy beautiful." I cringed as her hoof crashed into the metal corner guard.

"Don't hurt yourself beautiful. Please, please medicine work."

"It's working." Mom said. "She's slowing down. Her head is lowering. The medicine's working."

I felt Trixie's quivering lessen under my hand. Her hoof stopped in mid-kick, and slowly dropped back to the floor. I leaned in against her side and sighed. The pain had finally ceased.

Violently shifted by her struggles, the blankets now twisted around her body, one lay way back on her rump, half wrapped around her legs, the other lay on the floor. Her orange blanket hung in pieces, ripped halfway down the back stitching. I felt her skin. She seemed dry and warm. I pulled the ruined blankets off her.

The stomach tube hung halfway out and nearly dragged on the floor. I pulled it the rest of the way out. Better my doing it, than her stepping on it, and ripping it out the painful way.

I took a deep breath. The barn smelled of silage, rotten and pungent from Trixie's stomach water. "Let's try to get her out in the fresh air. I want her to be out when the sun comes up."

"How?" Mom asked. "She's swaying where she stands. She isn't lined up with the door. She won't be able to turn without falling."

I looked at the door. Mom was right, but if Trixie moved over just a couple of feet. Side-step, I hadn't asked her to side-step in at least ten years. I put one hand on her neck, the other on her side, and pressed.

"It's been a long time girl but I know you can do it. Side.... Zzzz. Side... Zzz. Side..... Zzz. Side.... Zzz." Her head came up some. "That's a girl. Side..... Zzz. Side.... Zzz. Side.... Zzz." She took a faltering step to the side, then another away from me. I kept the pressure on her side until she stood lined up to the door. I took my hand off her side and leaned against her neck crying.

"Oh, beautiful, beautiful girl. My smart, beautiful, girl. You're such a good girl, such a beautiful, good girl."

I led her out into the false dawn, one so slow step at a time. I talked to her the whole way. "Let's get you out where you can see the sunrise. That's it, my brave girl." I ground tied her by simply dropping the lead rope.

"I'll come right back beautiful." I went and grabbed her brushes. She was sweaty and dirty from all of the rolling that she'd done. We stood out under the open sky as it brightened, sharing our old ritual, Trixie dozing off as I brushed her and talked to her.

Mom chuckled as I dropped the brushes to the ground and just began rubbing my hands all over Trixie's neck and sides.

"You bring out the brushes and then use your bare hands."

"Sometimes the brushes fail to break up the dirt good enough. Trixie likes it better when I rub her." She did indeed like it. Even in her drugged state, she leaned against the pressure of my hands. Plus, all though, I refused to admit it out loud; giving her that shot meant I'd given up hope. I was going to lose my girl and I wanted my hands on her one last time.

The vet showed up and examined her. Trixie made no belly sounds at all. Her intestines were even more distended and her heart rate had increased even with the sedative.

"She probably only stands about a thirty percent chance at surviving surgery now. Her intestines are dying; parts of them would need to be removed."

I shook my head. "No surgery, she'd be terribly scared. She became very frightened when she stayed at the clinic before. No surgery." I knew only one option remained.

I stood there crying, my nose running. Mom and I had used up all of the tissues and paper towels in the barn. My jacket hung on me, soiled and heavy, totally soaked with a sickening mix, of Trixie's stomach water, her slobber from pulling out the stomach tube, and my tears. I don't think that I ever looked worse in my life. I knew that I had never felt worse. I felt like asking the vet, if I could get a sedative for me. I felt like curling up in a ball and never moving ever again. But Trixie needed me. She had always been there for me. Now, I had to be there for her.

The vet looked at me, patted Trixie, and spoke slowly. "We have no option but to put her down. She is burning off the sedative fast. Within an hour, the pain will return two-fold."

"No more, pain." I stuttered. "No more."

"I'll go get what I need." I leaned against Trixie, crying and rubbing her neck.

Mom leant against the barn crying. "Thanks, Mom. Thank you for coming. I know you left work early to get here. I hope they didn't give you a hard time." Mom shook her head.

"You raised us both, you know. You're as much Trixie's Momma, as Dixie and I am, she liked seeing you. I needed you to be here, thank you." Mom hated to have animals put down. She had just lost her cat a couple of weeks ago. I knew this was terribly hard for her. It probably hurt her nearly as much as it did me. She'd watched Trixie grow up alongside me.

The vet came back in moments. "Do you want it done here?" She asked.

I looked around. "There in the clean snow, where the sun shines through the trees." I tried to get Trixie to back up.

"Lead her forward in a gentle turn until you get there." The vet said.

"Ice lies under the snow. I don't want her to slip."

The vet looked at me and her lips curled up in a tiny wry smile. I realized how foolish I sounded. I was having Trixie put down and I still worried about her slipping and getting hurt on some ice. I led her in a gentle turn onto the snow. She followed me with a halting step, trusting me not to lead her astray.

The vet tried to find the artery on the left side of Trixie's neck, but couldn't. She moved to the right side and found it. "This will go right to her brain first. She won't feel any pain. Her legs will buckle real quickly. She'll take a couple of deep breaths and it'll be done. Are you ready?"

I'll never be ready. But I saw Trixie flick her tail, the sedative had started to wear off, soon the pain would return. She shouldn't have to feel pain. I closed my eyes and gave a small nod.

When Trixie's legs buckled so did mine, I landed in the snow beside her head. I saw the fear come into her eyes. "Don't be scared, beautiful. Please don't be scared. You go to the green pasture, okay, the green pasture in the sky." The fear receded and her ears came forward as she listened to me.

"You go up to the green pasture, the one beside the

gentle flowing stream that has a warm morning breeze." Her breathing slowed. I leaned over and kissed her beautiful rose-petal nose.

"You deserve green pastures girl. You deserve the best. You go to that green pasture, okay."

Trixie took a deep breath. The vet stretched her finger out towards Trixie's eye. I instinctively hunched a shoulder to shield her. I realized how absurd that seemed. I tried to pull my shoulder back. It refused to listen. The vet reached around me. She touched Trixie's eye, then patted my shoulder.

"I'm sorry." She said, got up, and walked away.

I leaned over Trixie's ear. I whispered to her.

"When it's time girl, my time, you call and I'll come running." She took another deep breath and then she was gone.

Epilogue

Life without Trixie was difficult. Joy became so much harder to find, laughter so much rarer. For weeks, sleep seemed like a near impossible thing to do. I always woke up after a couple of hours and jumped up in bed with one thought on my mind, I forgot to take care of Trixie before I went to sleep. I'd leap out of bed, jam my slippers on, and then I'd remember she was gone. I'd lie back down and cry, but sleep refused to come again.

It felt like so many things needed to be done after she was gone. I cleaned the barn, totally. I scoured that horrible silage smell from it. I washed her pails spotless, put down fresh shavings. Her halter and bridle had to be hung, just so in there spots. I scrubbed her dirty lead rope. I refused to wash her halter though, that carried her hairs on it. Its dirtiness meant something special to me, a small remaining piece of my girl. I left the smudges on the plexi-glass in the barn door. My beautiful girl had made those with her nose.

The electric wire fence needed to come down. Trixie was free of that now. Most of me believed that she now lived in a heavenly green pasture. She deserved heaven more than most people I knew. But a small part of me still felt her around me. I refused to have any part of her bound any longer. She needed to be totally free so I took the fence down.

The back barn door has never been closed, since April 1. What a cruel joke, Trixie left this world on April 1. We had just celebrated our twenty-fifth anniversary on Easter, the week before.

It seemed both fitting and heartrending, that I finished writing the first draft of this book as the sun dawned on another June 1. Twenty-six years had passed since, Woody Brown looked out into his pasture, to see something brown running behind his Pinto mare Dixie. Twenty-six years had come and gone since, my mother took me for a trip to see a newborn foal.

I arranged to have a barbecue on June 4 to celebrate Trixie's life. I invited the people who were instrumental in our life's. I bought flowers to plant in her memory. I had stories to share, food to eat, and tears to shed. Mary and Woody Brown planned on coming.

In her reply, Mary sent me a short story explaining how Dixie came into their life. She told me about Trixie's father and about their decision to give Trixie to me. She said we had come full circle.

That got me thinking, full circle. *How do you find the beginning on a circle? Is there an end on a circle?* No one point forms the beginning or end. I could point to the spot, where it started for me, but before that lay the spot where it started for the Browns and for Dixie.

I wondered if that circle was built like an onion, layer on

top of layer, going back deeper and deeper into the past. I thought it had to be. Why did I think that? Because I realized, there was no end. I knew the day Trixie's spirit left this earth. But that didn't make it the end. As long as I lived and breathed, there would be no end to Trixie and me. I was her girl. I knew how to persevere, how to fight, and how to love with every fiber in me. I learned it all from the most special horse in the world. I would carry her inside of me until I rejoined her and we thundered across the heavens together, soul-mates and best friends flying on the wings of a horse and the prayers of a child.

*   *   *   *   *

Now, over seven years after Trixie's death, I'm still coming to terms with her absence. At first, I felt overwhelmed by the emptiness within me. I sensed a huge, gaping hole in the fabric of my heart and wondered if I'd ever be whole again. Then slowly, I began to comprehend that Trixie had not only influenced the physical aspects of my life.

True, the people I met through her, the jobs I got to take care of her, and even the house I bought so we could be together year-round were the most obvious alterations she brought into my life. They were not however the most important gifts that she gave me.

Trixie shaped my very spirit. She opened my eyes to the natural world, to compassion, to love. I often find myself stopping because I sense something waits for me to notice it. And when I take the time and actually look, I always find something; a fox trotting across the back lawn, a hummingbird sipping nectar from the lilac bush, a doe and fawn grazing in my girl's pasture.

On many days, I find myself wandering out to the barn. I trace my hand lovingly over a faded blue halter, sweeping away cobwebs and dust, trying to turn time backwards. And as I look out the barns open back door I feel an urge to call out.

"Trixie girl! Come on beautiful!"

But I never do. Because I know that the absence of an answering whinny and the rhythmic pounding of galloping hooves would break my heart.

People often ask me. "Kim, why don't you get another horse?"

I find it impossible to explain to them. But the closest I've ever come is simply we are each destined to find one true love during our lifetime. I found mine and now she's gone. There's no way to replace that. And while I realize the world holds other loves, different loves for me to discover. I also know my heart must heal from the loss of my girl before it can expand, find, and welcome another love.

All of the deepest parts of me existed because of or with Trixie. The things that made me feel the most profound emotions in my life, all involved her. My darkest fears occurred while riding to a vet clinic, wondering if she would have to be put down, and before a certain hunting season, when I needed to find a safe place for my girl. My most fulfilling joy came to me as I stood on a hill and called Trixie. And as she ran to me, I rejoiced to be living my life. I have never again felt as free as I did when she flew me above the Earth. Her strength, her power, and her will my wings.

My father was a huge, rough stone who threw himself about in my life. He caused wave after wave of turbulent water, great surging ripples that nearly drowned me under their dark weight. But Trixie lifted me up to the surface, up to the beauty of light sparkling across the wave's crests, up to the joy of the breeze blowing through my hair. She showed me how to ride the waves of life, how to survive the dark dips and rejoice in the heady swells.

She is with me still, a light in my darkest hours and a companion in my glorious moments. On June 1 of 2006, Trixie's pasture bloomed with a teeming profusion of buttercups. I'd never seen those flowers there before. I felt it had to be a sign from my girl and I wanted to know what it meant so I looked up the meaning of the flower. The symbolic qualities of the buttercup flower are self-worth and the power of words.

I got the message, girl, loud and clear.

Trixie flew me high enough to touch the stars. Together, we soared above the world. And as she gifted me with flight, I wish to share it and her with others as a tribute to her generous spirit. The only memorial I can give her that comes close to what she deserves is to help others understand how beneficial and encouraging horses are for those who struggle through life's hardships. If Trixie's story inspires kindness, loving attention, and proper care for and towards animals, it will be worthy of my girl.

My friends often try to correct me when I call this book Trixie's story. They say it is my story as well. In a way, they are right. But if not for Trixie, my story wouldn't have turned out well enough to merit sharing it. So while I'm also on these pages, she made me worth putting there.

Over time, I have discovered that the deeper you go into me, the more you find Trixie. So there will never be an end, not as long as I'm here. I carry on and I won't forget the laughter, the smiles, the joys, the freedom, or the tears we shared. I won't forget her loving spirit, her adventurous soul, or her loyal heart, and I won't forget to go running when she calls me.

Until then, the circle continues to go around, layer on top of layer. Those I touch will carry on after I'm gone. Since I am and always will be Trixie's girl, they won't be carrying just a part of me forward. They will also be carrying, a part of the most beautiful, precious, and special horse in the whole world.

*   *   *   *   *

Please, if you enjoyed this book, take the time to write a review on Amazon or Goodreads. You can write a review even if you borrowed the book from a library or friend. Reviews are vital to not only the author, who gets more marketing from pages as their review numbers increase, but also to fellow readers who are trying to choose which book to read.

If you want to learn more about me, here is my FB author page:
https://www.facebook.com/ComeRunningWhenICall

If this story has truly touched your heart and inspired in you a desire to make the world a better place for horses or animals in general, please follow these simple steps to help them.

1. **Spay or neuter your pets.** Indiscriminate breeding of animals puts a huge financial strain on animal shelters and charitable organizations.

2. **Adopt, never buy your animals.** Adopting your animals means you not only save a life it also has the added benefit of allowing you to discuss which animal to get with someone who honestly wants the best outcome for both you and the animal, instead of someone who merely wants you to make a purchase.

3. **Always report any animal abuse or neglect that you witness.** Never assume that someone else must have reported it. Horses have been known to slowly starve to death over a period of months directly beside busy streets because everyone assumed someone else must have already called in the neglect.

4. **Volunteer to help at your local animal shelter or horse rescue organization.** It doesn't matter what your skill set is. These worthy charitable organizations can usually use help in everything from mucking out stalls, exercising and grooming, socializing traumatized patients to car maintenance, house repair, and keeping the paperwork in order.

5. **If you have extra funds, please donate it to an animal cause.** Animals and children are truly those who can't help themselves and in these financially difficult times the shelters and organizations that see to their welfare are struggling. Any help large or small is much appreciated.